BEYOND BORDERS

BEYOND BORDERS

The Perils and Pleasures of Two Hitchhikers on a Journey Through Central and South America

TERRANCE BROWN, FAIA

DANELLE CROWLEY

Clovercroft Publishing

Beyond Borders: The Perils and Pleasures of Two Hitchhikers on a
Journey Through Central and South America

Published by Clovercroft Publishing, Franklin, Tennessee
ClovercroftPublishingGroup.com

Interior Design by Suzanne Lawing

Printed in the United States of America

ISBN: 978-1-956370-49-2 (print)

Terry's Preface

After graduating from Texas Tech University with a Bachelor of Architecture degree and a commission in the US Army as a 2nd Lieutenant, I desired to travel in Mexico. So, I requested a six-month delay from my entrance into the Army. At the same time, friends and family members convinced me that traveling in Mexico might not be safe. Instead, I hitchhiked for a second time through Europe and helped a man from Kuwait drive his new Mercedes Benz car across Germany, Austria, Yugoslavia, Bulgaria, and Turkey. I was turned back at the Syrian border because the Syrians were mad at America for selling jets to the Israelis. So, I traveled by taxi to the coast of Turkey, flew to Beirut, Lebanon and steamed in a passenger boat along the Mediterranean Coast to Greece and returned to Germany via train. Then I entered the Army and served a year in the states and 10 months in the Vietnam War (1960-1971).

Shortly after mustering out of the Army, I received a letter from a college friend, Danelle Crowley, asking me to travel with her and a friend named Bill M. to South America. I was 26, unmarried, and didn't want to be "tied to a drafting table" in an architect's office. I was pleased with the opportunity she offered. Since I had been to war, I was not as concerned about the safety involved in traveling to Mexico and South America.

Thus began what we called our Patagonian Adventure. In brief, it entailed traveling through Mexico, every country in Central America, and the majority of the countries in South America, including the Andean countries of Colombia, Ecuador, Peru, and Bolivia. Then we continued to Argentina, Chile, Uruguay, Paraguay, and Brazil. Our goal was to live on $1.00 a day. Our travel expenses hitchhiking for three months around the Patagonia (Southern tip of South America) came to $30 for me and $20 for Danelle.

Action began the moment I landed in Colombia and had my passport stolen by a fast-fingered thief. Getting bored with hitchhiking and desiring to return to the US was a constant companion, but I mustered the energy to continue to "the end of the earth." Having a wild driver nearly ran us off a cliff, and helping a car owner repair his vehicle, were just two parts of this adventure. There is more, much more, that you will read in this account.

Our Patagonian Adventure began on November 27, 1971, when I laced on my Vietnam combat boots, grabbed my backpack, and drove from Montana to meet Danelle and Bill in Lubbock, Texas. From there we headed to Mexico in Bill's van. In a peculiar way, my boots and boot strings tie this journey together. My feet are too big for Latin American shoes, so I relied on my sturdy jungle boots for traveling and hiking. I made a pair of sandals in Guatemala, but they were not usable during our travels in the cold Andes and in Patagonia.

We explored various pre-Columbian archaeological sites including Tula, with its majestic 15-foot-tall Toltec Warrior Columns, the ancient ruins of Teotihuacán near Mexico City, and Monte Albán in Oaxaca. These complexes were built hundreds of years before the arrival of the Aztecs.

We had a great desire to see the Pacific Ocean, so we traveled to the village of Puerto Angel. Bill parked along a gravel road near the ocean, and we unrolled our sleeping bags on the beach. The next morning, we found thieves had broken into the van and stole all our belongings except for my combat boots. Fortunately, we had our sleeping bags, the clothes we wore to the beach, money, toothbrushes, a few personal items, and our passports with us on the beach.

Pre-Aztec Toltec Warrior Columns

Bill returned to California with mechanical troubles, but Danelle and I continued our journey hitchhiking east across Mexico to explore Mayan ruins in Mexico and Guatemala. We caught a ride with two Mexican students driving a VW Beetle and told them we were heading to Belize. They said they too would like to visit Belize, and we headed to the Mexico-Belize border. When we arrived, the Belize customs official told the students he would not let them enter the country and would not explain why. Then he told me to put my luggage on the table for examination. I placed a small cloth flour sack with a few personal items and my rolled-up sleeping bag on the table. The official asked, "Is that all you have?" I answered yes, and he said he was not going to let me in his country.

Angrily, I raised my voice, even yelled. "Mexican bandits robbed me, and this is all I have left," I said. "I was an officer in the US Army and served in the Vietnam War, and I can't believe you won't let me visit your country." He asked to verify that I served in Vietnam, and then asked for my passport and went to the back room. When he returned, he handed my passport back with a five-day visa—enough time to travel across Belize.

The same guard then hassled Danelle because of small bones decorating the front of her dress. She said she was a teacher. Eventually, he also gave her a five-day visa. He was glad to get rid of us. We said goodbye to the students and took a bus to Belize City where we spent the night in a budget hotel.

It is interesting to note the city's location on the Caribbean coast makes it vulnerable to hurricanes, storm surges, and flooding, so many of the buildings were raised on poles to keep them above the flood plain.

The next day we headed via bus to Guatemala and passed through Belmopan, Belize's new capital city. It had only been founded the year before.

In a thick jungle near the Guatemalan border, we came to a bridge and arranged for a boat driver to take us upriver to visit a young man Danelle had known in college. It was raining as we motored to a muddy landing along the river's edge. The boat driver told us to follow the cattle trail; he said it would lead us to the farm. We were anxious to locate the house before dark because we didn't have a flashlight.

Danelle's friend and his family did not know we were coming and, obviously, were surprised to see us. They graciously invited us in and visited for a while but told us they did not have a place for us to stay. They asked us to go with a boy who came to take us by boat across the river to his home. His family provided us with friendship, dry clothes, and a room. We stayed overnight, then returned to the bridge and bused to the border.

We walked across the border to Guatemala and hitchhiked to the magnificent Mayan Tikal ruins, one of the largest archaeological pre-Columbian centers in the Americas. We were surprised to see the enormity of this ancient jungle-shrouded complex and its tree-topping pyramids.

In a roadside *tienda* (store) near Tikal, I bought a small notebook to use as a journal. I had experience writing a journal during my service in the Vietnam War and wanted to record this journey. (My illustrated Vietnam journal is published by Sunstone Press in Santa Fe, New Mexico: *A Vietnam Journal—Life at the End of the War*.)

Danelle began her journal a little more than a year later when we departed Buenos Aires, Argentina for Chile on December 21, 1972. (You will read more about this in her preface to this book.) Interestingly, her handwriting is minuscule; she squeezed three lines of writing between each ruled line of her notebook. A page of her handwritten journal can be seen in the photo section of this book. Her journal entries in this book are clearly noted and add to the texture of our stories.

We hope you enjoy—and get to live, just a bit—this Patagonian Adventure with us.

Drawings, illustrations, maps, and photographs in this book are by Terrance Brown, FAIA. Charles "Chuck" Eilers provided the photos of our group traveling on the Inca Trail and Machu Pichu. John Buster provided photos of Terry and Danelle in Buenos Aires, Argentina.

—Terrance "Terry" Brown, FAIA

Danelle's Preface

While Terry was in the Vietnam War, I was serving in the US Peace Corps in the village of Los Olivos, province of Los Santos, in Panamá. After my two-year stint, I planned to travel through South America before returning to the US, so I left Panamá and went to Colombia to begin the journey. However, I learned that my brother Dan was going to get married, and I returned to attend his wedding, held in Arizona.

After a month or two in the US, I contacted Terry, who had completed his tour of duty in Vietnam, and suggested he travel with me to South America by land. Both he and Bill M., a friend with whom I had traveled from Greece to Germany, decided to go. Bill eventually returned home from Southern Mexico while Terry and I continued to Guatemala.

In the *pensión* (inn) where we stayed in Guatemala City, I met Juana, a Native Mayan woman who had just given birth to her son Carlitos. She had severe breast inflammation and had to get medical help in the hospital, so I offered to move into her room in the inn and take care of the baby until Juana returned. A social worker, a woman, came from the hospital, got my information, and had me sign a guardianship form saying I would be responsible for the baby if Juana passed away. I already loved Carlitos and did not mind signing this form at all. Several people living in the pensión would help me if needed. All went well. Juana returned and asked me and another friend in the inn to be godparents/ sponsors at the baby's baptism.

Not long after the baptism, I contracted typhoid fever and spent some time in a hospital. After I left Guatemala, I did not see Juana or Carlitos again for three years.

During the time I was helping Juana, Terry had studied Spanish in Antigua and continued traveling to Panamá and across South America to Argentina, where he got a job with an architect in Buenos Aires.

I made my way to Nicaragua to visit a Peace Corps friend named Barbara who was serving in an isolated mountain village. For a while I helped her with adult literacy lessons she was conducting. She once told me that in the US boys never asked her to dance. However, in Nicaragua I saw that when she walked through the village in the evening, anyone who had a musical instrument would grab it and throw a party in someone's front room so that all the single guys would have a chance to dance with Barbara. She eventually chose the most handsome man, but she wanted to see Perú before the wedding. She later met me in Quito, Ecuador, and we traveled to Perú by hitchhiking, bus, train, or—this is common in the Andes Mountains—in the back of trucks.

I was sick the day we planned to travel from Cuzco to Machu Picchu. Barbara reminded me that I might never get another chance to see those ancient Inca ruins, so I went with her. After arriving in Machu Picchu, Barbara went to get a room in the inn for herself. I walked a short distance up the Inca Trail from the main ruins, slept in my sleeping bag on the ground, and woke up the next morning on my 27th birthday. I honestly thought I would never live to see my 30th. As of now, while I write for this book, I have made it to 78 years of age.

After recuperating for a while in Cuzco on a diet of chocolate-and-nut candy bars, I continued alone through Bolivia and Northern Argentina to Buenos Aires where I found Terry. A short distance away from where he worked in downtown B.A., I found a makeshift room on the roof of an old hotel which I rented for less than fifteen dollars a month. I loved living there in what one might call a mini slum in the heart of the city on one of its most fashionable streets. I would go to the artisans' market in the park once a week and sell enough of my beadwork to buy a loaf of bread.

I became acquainted with several truly kind and interesting people, including the daughter of a surgeon who asked her father to take care of me when I began to have pains in my abdomen. The timely surgery he did for me repaired an inguinal hernia and removed my appendix, which was on the verge of rupturing. After that, Terry and his Argentine friend, Marta, who was shocked by my living conditions, rescued me from my beloved slum.

Along with Terry, Marta drove me to Terry's lovely *pension*, Hotel Victory, in the suburbs, where I recuperated until I was ready to travel to Tierra del Fuego. I began my journal when Terry and I departed Buenos Aires and set out for our epic journey to Tierra del Fuego and then back to Buenos Aires.

—Danelle Crowley

Danelle's entries will be labeled "DC"
and Terry's entries will be unlabeled.

Terry departs Montana
sidney, montana
UNITED STATES
Lubbock
Terry joins Danelle in Lubbock, TX and travel to Guatemala
MEXICO
HONDURAS
GUATEMALA
EL SALVADOR
NICARAGUA
COSTA RICA
PANAMA
VENEZUELA
Danelle's travels in Brasil
Terry and Danelle traveled independently from Guatemala to Buenos Aires, Argentina
COLUMBIA
ECUADOR
Terry flys back to Guatemala
PERU
BRAZIL
brasilia
BOLIVIA
PARAGUAY
CHILE
N
NW
NE
W
E
SW
SE
S
URUGUAY
ARGENTINA
Buenos Aires
Santiago Chile
Terry and Danelle's journals record their travels in Patagonia
ROUTE OF TRAVEL
CHILE
Ushuaia-tierra del fuego

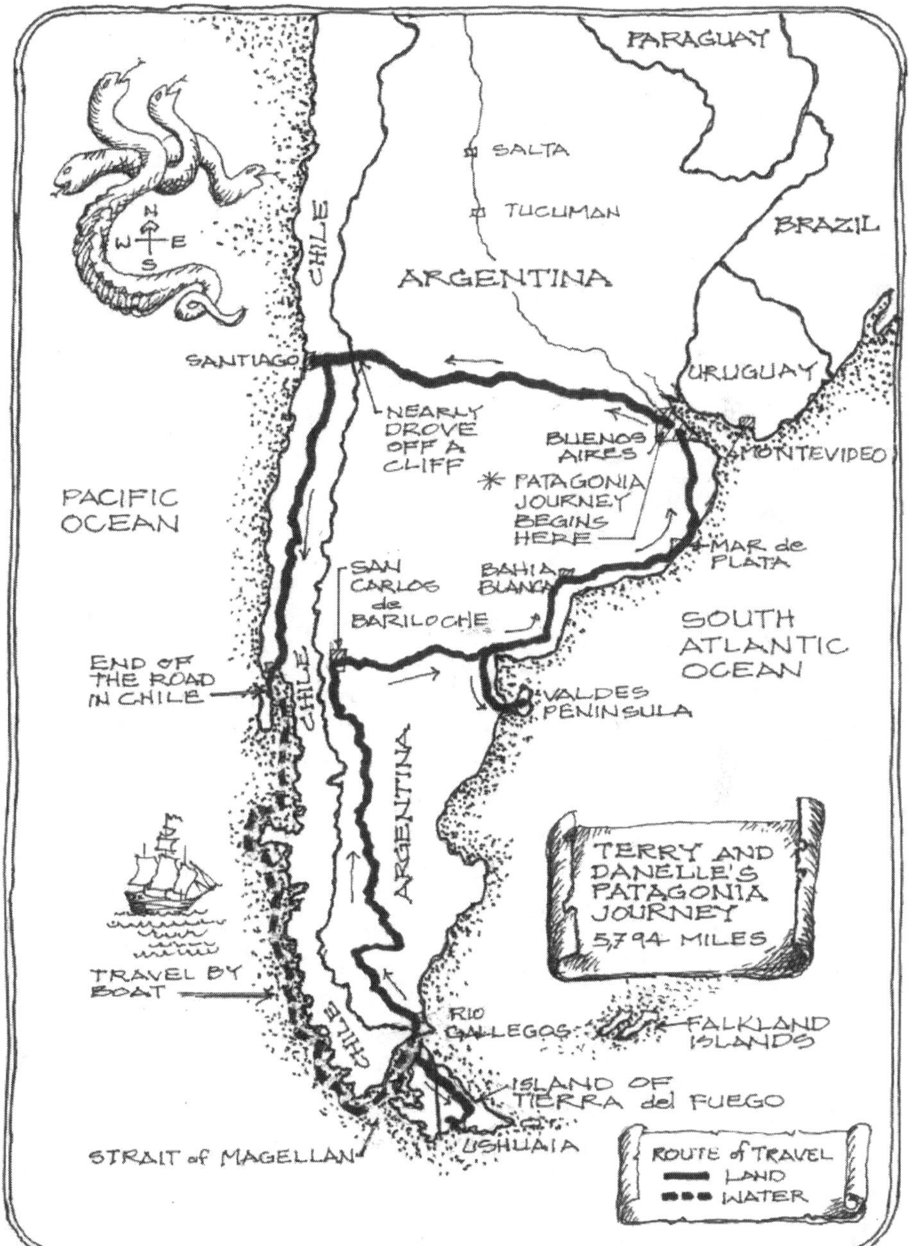
PARAGUAY
SALTA
TUCUMAN
BRAZIL
CHILE
ARGENTINA
SANTIAGO
URUGUAY
NEARLY DROVE OFF A CLIFF
BUENOS AIRES
MONTEVIDEO
PACIFIC OCEAN
PATAGONIA JOURNEY BEGINS HERE
MAR de PLATA
SAN CARLOS de BARILOCHE
BAHIA BLANCA
SOUTH ATLANTIC OCEAN
END OF THE ROAD IN CHILE
CHILE
VALDES PENINSULA
ARGENTINA
TERRY AND DANELLE'S PATAGONIA JOURNEY
5,794 MILES
TRAVEL BY BOAT
RIO GALLEGOS
FALKLAND ISLANDS
CHILE
ISLAND OF TIERRA del FUEGO
STRAIT of MAGELLAN
USHUAIA
ROUTE of TRAVEL
LAND
WATER
N
S
E
W

A Patagonia Adventure

The journals of Terrance (Terry) Brown and Danelle Crowley's travels through Central and South America

Terry's Journal:

PETEN JUNGLE, GUATEMALA - JANUARY 20, 1972

Our journey across Mexico to Guatemala has been stimulating. Danelle and I have been hitchhiking whenever possible; but sometimes the long wait for a ride and rainy weather force us to buy a ticket on a bouncing, rattly, "chicken bus" (bus that allows people on with chickens and other small animals).

The road through the Petén jungle of Guatemala is jarring, full of ruts; and, in places, only wide enough for one vehicle. The jungle brings back memories of my service in the Vietnam war. The Native Mayans in the jungle live close to the dusty artery in handsome, thatched-roof houses with walls of thin poles standing on end. Pigs are not only their necessity of life but constant companions along with chickens, ducks, and especially dogs. Every man who goes into the jungle to hunt or clear his fields travels with his machete and favorite dog.

The night before Danelle and I went to see the Mayan ruins of Tikal, we slept in an Esso gas station at the road intersection. The floor was covered with diesel fuel; so, Danelle slept on large sheets of cardboard, and I slept on the narrow countertop. I hoped that I would not sleep too soundly and roll off in a stupor. I did not sleep well.

We caught a ride to the ruins with three Spanish priests the next morning and spent the rest of the day climbing up and around those towering ancient structures. Unfortunately, it was raining off and on and dampened our spirits. The views from the tops of the pyramids, looming high over the tops of the jungle, were most impressive and beautiful. The ancient Mayan priests must have labored in their ornate costumes climbing the steep stairs to the top of Temple I.

After touring the ruins and small museum, the priests took us back over the bumpy road to the nearest town where we slept on a stone floor for fifty cents apiece for the night.

Today we made it through the jungle by hitchhiking and bus. Along the way we saw the Guatemalan army traveling the road and checking identification and personal belongings in hopes of putting a squeeze on the Communist guerrillas in the mountains. We were told that a guerrilla gang machine-gunned a truck full of National Army troops on the same road we came on. I felt like I was back in Vietnam.

Today, I saw a dog swim about sixty yards to the middle of a river and back. He must have been one hell of a strong dog.

We are about 150 kms from Guatemala City, so with any luck at all we should be able to hitch there in the morning. As I am writing this, a group of teenagers are all looking to see what the "stranger" is doing. I am the biggest attraction since the last bus to "the city" came through. When the bus stops, all the little girls and their mothers rush up to the sides of the bus offering to sell their snacks and food, usually consisting of boiled eggs, tortillas, and peppery sauce.

One of the ladies is letting us sleep under her porch roof beside her shack. She is the second person to offer us her house or her yard to sleep in. These people are uniquely beautiful.

ON THE ROAD THROUGH THE PETEN JUNGLE - JAN. 21, 1972

I did not sleep well here either. Dogs were barking at the pigs, and the pigs were rooting around my sleeping bag. Adding to the confusion were the odd passersby in cars and trucks who stopped to buy a snack.

GUATEMALA CITY - JAN. 23, 1972

We found a cheap pensión (inn) which charged $1.00 a day including three meals. This was when I was introduced to cilantro in my soup, and I did not like it.

ANTIGUA, GUATEMALA - JAN. 26, 1972

I ate my first french-fried bananas today, and they were delicious. They were sliced very thin and fried green, which made them crisp like potato chips.

I decided to stay in Antigua for a month and study Spanish in a linguistic school called Proyecto Lingüístico Francisco Marroquín (PLFM). It will cost $250 for the month's course. It is highly concentrated: 5 days a week, 7 hours a day of study. I will also be living with the Okrassa family in the central part of Antigua, which will add to the total immersion into Spanish. A single Guatemalan teacher will be my instructor, and I will have a different teacher each week. I am looking forward to learning a second language, so I can converse with all the beautiful people I have been meeting. It is difficult to imagine traveling for a year or more in Central and South America and not being able to speak Spanish.

This drawing was done from Cerro de La Cruz (Cross on the Hill) which provides a suburb view of Antigua, a small city nestled in a valley surrounded by three towering volcanos named Agua (Water), Fuego (Fire) and Acatenango (Hill of Reeds). It served as the Spanish Capital of Central America. Many of the buildings have been restored following a 1773 earthquake that ended its 200-year reign as the Spanish Colonial Capital. Earthquake-ruined churches are found throughout town and serve as a reminder of future quakes. Most of the buildings have thick adobe walls punctuated by Spanish Colonial protective steel bars.

PANAJACHEL, GUATEMALA - JAN. 28, 1972

The Peace Corps volunteers that we have been meeting have been the most hospitable and friendly people Danelle and I have ever met. We have been total strangers; and yet they took us in, fed us, and offered us their surroundings as if we were family.

I have just finished polishing off a 50-cent meal that was one of the best I have ever eaten, at least for the money. "Mama" Leonora is the cook, and she is "world famous." Everyone we talked to who has eaten here told us about the delicious "all you can eat" meals. To a traveler on a $1.00-a-day budget, this is music to my ears. We had steak and sauce, fried potatoes, boiled carrots, another vegetable, tortillas, and a dessert of orange slices and bananas. A genuinely great meal!

Today Carol, Danelle, and I hitched up to a small village high above Lake Atitlan called Sololá, where Native Mayans, in their very colorful traditional clothing, come to sell their goods. The women carry jugs of water and large baskets of goods balanced on their heads. Their long black hair is braided with long bright strips of cloth woven within the braids and wrapped around their heads forming a broad brim. The women wear very intricate, colorful, hand-woven blouses called "huipils" which are tucked into full-length, heavy skirts wrapped around their waists and tied with a long sash. The men wear equally colorful clothes; but their striped pants are knee-length, loose around the legs and embroidered with small birds. They also wear an apron and a wool jacket. The girls dress like their mothers, the boys like their fathers, and everybody looks like everyone else.

This village called Panajachel, is surrounded by three beautiful volcanos and rests on the shore of one of the most impressive, clear-water lakes in the world. Two cheap places to stay in Panajachel are La Tienda Miniatura (Miniature Store), which charges fifty cents per night, and Casa de Viajero (Traveler House), which charges $1.00. The best of the two is La Tienda Miniatura and is on the main road through town. It looked like a decent place with a nice patio on the interior. All reports say it is the best for the money.

We bathed in the hot springs along the lake's edge today. It was very refreshing.

CHICHICASTENANGO - FEB. 29, 1972

We are staying in a hotel for $1.25 apiece which is not bad for a tourist town. We ate a meal for 15 cents tonight consisting of rice, refried beans, and a hunk of stewed beef. I had to eat two orders to fill up.

We had good luck hitching today. It only took two rides to get here from Panajachel. Both were with Americans. The second ride was with a Church of Christ missionary who told us about this place we are staying in. Tomorrow morning, we will visit the colorful market and hitch back to Antigua.

ANTIGUA - FEB. 28, 1972

This past weekend, five of us Americans and five British volunteers, all students in the Proyecto, climbed Volcán de Agua (Water Volcano) on the outskirts of Antigua. We slept on the rim of the crater which gave us a ring-side seat for an astonishing view of the country at sunrise. The climb up was sheer misery and took six hours to reach the top; but the minute I looked out over the world and was able to see both oceans, I knew it was worth it. It took two and a half to three hours to climb down. When I returned to Antigua, I was one tired man with a contented look on my face. Life in the land of the sleeping giants (volcanos) is a wonderful experience.

ANTIGUA - MAR. 8, 1972

I find a special place in my heart for the Mayan people of Guatemala, much as I do for the Native Americans I grew up with in Montana. It is amazing that these beautiful people have been able to keep their centuries-old costumes and customs. God only knows how they survived the Spanish conquest and Inquisition. Their spiritual and physical strength is overwhelming. They smile with their eyes. When you look in their eyes, you know they are seeing you for what you are and not for what you look like. We have a great deal to learn from these wonderful people.

I have been busy with my own little projects. I have been successful in getting four people interested in making articles out of leather. I am helping a teenage boy cut out the design for a pouch this evening. It is a warm feeling to watch people get into a new hobby; and it is great to be able to say, "I made this with my own hands."

It is becoming easier to speak Spanish and talk to my family with short sentences. It is nice. I am getting too settled here with three square meals a day. That will make it difficult to leave after I complete my language lessons.

ANTIGUA - MAR. 13, 1972

The cats are fighting on the corrugated metal roof, and it sounds horrible. They make such a racket screaming, running, sliding, and smashing against the thin metal roof. It hardly seems possible either of them will come out alive. This happens at least once a week. Sometimes they are at it so ferociously that we cannot even talk and be heard above the racket.

I saw a Mayan girl walking down the street today with her family. She was carrying a large iguana held tightly against her breast. Kind of a strange sight!

ON THE BORDER OF GUATEMALA AND EL SALVADOR - APR. 4, 1972

Yesterday I said goodbye to my friends in Antigua and headed for El Salvador in a VW Minibus owned by friends Derek and Hjordis W. from Canada. They invited me to travel across Central America to Panama with them. I had met them in Mexico City. Later they looked me up in Antigua and studied Spanish for ten days.

As one of my friends said, "Travel adds appreciation of home and appreciation of where you've been when you get home." I have been thinking about home lately; I would like to be there, but I know that traveling to South America must come first. Staying planted in Antigua for two months, after traveling hard in Mexico and in Belize for two months to get here, added to my longing to return home. I almost let my feet get planted again. Now they have been ripped out of the ground and I am on the road for Panama.

We are waiting at the El Salvador border because Derek had to go back to Guatemala City to get the papers on his VW Minivan extended. He tried to exit Guatemala two days over the allowed 30 days. It was either pay a $50 fine at the border or travel by bus back to Guatemala City to get his paperwork for free. That was an easy decision. Hjordis and I are patiently waiting for Derek's return. The border guards let me sleep in their bunkhouse, and Hjordis is sleeping in the van. One

of the young border guards drew this portrait of me and I illustrated the border. It's a good likeness.

It is hot and uncomfortable here and difficult to get used to after the wonderful cool days of Antigua. Danelle is in Panama now and is in no hurry to leave. She has a lot of old US Peace Corps friends to catch up with. I am going to take it easy traveling through Central America. It is possible that she and I will go to Colombia together if her timing is right. I am eager to get there.

I spent my last 4 days in Guatemala at Lake Atitlan, one of the most beautiful lakes in the world. I traveled there with a wonderful young lady named Bonnie, whom I had met at the PLFM. We had a wonderful time together. It was a beautiful feeling to swim in such a beautiful clean lake surrounded by volcanos. It is a rare treat to swim someplace where neither salt, pollution, nor chlorine burns your eyes.

As I think back over my stay in Antigua, I can vividly remember hundreds of events, different fruits, colonial churches, cobblestone streets, and volcanoes ringing the town which all impress me. When I first went to live with the Okrassa family, I could not say anything in Spanish to them; so, I usually sat quietly eating with Grandfather Don Roberto Okrassa as we ate our dinner, usually in the dining room. Whenever he was not there, I ate alone. At one point I counted fifty-seven spoonful of bean soup which I tediously spooned into my mouth. It was tasty but watery. We had a variety of interesting food, especially at lunch, often served with vegetables, soup, and fresh fruit juice. For breakfast, I had black beans, bread, one egg, coffee, and sometimes orange juice. Supper was always beans, rice, and bread. Occasionally I fried bananas or chochos (sweet tamales). During my second month I always ate in the kitchen while Elena cooked, which was comforting because I was not eating alone. I could practice my Spanish and learn more about the family.

Don Roberto does not live in the house but is provided his meals with me at noon. He is 69 years old and plays a stringed instrument he calls a "sitara," which appears to be a zither. It has over thirty strings and he uses all his fingers to play beautiful music. He is the son of a German immigrant who obtained a huge trunk of hardwood years ago and fashioned the large living-room table we eat on. The table and chairs are carved and finished by hand. A photo of this old man is framed in a fancy, hand-carved picture frame. He also built and patented the coffee bean separator, grinder, and toaster in the back of the house. It is a beautiful machine run by leather belts from a gasoline-powered motor. The original motor was steam driven. Elena

said the coffee equipment is maintained by her 30-year-old alcoholic brother, Roberto.

The Okrassa house is simply furnished with handmade furniture and unique in its appearance. Everything in it appears to be handmade and antique, including the ancient coffee separator and coffee grinder. Elena cooks on a gas stove or charcoal burner while her husband, Antonio, is out in his VW Safari traveling around the country selling tractors. Elena will have a baby in about a month.

What I found most interesting about the house is that it was previously a large house with broad open patios. Now the house and patios are divided in two equal parts by a heavy masonry wall. Different family members share each side.

Maurina is the 15-year-old house cleaner and helper who makes $8.00 a month and works her butt off. Her room and board are free. Lyncho is an older man who lives somewhere in the house and works on anything needing repair or helps with the coffee grinding and separating. He is a good man. I have not been able to figure out where he sleeps, I think somewhere with the coffee separator. He always gets up when I do. I see him with his tousled hair washing his face in the large water tank where chilly water is drawn for washing bodies, clothes, and dishes.

The shower compartment I was instructed to use was open to the sky and only had icy water. I normally waited until the sun was directly overhead to make the space a little warmer before I showered.

The Easter processions along the cobblestone streets of Antigua are magnificent Catholic religious events. A statue of Christ carrying a cross is supported on a massive wood base and is supported on the shoulders of men dressed in long purple robes. The men walk rhythmically through the streets of Antigua for 12 hours. These parades are always a big event for "my family." These huge floats are so heavy that it requires eighty men to carry them. They pay about $2.00 for the privilege of carrying the "weight of Jesus" for one block, then switch carriers. For Easter, there was a team of more than 2,000 men who carried the float at various times. At nighttime, the float looks like a huge ship sailing slowly on the shoulders of the crowd, clouded in incense as it passes down the narrow cobblestone streets. And suddenly there is "the Electric Jesus," all aglow with neon lights powered by a noisy gasoline generator. The generator noise competes for volume with the funeral band walking behind the float. The generator is pulled by hand behind. Jesus is paraded through the streets repeatedly every Sunday in March until the last momentous day of his judgement, that of Easter Day. Thousands flock to see this. Families spend all night making grand, ornate, multicolored carpets in the street with dyed sawdust. At times they also use flowers for decorations. The carpet is obliterated by the shuffling feet of the float carriers as the float passes over the beautiful carpet. Families of lesser wealth simply cover the streets in front of their house with pine needles bought to town by Native Mayans, or they simply sprinkle the street with water.

LAKE COATEPEQUE, EL SALVADOR - APR. 5, 1972

We drove forty-six miles today and wound up at the edge of Lake Coatepeque. It is a beautiful crater lake where one can see the bottom. It was a sweltering day, and the water was therapeutic both to the body and the mind. We talked to the caretaker of the El Salvador Automobile Association Recreation Club on the edge of the lake. He is letting us camp here tonight at no charge. We are the only ones here. He says members usually arrive on the weekends. A beautiful day!

EL TRIUNFO, HONDURAS - APR. 8, 1972

I feel like I am in an inferno. We are staying the weekend at a friend's place to not have to pay exorbitant prices which are raised on weekends at the border. The people we are staying with are an English Peace Corps volunteer and his Jamaican wife. He is teaching agriculture to the natives: mostly how to improve their crops. The heat builds to a high peak in Central America with its high around the time of Semana Santa (Easter week) until the monsoons begin in May.

As I think back over the linguistic school at Antigua, I only find favorable comments. Where else can one study Spanish 7 hours a day, 5 days a week, with a one-teacher to one-student ratio. They also offer instruction in English and the Mayan languages of Guatemala including Mam, Quiche, and Cakchiquel. The Proyecto Lingüístico

Francisco Marroquín is also doing unique, independent research on Indigenous Mayan languages.

PALMARES, COSTA RICA - APR. 11, 1972

When I last wrote, I was staying the weekend at a friend's place in Honduras until Monday. On Monday we tried to cross into Nicaragua on the new Pan American Highway, but they would only let pedestrians across, not cars. They said we might be able to cross in two months. So, we had to double around and enter "Nickers" at another border station where we expected a fleecing like we got when we left El Salvador and entered Honduras. To our surprise, they did not charge us a penny.

Managua, the capitol of Nicaragua, could have been a bummer because the friend we had met in Guatemala could not be located anywhere; and we really had no place to stay. As it turned out, a wonderful lady in the British Embassy invited us to her house for the evening and gave us spare beds for the night. Her name was Meekle (Minks)

Bowie. She said she was fifty, but I thought she looked about forty or in her late thirties. She had five grown children, was a grandmother and was quite a lady. It is hard to find someone as trusting and hospitable to strangers as she was. She made us completely at home in her house and kept pouring us wonderful rum and cokes. She was from Jamaica but had lived in "Nickers" most of her life. A genuinely good person!

Today, we crossed into Costa Rica at what I thought was the most efficient border yet. We are camping beside a boulder-lined, clear-water river tonight. Tomorrow we will head for the capital for business at the embassies. I must buy malaria tablets in preparation of traveling

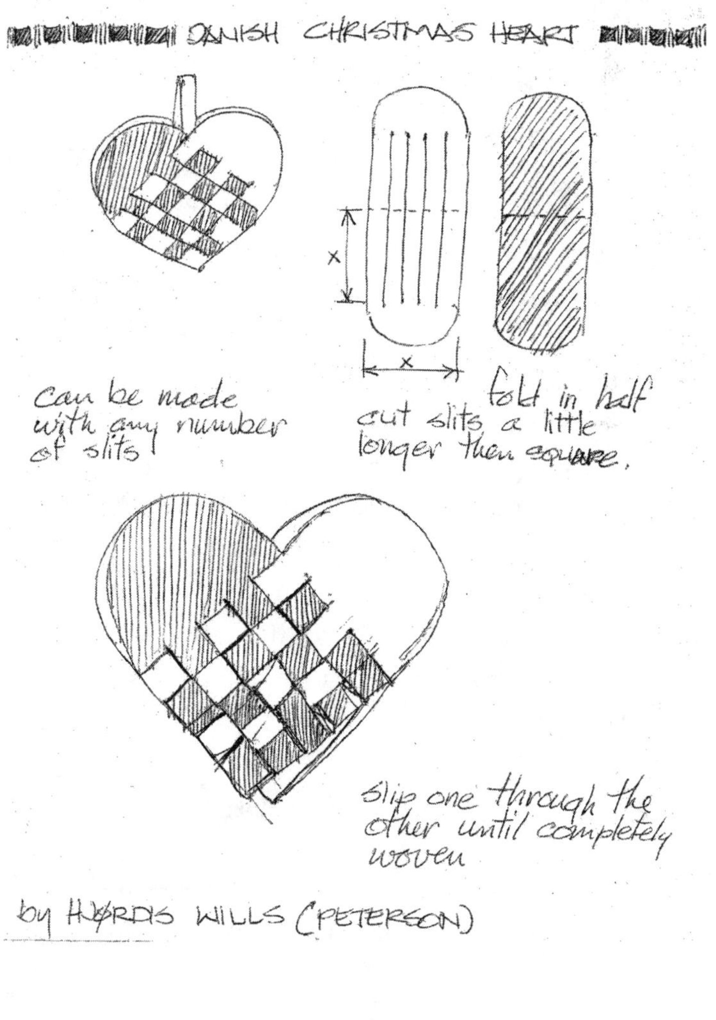

in Panama. The sky is still mostly clear as darkness descends, but I am watching a large white cloud, with brilliant lightning inside it, grow ever larger on the other side of the river.

The most challenging section of the Pan-American Highway is in Costa Rica and has the ominous name Cerro de la Muerte (Summit of Death). At 10,942 ft. it marks the highest elevation on the highway.

Hjordis cooked a modest meal tonight consisting of rice, tomatoes, eggplant, and eggs. It sure was good. We had delicious slices of fresh pineapple for dessert. I hope it does not rain on me tonight. While we ate, Hjordis showed me how people in Denmark made a simple Christmas decoration.

SAN JOSE, COSTA RICA - APR. 12, 1972

Living fence posts seem to be the norm in Costa Rica. The farmers jamb tree limbs or small tree trunks in the ground as you would with any other fencepost, except these limbs spout branches and grow into trees. That is a strange sight for a man who grew up on the Western prairies of the USA where fenceposts often rotted at the base and fell over.

The terrain and climate change rapidly as we travel across these small and varying Central American countries. Last night I went to sleep hot, sweaty, and fighting mosquitos. Tonight, I must wrap my sleeping bag in a plastic sheet and sleep with my clothes on to keep warm.

As we traveled through Honduras and "Nickers," we constantly saw beautiful trees blooming brilliant yellow flowers. They were completely covered with flowers leaving no visible green leaves. They perked up the view of the arid countryside.

ABOUT 20 MILES FROM THE BORDER OF PANAMA - APR. 13, 1972

I am sitting in the front seat of our minivan reading and writing while Derek and his wife are "sacked out" in the bed. They usually nap a little after they eat and get up later to write in their journals and have a cup of tea. A little on the English side there!

I have been trying to finish a fascinating and thought-provoking book called *Future Shock* by Alvin Toffler. He discusses change, what happens to people when they change, and how they do or do not adapt to change.

It has taken us about nine hours to travel two hundred miles today. The road was terrible with alternating sections of paving and gravel. We had to drive over huge, rough rock which I thought for sure was going to tear the tires apart. In places the jungle threatened to grow over the road. Landslides were a common scene where the road had dropped away or sunk. This is the sad state of the Nicaraguan section of the Pan American Highway. We passed through the rainforests where trees are constantly bathed in moist clouds and enveloped with moss and parasitic growth.

Costa Rica's mountainous terrain appears comparable to Switzerland's deep green valleys and mountain beauty. Unfortunately, the people here are too poor to build large, beautiful houses such as those seen dotting Swiss countryside. The rough roads made it difficult for me to observe the immense beauty of the country. We were so jostled that my insides felt they were being jarred loose. Nevertheless, the "Alps of Costa Rica" are a striking sight.

It's raining now, so I don't know what I will do about sleeping. I was going to wrap myself in a plastic sheet; but if the rain keeps up, I may curl up on the floor under the bed in the van.

SANTA CLARA, PANAMA - APR. 14, 1972

We are spending an evening on the beach of Santa Clara, and that's where the fun began. I was strolling along the beach and saw two girls coming out of the water. Oddly, they were swimming with their clothes on. As I passed, one said, "My hands are wet. Will you roll a joint for us?" I, thinking it would be enjoyable to hang out with the girls, ignorantly agreed. We sat down in the sand, and one of the girls handed me a small cloth sack of grass and papers. As I am rolling the joint, she said she better put the bag in her purse because her "old man" might be around and that he was a narcotics officer. I handed her the joint after I finish rolling it, and I see some guy walking towards us at a fast clip. My mind flashed "HER FATHER;" and he was upon me with his fist doubled saying, "What did you hand her?" Before I could answer, as if he thought I was going to tell him, he hit me on the side of the head saying, "Get the hell out of here," in so many words or less. I took off running along the beach. My feet were really spinning, and I ran a long way before I looked back.

So, there I was, exiled, not knowing what to think except how stupid I was for getting myself into such an irresponsible situation which could have turned out terrible. I waited for an hour before I made my way back to the van under the shadow of darkness. When I got back, Hjordis had supper ready, and they were almost finished eating. It was good to find no one waiting for me, such as police officers or the Army, or even the "old man."

I was utterly amazed at seeing Panama for the first time. I had expected lush jungle covering the countryside, but it was dry, ranch land much the same as the semi-arid ranch lands of the American West. The highway was all smooth concrete and a beautiful change from Costa Rica's miserable road system. Sleeping in the jungle last night got my sleeping bag sopping wet, but it dried out well. I hung it over the guard rail of a nearby bridge built with USA money, as were all the bridges we crossed in Panama and Costa Rica.

I finished reading *Future Shock* by Alvin Toffler, and in one bold statement he says:

> By now, the accelerative thrust triggered by man has become the key to the entire evolutionary process on the planet. The rate and direction of the evolution of other species, their survival, depends upon decisions made by man. Yet, there is nothing inherent in the evolutionary processes to guarantee man's own survival.

He also brings out the point that man must anticipate and design the future instead of rising in revolt against it. He says, and I agree, that our present school systems are organized and run on the level of the old industrial revolution and not for the fast, ever-changing society of today or tomorrow. There are going to have to be some broad changes soon or everything and everyone will burst at the seams.

Derek just figured out that we've been spending $1.70 a day apiece for food and gas for the two weeks it has taken us to get to Panama City. That's about $18.00 apiece for the 2-week's travel from Guatemala. We've been eating two good meals a day on that. Pretty darned good!

PANAMA CITY - APR. 20, 1972

Panama City is an attractive city and exciting one. It isn't as beautiful as cities like Paris or downtown Mexico City, but its total beauty is exceptional. This tropical city curves gracefully around a bay dotted by anchored fishing boats.

The "Bridge of the World" and the Panama Canal are fascinating. They are among worldly sites which I have always read about but never thought I would get the chance to see. The Canal Zone is five miles wide on both sides of the canal, and is fenced, but the jungle in those fenced strips has not been denuded. I had an enjoyable time hiking along a trail through the luscious jungle growth. It was pleasant to be able to walk through the jungle and not have to worry, like I did in Vietnam, if my foot was going to be blown off.

As I entered Panama City, I could not help but be amazed at the banks and ritzy buildings on one side of the street and old French Quarter slums on the other. I've never seen so many shoes and shoe stores in my life, not to mention the camera shops selling duty-free cameras and stereo equipment. On the outside of these flashy dream stores are your hucksters shoving stolen wrist watches and whispering that they have hot cameras for sale. Just think, a $195 camera for $75. Pretty tempting!

A guy in front of a camera store offered the same to me yesterday as I walked out of the store. I saw him today while I was downtown with a friend named Jim S. We decided to try it. He said we'll go in his taxi about 5 or 10 minutes away. We followed him to a side street and climbed into the back of an old Chevrolet. The huckster and another guy climbed into the front, and we were off. At that point I was beginning to feel foolish and unsure of doing this. I tried to open my door handle but horrors! It just spun around, and there I sat with a million things going through my mind and $275 in cash in my pocket. I motioned to Jim to try his door handle, and we were in luck. It worked, and we were out of the car in a flash when the driver stopped at a stop sign. We had ridden three blocks, and I told the guy the deal was off.

He said we'd have to pay $2.00 for the car ride. We refused and started walking off in the rain back to where we started, and here comes the guy waving a 3-foot-long, 2 x 4 board. He was hollering for a police officer, and so were we. I thought I heard him call the police officer by his first name. The police officer said, after hearing both sides of the story, that we were in a special taxi; and it was his prerogative to charge more. We argued, and the guy said $1.00. We called him a crook and worse but gave him the dollar to get out of there. The police officer said no, we couldn't go yet, and that he had to talk to his jefe (boss), who said the same thing as the other police officer but said we could go.

It was a scary experience, and I'm sure relieved I didn't go through with it. If nothing else, who knows what he would have charged us for a 10-minute ride in his taxi, not to mention what else I could have lost. It seems that Panama is quite the place for excitement, at least for me. This is an exotic place.

IN ROUTE TO BOGOTÁ - APR. 22, 1972

Well, I'm finally in South America taking a 15-hour bus ride (for $3.25) from Medellin to Bogota. As soon as I arrived in Medellin, I had my passport and shot record stolen out of my pouch but no money. Everyone knows how bad the thieves in Colombia are, but I never really thought they would get me so soon. I had thought my pouch looked empty. It was.

While in Panama City, I had resided at the Hippodrome, a sports park built for the Pan American games a few years back. Lots of travelers stay there, and some have even been there a month sleeping under the tin roofs put up around the parking lot. I lived on the band stage with thirteen other people. We could leave our possessions there, and no one would touch them. It was quite an experience to meet people traveling in all directions. There was a father and teenage son traveling with two monkeys and some snakes in an old army first-aid truck. They were from Uruguay and had been on the road for two years.

They had traveled all the way to New York and Canada. Then there was the ex-Air Force Captain who was going to South America in his van, as well as others who shipped their vans to a port in Colombia and flew to meet them.

The missionary came wheeling in with long white hair and beard. He had four kids with him and his wife. They were living in a huge bourgeois camper on the back of the truck. The whole family would dress up in their long white robes and walk around together handing out leaflets and trying to get people to believe in whatever religion they espoused.

There were people waiting to go to England or Australia. Some people wanted to sell their beloved motorcycles or vans to get to South America.

BOGOTÁ, COLOMBIA - APR. 23, 1972

I arrived at 2:00 AM after a long, freezing, churning bus ride. I felt like I was riding in the back of a vehicle taking me to a Siberian Prison Camp. I don't feel completely safe because I've heard thievery is ramped up here, so one never knows when he will be hit.

Three young women on the bus helped me get a taxi and took me to a safer hotel than what was available around the bus station. They were very nice people. I feel a great deal better this morning.

Just before I left yesterday, I sold one of my sleeping bags for $10 to a girl who needed one. I had a tough time deciding to do it until I rolled up all my clothes and sleeping bags and saw how big the roll was. It was so fat it was obnoxious to look at. Unfortunately, what little money I made on selling my pouches and sleeping bag will have to be used for getting a new passport.

From what I can see from the balcony of the Hotel Bogotá, this is a big, dirty city. There is really nothing worse than a dreary looking, cold feeling city, in a cold climate.

BOGOTÁ - APR. 25, 1972

I have never seen so many people crowding the streets of a city since Saigon. This constant flow of the masses begins early in the morning and carries on into the night. The streets are not only teeming with people going somewhere, but up and down every block are street vendors trying to sell their goods by demonstrations with a convincing voice. Some are selling ink to refill expended ballpoint pens; and some are selling knife sharpeners, apples, tables, place mats, spoons, dogs, fortunes, watch crystal polishers, American cigarettes, and magic tricks. Bogota is a city where the ordinary blind beggar does not have a chance. Legless men are scooting along on roller-skate-wheel carts and freaks of all types are trying to eke out a living. In a city where a supper costs 25 to 35 cents, it seems like an impossible task. It's difficult to look at those poor disfigured people as human beings; but it is important to keep in mind, even the man who walks on all fours is every bit as human as I.

The police here appear to be dressed as if they were out of a Buck Rogers comic book. They wear helmets with transparent plastic face visors and carry shields and clubs. The students at the University are always uprising in protest to the present government.

Jim and I took a cable car to the top of a high mountain overlooking this grand city. On the top is a simple, unadorned church with a statue of Christ, all bloodied and beaten, in a glass box on the altar. In the passageway near the statue are a staggering number of crutches, canes, and thank-you plaques on the wall given by believers who were cured of their ailments.

BOGOTÁ - APR. 17, 1972

I am still waiting for confirmation of my citizenship so I can apply for a new passport. It was supposed to be here today; but as I expected, it did not arrive. I even had trouble getting the photo studio to print the right size picture, 2 ½" x 2 ½." Twice they printed them the size required for a Colombian passport.

Michelle L., a young lady I met in Panama, arrived today. Jim, Michelle, and I will all travel south together. This afternoon we sat looking out the second-floor window of a coffee shop located on a terribly busy intersection, and I mean busy. Within the period of 15 minutes, we saw a pickpocket stealing a man's wallet and saw unbelievable traffic jams. The wide streets were packed bumper-to-bumper with smog-belching buses. We saw two young boys try to jump on the rear end of a truck; but the tailgate fell, and boys went sprawling on the pavement with thick traffic flowing all around them. It is hard to believe they did not get run over. That incident made the car wreck we saw look innocent. Everybody runs to catch the bus: old ladies, disabled people, babies, pretty girls, and businessmen in dapper suits. If they do not hustle to the bus stop, the driver keeps going. Catching a taxi offers the same problems.

We spent a fantastic afternoon in the Museo de Oro (Gold Museum) where we saw thousands of artifacts made of gold. The shimmering gold was simply ineffable. We were ushered into a dark room through a doorway with a two-foot-thick sliding door. The room lighting was dim. As we stood in the darkness, a rheostat gently brought the room lighting up. All around us were 9,000 glittering gold objects on the walls and ceiling behind glass panels. Seeing that amount of gold art in one room was a stunning spectacle. We were told the guards have no orders to arrest or apprehend anyone trying to steal the gold, only shoot to kill.

The beauty of the glittering gold artwork I saw today is equal or unsurpassed by any of the historic pieces of art I have ever seen. These pieces were objects buried with the dead. God only knows what the Spaniards melted down. The Inca gave them all their gold artwork, and they never made any more.

BOGOTÁ - APR. 29, 1972

Well, we are stuck here for the weekend; and wouldn't you know it, Monday is a holiday. So, the soonest we will be able to leave is next Wednesday. With inefficiency at its highest, I cannot even be sure about that. I was supposed to have everything in order last Thursday, but the wire to Washington, DC, did not come back; and the Colombian Bureau of Investigation sent for proof of my entry visa. After waiting for 3 days, I discovered they had my name spelled wrong and had the wrong date for my day of entry. The secretary says, "Please have patience," after telling me I would have to wait four more days.

Sparkling green emeralds are very abundant here, and Jim is in the market for buying several. He says you can buy them here at decent prices and sell them for more in the USA. He bought one good uncut stone for about $10. Today a guy, very sleazy-looking and sneaky, asked Jim if he wanted to buy emeralds. He showed him three large cut "stones." Jim bartered him down to $10 for the three and decided to chance it. Of course, Jim was dreaming about getting a great deal. I suppose the sleazy little guy was too. After making the payoff and getting back in our room, we both, after careful investigation, decided he paid $10 for three pieces of colored glass. Such is life.

We have been staying in the Hotel Lido on Eleventh Street. The meals here are cooked by a little lady who slaves away all day behind a huge charcoal-burning stove. Breakfast costs six pesos, dinner six pesos, and supper six pesos. It is hard to believe the quantity of food she serves for six pesos or thirty cents, and well-rounded meals at that. The cook has a yellow and black bird that is 20 years old in a cage. He is crippled, but his singing voice is clear. He is a beautiful whistler.

BOGOTÁ - APR. 30, 1972

About the only pressing problem I have now is a sore throat. I need to buy new socks. My one pair has a three-inch hole in one heal and two big holes in the side of the other. They are really beyond repair.

I now have three pairs of pants, two long sleeve shirts, a tee shirt, one pair of shorts, and two pair of socks. I also have a sweater, a pair of sandals, a pair of Vietnam Army boots and a wool Mexican poncho. These are my only clothes. I also have my sleeping bag, two books, toilet articles and a gourd water bottle. Oh yah, I have a camera which I bought in Panama.

My things are starting to wear out, especially my clothes, boots, and sandals. I keep mending them, but there is always a limit when the patches become more than the article patched.

I am happy with what little I have. It is a certain security to know I do not have much; and because of that, I do not have much to lose.

BOGOTÁ - MAY 4, 1972

We are still here waiting, waiting, waiting. The information from the Colombian Department of Investigation came through, but proof of my citizenship has not arrived. I was a fool for not having written home for a birth certificate at the same time I sent the wire to Washington, DC, because the wire still has not come through. The Military Attaché sent a tracer out for the wire yesterday, but still no word. I sure hope it arrives tomorrow or else Jim and I will be stranded another weekend in Bogota; and we both are getting itchy feet to move on.

Two days ago, we went to Izaguirre, a small town north of here that has a huge, underground salt mine with a Catholic Church built within the tunnels of the mine. The amount of salt from this mine is said to have fed the earth for one hundred years. Digging the cathedral took ten years, and its grandeur is overwhelming. The columns of black rock salt, which support the earth above, are 30 to 35 feet square at the base. It was a huge undertaking. I wonder how many men died digging this mine and had their lungs poisoned by breathing the noxious fumes in the black dusty air.

What started out to be a phenomenal piece of unadorned architecture was ruined by the addition of classical, mundane, church details. The lighting was terrible. They used neon lights with exposed bulbs that assaulted my eyes. Indirect lighting could cause this grand underground cathedral to be one of the most moving spaces made by man.

BOGOTÁ - MAY 7, 1972

Jim bought a packet of marijuana last night that he said was amazing. He bought it in a place called La Calle, where hippie types hang out. La Calle is a block square and is just behind the new Hilton Hotel. You only need to stroll through the square, and everybody will ask you if you want to buy grass. Police officers do not come in, and everybody smokes in the street. This all seemed too good to be true, but it is.

We are sitting in Bogotá waiting for my passport. The wire I was waiting for finally came through. The reason it took so long is because they sent the answer back in a letter through the mail. After all that waiting, the wire did not say I was an officer in the Army. It said, "Our records show that he is a US Citizen;" but that really does not prove it. The Council said to come back Monday. He said, "The problem is we have all these books with these darned rules to follow."

BOGOTÁ - MAY 9, 1972

A good place to change money is with Raul Mosquera Perez, a money changer in room 504 on Carretera 7, #17-64. He gives twenty-two pesos for $1.00.

I received the letter from the Army proving my citizenship, but the US Embassy guy still is not sure I am me. He thinks I am trying to pull something over on him and that I faked my IDs. He cannot understand why he cannot get a birth certificate from me. Trying to save $10.00 is inconceivable to him.

Last Friday after receiving the letter, which should have been sent by wire, I talked to him. Amid four or five lengthy interruptions, he told me, "We are closing," and that I would have to come back on Monday to approve my application, and that the Embassy would be closed on Thursday and Friday of next week.

So, when I came back on Monday, he said, "I am sorry, I cannot do it. I have no proof you are you." I said, "I have identification and one with a picture of me on it." He said, "You told me you didn't have any ID, that they were destroyed." I reminded him that during our first meeting I said my social security card was destroyed in the wash, but I had a draft card; and he had told me that was "nothing, nothing at all."

All is against me. If I am lucky, which I have not been, the wire will come on Wednesday, and I will get my passport then. If not, I will have to wait until Monday because the Embassy is closed on Thursday and Friday to move to a new building. It is difficult to imagine having to stay in Bogota longer. I have been here three weeks now. The only thing that is keeping Jim and I going are Sophia's fantastic thirty cent meals. Other than getting a passport, her food is the only thing we look forward to.

BOGOTÁ (AGAIN) - MAY 10, 1972

This is really beginning to get ridiculous. Jim is sterilizing his toothbrush in a glassful of his favorite Scotch, and I am sitting here with nothing to do. We have made ready everything we need for our journey south. I mended my sleeping bag and aired it out, made my side pouch more secure, made a pouch for my leather tools and a leather neck case to hang from my neck for my passport and money. We have everything organized and sent home the things we do not need. We are down to the bare minimum. If that wire does not come through today, we will have to stay here for four more days. I shudder at the thought of it. Both of us feel like we are planted here.

In 45 minutes, we will be able to go down and eat another delicious Sophia meal. The wire transfer did not come through, so we have no choice but sit in Bogota five more days with nothing to do.

BOGOTÁ - MAY 13, 1972

Both Jim S. and I are depressed that we must wait a week more to get on the road. We are sitting here waiting and waiting, so we spent the last two days and much of this one drinking wine. Jim had gone to a nearby corner store and bought three bottles of wine. This was last Wednesday after I found out we would have to wait for five more days.

I have been reading three books. I gobbled up *The Adventures of Huckleberry Finn* by Mark Twain which was a fun read. It is hard to imagine that I have waited for over 26 years to read any of Mark Twain's books. His vivid description of life along the Mississippi sounds real. Mr. Twain sure knew his river and how to reach the hearts of his characters, and his readers.

Across the street is a large store called TIA, an equivalent to the five-and-dime stores in the USA. Every time I go in, it is packed with people. The vast number of people in this one store alone is unbelievable. It is bad enough having thousands of people jockeying and shoving; but to make things worse, there is a guy talking rapidly on a battery-powered megaphone. Nobody listens and can phase out the assaults to their body, ears, and mind. On the street the people ignore tons of diesel exhaust, and crowded buses, and always walk dodging everybody else, including the street vendors, and greasy street photographers who snap thousands of pictures, mostly of girls walking along. The photographer hands them a piece of paper listing where they can buy the picture.

BOGOTÁ - MAY 14, 1972

Jim and I hopped a bus to La Nueva (New) Guatavita to see a bull fight and the new city which was built alongside a man-made

lake which flooded the old village. The new village was designed in a remarkably interesting and attractive Spanish Colonial style, thus in keeping with the historical background of Colombia. The market, done with an exposed timber ceiling and rough brick masonry, was one of the strongest architectural statements I had seen in Colombia.

The bullfight was a farce. The first matador spent more time being thrown in the air by the bull than he did on the ground, or he was under the stomping hooves of the bull. He was thrown five times and got run over. All the matadors were young kids in their teens and were an example of mass confusion. There were twenty young matadors waving capes in the face of the bull. At this point, thoroughly confused, the bull would usually run out of the ring. That sight was enough to make Hemingway cringe under his seat.

One young matador-to-be knelt in front of the entry chute near the center of the arena, and the bull came charging at him. The kid pulled aside, and the bull went right by him with a flash of the red cape. But, as the kid was turning around, the bull turned fast and ran over him. The "crowd" of about three hundred people was laughing in the aisles and went wild when a 10- or 12-year-old kid waved his cape a couple of times in front of the same bull and got run over.

An 18-year-old female matador tried her hand at it but had the misfortune of having all twenty others waving capes in front of the bull at the same time.

It was funny all right, but those big critters are nothing to be played with. I am glad the bulls were not killed.

BOGOTÁ (ONE MORE TIME) - MAY 15, 1972

I finally received a new passport at the cost of $22.00. We are as good to go. I must take care of last-minute things and check the bus schedules for Cali. Tomorrow we will be looking at Bogota in the rear-view mirror. Having to stay twenty-four days in Bogotá to obtain a new passport was huge waste of time.

Bogotá is still going as crazy as usual. While walking to the bus stop, I saw two little boys about five or six years old hitching a ride hanging on the back of a minibus. While I was in the bus heading for the new US Embassy, I saw a guy in a suit sprawled out on his back on the sidewalk with blood running out of his mouth. People were standing around looking at him; and all appeared to wonder, "What should I do?"

While at the Embassy, I talked to an American guy who was making application for a new passport. He said he was robbed by two guys. One had a gun, and the other had a knife. A shudder went down my spine when I heard that. Just when we think we have our "shit together," we hear a story like that. I have fixed it by sewing a flap on the inside of my boot top to hold my money around my leg above my ankle.

Jim bought another emerald today. This brings his total to eight: five cut stones and three rough ones, about $70-worth. That is not counting the $10 he paid for the three fakes. Frankly, they are all fakes.

CALI, COLOMBIA - MAY 18, 1972

It feels good to finally leave Bogotá and be on the road again. We rode in a comfortable bus through beautiful country. The bus cost sixty pesos, or $2.73. It took 11 hours to get here. We met a girl on the bus named Anne B., an American, who has decided to come with us to Lima, Peru. She said she spent two years in Turkey as a Peace Corps volunteer, so we talked about my travels in Turkey. Turkey is a stimulating country, and it was interesting to hear more about it. Michelle disappeared shortly after meeting us in Bogota, so I have no idea where she is. She must have taken off with others.

Cali has beautiful weather. Not too hot, not too cold and a refreshing breeze is always washing over us. It's a much quieter city than Bogotá, but you wouldn't know it by sleeping in this room. There was something constantly happening somewhere on the street below. Radios blaring, vendors barking and just plain old city noise which couldn't be kept out because our windows are nothing but louvered doors. We're going to have to get another room.

Yesterday a sleezy little man, with a white handkerchief in one hand and a double-edge razor blade in the other, made two passes at me. On the second, I recognized his moves as a "rip-off artist." As he walked close by me, I pushed him out of the way and noticed the razor blade. I said, "Hey, that dude has a blade!" He looked extremely nervous and quickly went to look at the nearby window displays. The reason I was wise to him was because the same thing happened to me in Bogotá. A guy had made two obvious passes at me by running into me like he didn't see me or faking like he was trying to get around me. If this happens twice to you by the same man in a matter of a few minutes or seconds, watch out. The guy with the blade really scared me. They don't care what they cut to get what they want.

While we were at the bus station yesterday, a man fell to the floor in an epileptic seizure, jerking and banging his head violently on the floor. Everybody was standing around watching, so Jim and I jumped in and held him to keep him from hurting himself. After he relaxed a little, he asked for water. Jim went to get it; and when he returned, the guy pulled out a bottle of pills from his shirt pocket, took one pill and seemed to improve. I was sure glad to be able to help him, but I wish I knew how to help someone having a seizure.

Tonight, Jim and I dyed a few clothing items blue so they would not look so faded. The lady here let us use her archaic kitchen to cook with her two kerosene burners. It was genuinely nice of her.

We took in a flick this afternoon, *Andromeda Strain*. I was thoroughly amazed at the money and equipment those scientists had to use to isolate a destructive biological organism from outer space.

CALI, COLOMBIA - MAY 19, 1972

This hotel we are staying in has huge rooms, and the showers are so big I had to take a step or two to get to the shower handle. Unfortunately, it only provides chilly water. Often in these hotels, the showers are so cramped it is difficult to maneuver. Here, I can dance in it. This place is called Hotel Cordoba, and it is on Carretera 7a, 12-60. They charge twenty-five pesos for one and forty for two. It is old but not bad, and the people are friendly.

I really splurged these last couple of days. Yesterday, I had some ice cream and yogurt and went to a movie. Today I again ate ice cream and had a couple of beers.

I talked to the guy in charge of the Meyer Language School and found him to be an agreeable, 24-year-old South Carolinian named Walter.

POPAYÁN, COLOMBIA - MAY 22, 1972

Today we will travel about three hundred miles to Pasto, which is near the Ecuadorian border. An Australian girl, whom we had met in the language school in Cali, is traveling with us now; so, overall, there are four of us. Anne is with us too. It sure is nice to travel with women, at least at this point. We met a few other Americans yesterday, and one of them was traveling north from Peru. He had his camera stolen on the train, just following the trend, another rip-off in Latin America. It was good to get some information from him about Peru.

PASTO, COLOMBIA - MAY 23, 1972

Yesterday we went 270 miles in 12 hours. Our bus couldn't have been going more than 20 mph, and it broke down twice. The engine support gave out, and the fan was hitting the radiator. The second time it went out, we were high in the Andes, one of the most beautiful areas I have ever seen. The steep green valley's varying shades of blue and green with each receding rugged ridge. It was on the grandeur of the Grand Canyon, except everything was green, green, green. As I stood on the edge of the road, I could hear the rushing of fresh waterfalls crashing over the steep cliffs far below. Some of the poorest people in the world live on the edge of these cliffs and see these commanding views each day. I think it's only fitting.

That was it for our bus. After waiting for hours, we wound up boarding another bus from the same company to finish our journey.

We arrived about 11 PM in a drizzling rain and scurried around looking for a room, but most places had no vacancy. We got to sleep about 2:00 AM in a grungy old room for 65 cents apiece but were rudely awakened about 4:00 AM by a blaring radio. I complained twice to the manager, but it didn't do any good. The guy with the radio left for work when he was ready. At the same time, a strange girl was asking about clothes or something and pointing at the corner of our room. Jim finally figured out she was asking about the panties she had

left the night before. I still can't figure out why she was asking about them at 4:30 in the morning. The whole thing seems like a bad dream.

I just had a rare hot shower and was it ever nice.

QUITO, EQUADOR - MAY 27, 1972

The road from the Colombian border to Quito is a torturous, single-lane road paved with hand-placed rocks. It winds its way across the Andes Mountains, clings close to the mountainside, and crosses steep valleys as high on the side of the valley as possible. We often crossed exceedingly narrow bridges, barely wide enough to accommodate the bus. The road drops off at almost a 90-degree angle, without guard rails, to what seems like bottomless chasms. When the rear wheel of the bus nearly drops off the cliff edge, it gets a little hairy.

As the shadows grow longer, fog pushes over the mountain tops and slides into the valleys with stealth, appearing as if it were alive.

Quito is a beautiful, clean, city with no smog and exhaust-spewing buses. It is a pleasure to be in this capital compared to Bogotá. I feel safe walking the streets during the day and night. They have a beautiful central park which is only rivaled by the beauty of the central park in Antigua, Guatemala. The people here are friendly, and prices are very reasonable.

Any time I find a place of beauty in Latin America, there are always a bunch of young American kids hanging loose. Most, if not all of them, are heavy into the dope scene, especially grass and cocaine. The Colombian grass is the best around and the cheapest, but the cocaine is supposed to be the best. Jim had some grass yesterday that had a hallucinogen laced in it, and he was really floating. He said it was the best he's ever had.

Unfortunately, most of these freaks always group together in one hotel or area, almost like a foreign quarter of our big cities. That's where the problems begin. Hassles with police officers are no laughing matter in Latin America. They would just as soon bust one as not and pocket his money.

I had a chicken dinner for 48 cents last night which was tasty. I also saw a movie, *Straw Dogs* starring Dustin Hoffman which was excellent, and caught the last part of *Summer of '42* which was also a top-rated flick. I only had to pay 40 cents for the movies.

Today, we are going to move to a cheaper hotel. This costs us $1.00 a night. We want to get one for 60 cents a night.

Yesterday as we were standing on the street talking to some people, I heard someone calling, "Terry, Terry;" and as I turned around, there was Michelle getting off a motor scooter. It was quite a surprise. I did not think I was ever going to see her again. She said the reason she disappeared in Bogotá was she went to an Indian village out in the Colombian mountains. It was good to know nothing harmful came to her in Bogotá.

I want to spend a few days in Quito, but I'm sure getting itchy to get to Lima. I'm even looking forward to getting a job, which is a strange feeling.

QUITO - MAY 28, 1972

We splurged last night and went to see the movie *Lawrence of Arabia* and capped it off with a Chinese meal. The flick cost 24 cents, but we had to sit in the top row of the top balcony for that price. My

meal cost $1.05 for a plate of chop suey, with rice, and a couple of beers.

This morning Jim and I took a bath in a public bath house with hot water for 10 cents each. Jim said it wasn't anywhere near as good as the other place which charges 8 cents for 20 minutes.

Our new hotel is called La Buen Esperanza (Good Hope) and it's on Calle de la Ronda, one of the oldest streets in the city. It has old Spanish charm. We are paying 15 sucres, or 60 cents a night.

QUITO – MAY 29, 1972

The average day of this dedicated traveler seems to follow a regular pattern. I sleep in the morning until I wake up naturally, whether it's by the noise of people walking over the old wooden hall floor, or some guy whistling, or screaming kids in the courtyard. I may, or may not, walk to the public bath for a hot water shower, then spend the rest of the day finding places to take care of little business issues like locating and going to the consulate, picking up mail, and generally strolling around taking in all the sights on the way to and from wherever I am going. In the evening, I might drink a beer, see a flick, or generally sit around visiting with friends until I get tired and go to bed. Occasionally, I will open a map and think about my next route of travel.

QUITO - MAY 30, 1972

I just figured out, for the last 6 months of travel, I've been living on $4.80 a day, $33.60 a week or $134.40 a month. When I was traveling across Mexico and not having to pay to sleep anywhere, I was living on less than $1.00 a day. The figure of $4.80 a day shocked me, but that expense includes everything from sending gifts to the States, transportation, and sleeping accommodations. Budgeting $4.00 a day is a comfortable figure to use for backpack travelers planning to travel in Latin America. If I am careful and budget $4.00 a day for expenses from now on, I will only have until the 8th of September until I must dig into my $200 reserve.

I've been thinking about leaving Quito on the 1st of June and heading for Guayaquil, Ecuador. Then I will travel down to Lima, Peru, where I would like to find a job. I bought my brother a small hand-carved wooden figure of an old man carrying a burden on his back, which depicts a typical scene in this country. I bought it for his graduation from Texas Tech University which probably occurred today or will tomorrow. The store where I bought the sculpture is on Calle Yepez-Adan.

QUITO - JUNE 1, 1972

I haven't left yet. I guess I'm not in too much of a hurry. I met an Argentine girl across the hall who doesn't speak English. We hit it off, so I've been speaking a lot of Spanish with her. She has a Chilean girlfriend who knows a guy who works for the bus company and might

be able to get us a discount. I was planning to hitch south; but if I can get a decent discount on a bus to Lima, I'll take it.

I met a couple of guys from the States today and spent the afternoon shopping and translating Spanish for them. One of them said he had spent $10,000 on his travels through Central and South America, and they have only been gone from home for about 2 months. And I thought I'd been living comfortably on $4.80 a day!

I'm eating a banana and honey sandwich on fresh-baked, whole-wheat bread. What a feast! That is living good.

QUITO - JUNE 3, 1972

I'm sitting on my bed in my sun-drenched room reading a *Time* magazine cover-to-cover. The hotel radio is blaring all through the building with Andean music mixed with blaring advertisements and honky organ music. My mind is getting tight from reading and thinking and passing the time.

I am torn between wanting to see the rest of South America and going back to the USA and getting into something which I can really put myself into, both mind and body. I don't know why the US has such an attractive pull on me, especially when I read that President Nixon is planning to sell wheat to Russia over the next decade to make up for her meat shortage, not to mention selling sophisticated US industrial equipment and US credit to Russia. It staggers me how this can be done sanely while American young men are still dying in Vietnam from bullets fired from Russian weapons.

I like the United States primarily because I had a wonderful childhood. America has a great deal of bad points, but don't all countries? I'd like to discover America on an adult level now.

QUITO - JUNE 6, 1972

In about 3 hours I will be leaving this beautiful city for Lima. I was fortunate to get a discount on a comfortable bus for $19.52. A girl from Chile knows the guy who works in the travel office and helped me. I still wish I would have tried to hitch to Lima; but on the other hand, I am glad that I will get there in a hurry so I can get a job and start diligently studying Spanish. I am really hoping that with my optimistic attitude, I will find Lima a good place to live for a while. Most of the travelers only have dreadful things to say about Lima.

Once again I'm on the road. Quito has been a good place to stay for a while. I've met a lot of good people here from all over the world. I'm looking forward to Lima. Yesterday I walked up to a cemetery and was absolutely amazed at the gargantuan tombs people built for the dead.

Most of the tombs were far more substantial than the houses most people of Ecuador live in.

LIMA, PERU - JUNE 8, 1972

What I thought was going to be a short journey turned out to be one taking two days and three nights. The second night we stayed in a hotel in Tumbes named Hotel Escudero on the corner of Tarapaca and Abad Puell. It is the cleanest and cheapest place in town and costs 40 soles per person. It is really a wonderful place with good beds. The place seems out of place because it's so nice and is located on the corner of two dirt streets.

As we crossed the border of Ecuador and Peru at Aguas Verdes—a tired-looking, poor, dirty town—I met an obese, bleached-blond American lady about 35 years old who was wearing white short-shorts and a tight white blouse. She was a strange sight. Come to find out, she's been traveling for 5 years in North and South America, doing it all by hitchhiking with little or no money. She didn't even have enough money to get into Peru for the minimum of 3 days. One of the guys on the bus said he'd help her get to Lima and paid for her fare. She didn't think the bus would be fast enough, so she got out in the middle of the desert and hitched a ride. That blew all the natives' minds. She said borders are no problem for her because, if she must, she sells her body or gives it away. Her husband died 5 years ago, and I think that must be when she flipped out. She's pathetic and thinks the world is going to end soon because the Bible says so.

We changed buses at the border and are riding on an old, discarded Greyhound bus. It is impossible to sleep in the seats, especially at night as it bounces on these poor roads. On the bus I met a good guy named Milton Rodriquez who is a Brazilian. He's been attending the University of Texas for 5 years and is now a graduate student.

Just north of Lima I woke to a beautiful scene as the sun was coming up. We were traveling along the coast and saw sand dunes, soft in texture in the morning light. It was marvelous to see them with the ocean rolling up to the shore below. All colors receded to the sun.

I'm beginning to feel the effects of that tiring bus journey. I think I will sleep now. It sure was good to read all the letters I received.

I can add my sweater to the list of articles which I started out with that have been stolen along the way. Eva and I went to a movie late yesterday afternoon; and like a fool, I forget my sweater when we walked out of the theater. About a block down the street, I realized it was missing and rushed back in the theater to get it, but it was gone. Losing the sweater was difficult because my mother knitted it for me.

I found a suitable place to eat yesterday. It's called Comedor Municipal. It's a huge cafeteria run by the government. For 10 soles one gets a huge meal, cafeteria style. Hundreds of people pack the place. That's pretty darned good for 20 cents American: salad, rice, meat sauce, bread, soup, and an orange.

LIMA - JUNE 11, 1972

My impression of Lima changed today. The sun was shining for the entire day, and the weather was fine. This is a busy place. It is clean, friendly, and architecturally handsome. It's amazing what the sun can do to improve my feelings.

The girls here are exceptionally good-looking and are fine dressers. I'm really impressed with Lima. This morning, I bought 5 oranges for 10 cents which was a bargain considering they did not have seeds in them and were very juicy.

Eva and I ate in the municipal dining hall again this evening and was it ever good: rice, goulash, soup, bread, beans, and an orange. A little old lady sits outside on the sidewalk selling lime, salt, peppers, and spices to add zest to the meal, but it doesn't need any. Eva is an Argentine girl I met in Quito. She is on her way back to Buenos Aires. We had traveled to Lima together. She speaks no English, so I'm constantly forced to try to converse in Spanish. It sure is good practice.

and I went to the show late yesterday afternoon and like a fool I forgot my sweater upon leaving the show. About a block down the street I realized it was missing and rushed back in to get it but alas it was gone.

Found a great place to eat yesterday called Comedor Municipal. Its a ~~go~~ huge cafeterie set up by the government.

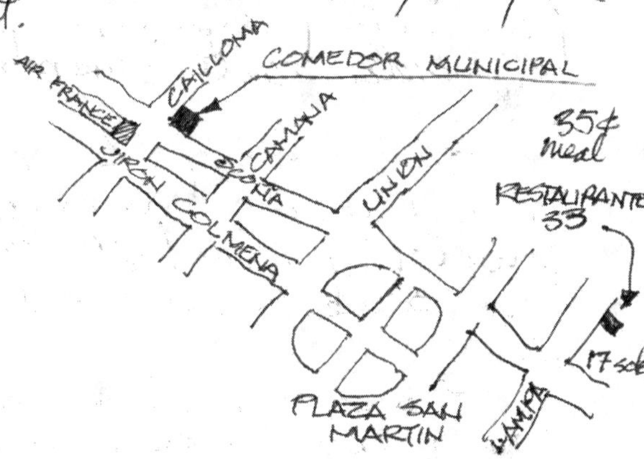

~~For~~ 10 soles one gets a huge meal cafeteria style. Hundreds of people pack the place. Pretty damned good for 20¢ American. Salad, rice, meat sauce, bread, soup, and an orange.

LIMA - JUNE 11, 1972

Another beautiful day in Lima! Yesterday was a nice sunny one also. I saw Eva off to the bus yesterday and took in a movie called *Carnal Knowledge*. Darned good flick! Today, Milton and I went to a friend's house on "the Point," a peninsula about ½ hour from here. It's amazing to see this city's edge so close to the beach. I never imagined it to be that way. We went walking along the beach and watched the pelicans fold their wings and dive in the water for fish.

This morning, I saw a man, walking on the sidewalk, nearly get killed. A truck veered off the road and hit the wall in front of him. That was weird.

LIMA - JUNE 13, 1972

I spent most of today in the Museum of Anthropology and just thinking. I decided to not look for a job here because of legal difficulties with the government. I must have a resident's visa which costs $100 if I stay in the country over three months. I don't know; I might go to the language school to see if they need somebody to teach English; but on the other hand, I think I will just split for Cuzco, get my butt down the road. Yesterday and today, I met three people who I knew in Quito. They are just traveling through.

In the museums they have some mummies from old Inca graves. Their sitting postures and facial expressions appear lifelike. The first thing I thought of were old folks in an assisted-living home. Very strange!

LIMA - JUNE, 16, 1972

I feel like a bouncing rubber ball. First I decide to split, then I decide to stay, then go, then stay. I don't know what I'm going to do. I'd really like to get a job, but the hassle is insurmountable. I'm going to check with a language school Monday as well as try to contact people who want to have private English lessons.

Last night a couple called the Speers took me out for a feast in a German Restaurant. We ate pork chops and German potatoes. The extra sausage with mustard was delicious.

Some friends gave me a couple of novels, and I'm reading about a guy traveling in the good ole USA. Today I splurged and bought a big bag of laundry soap for about 9 cents and a new padlock for a little over two dollars. My other lock, which I bought somewhere along the way, stopped working. It was a real cheap-o. It's the first padlock I've ever seen wear out. I could open it with my knife. Carrying a personal padlock is a good thing for the traveler because sometimes you get a room with no lock, and you want to simply keep everyone out, including the cleaning people.

LIMA - JUNE 17, 1972

I met a man named Sam from West Virginia who is also staying in this Hotel Venezia. He's a college student hanging loose down here for summer vacation. He and I changed some money on the black market with the doorman of the Hotel Bolivar which is one of the swankiest hotels in town. He gave us 50 soles for $1.00. It's 44 to 1 in the bank. We then went to "Restaurant 33" for a 34-cent supper. Not bad! Everybody knows about these doormen. I heard about them in Colombia. It's strange the police officers don't know about them.

Union Street, the main shopping area, is only five blocks long; but on weekends, especially at night, it's a pleasure to stroll along under the lights with lots of people in streets that are blocked off so cars cannot enter the area. Cars and people do not mix. It's beautiful when the people have the street and leisurely cross back and forth from store to store, not choking on exhaust fumes or dodging vehicles. People sell puppies on the street as well as necklaces and toy parachute men. The puppies of course are always an attraction.

Union Street is simply a lovely place to walk day or night. I really enjoy looking at the girls. Lima has a great wealth of beauties. I think that I can honestly say that for the first time in my life, I can feel a change within myself. It's a pleasant experience. I started to notice it in Vietnam and especially after traveling for seven months in Latin America. I feel comfortable with myself, and wiser. Change has constantly faced me for two years. I have felt great fear, almost death in a war, constant motion, and emotion and now the beauty of the road.

Jack Kerouac's *On the Road* and Tom Wolfe's *Electric Kool-Aid Acid Test* bring the road out in all its uniqueness. The road is quite an experience, different everywhere you go. One can't help but change. It's too much to absorb. It's so much I don't even want to stop. There are so many things to see in this world. Already my Swedish friend wants me to ride the Moscow-to-Peking train with him next year. Sometimes it's even too much to comprehend, but it becomes a part of you. When you become involved with all the fantastic people one meets every day, you're hooked. We are lucky to have such a beautiful opportunity to explore like this.

Lima is a beautiful city: clean, enchanting, and friendly. It's a city where one can see the dried-up body of the conquistador Pizarro, the murderer/founder of this city. He's laid to rest in a glass box in the cathedral of this once Spanish Colonial Capital of South America. The old Spanish buildings with lavish wood balconies still enhance the older parts of Lima. This was, and still is, a grand city of the desert. I sketched this scene from the second-floor balcony of my cheap hotel. The view of the historic bridge and Ciudad Vieja (old city) is enchanting.

RIO RIMAC LIMA

Sam and I walked a long way to the theater see a movie called *The Last Picture Show.* It was heavy on nostalgia in a small American town and could have been filmed almost anywhere in middle America, but it was situated in West Texas. When Sam and I arrived at the theater after a long, hurried walk, we found the theater sold out. Sam told the ticket taker I was from West Texas, and we still could not get in. Ha! The ticket scalp hunters on the sidewalk in front of the theater wanted 2% more for their tickets so we were out of luck.

About that time one of them we were talking to dropped something from his handful of tickets and money. Sam quickly picked it up, looked at it, snapped it, pulled it, and sure enough, it was 100 soles ($2.00). We turned around, bought two tickets from the same man who dropped the bill, walked in, bought a Pepsi and a big chocolate bar, and sat down to the tale of life in small town USA. It felt good scalping the scalp hunter. Even though the movie was in black and white, it was so good I could watch it repeatedly. I don't know if Peruvians could understand this flick without knowing small-town USA, but I guess small-town South America wouldn't be much different.

LIMA - JUNE 20, 1972

I finally decided to leave Lima tomorrow and head for Cuzco via Arequipa which is to the south. I want to hitchhike.

A pleasant thing happened to me as I was walking down the street. I ran into Milton, who I thought left a week ago. It was good to see him again. We talked over a cup of coffee and went our separate ways. Last night I walked about 2 miles. It was good for me; and besides, I couldn't get a bus anyway.

CHINCHA ALTA, PERU - JUNE 21, 1972

Well, I finally made it out of Lima, barely. I hitchhiked from the edge of town and caught two rides for a grand total of 200 kms. I met a couple of fine fellows from Argentina who are traveling to Alaska on a BJW motorcycle with a side car. They were my second ride and got me to Chincha Alta. I rode on the back seat of the motorcycle while the passenger rode in the side car. I met several of their friends who were providing them with lodging, food, etc., while they repaired their motorcycle. I'm staying with them tonight at a big egg farm. The owner of the farm is a young man named Miguel, who said I could work for him if I wanted to. I will have to talk to him today about it. It might not be a bad deal.

CHINCHA ALTA - JUNE 23, 1972

The job didn't pan out, but I've had a very interesting time here. There are many wealthy young guys here who have been feeding the Argentines and me in restaurants: steaks, Chinese food, the works. It's been good times here. Tomorrow morning I'm heading for Cuzco. Yesterday I rode around with Miquel with whom we are staying. We unloaded cotton at the gin, picked up food for his chickens, talked with his friends and generally got a feel of this agricultural community. It's like the little towns in Texas where the wealthy farm kids drive around in fancy cars or pickups with radios. They "drag the palm tree-studded square" in the evening, checking out the "mujeres" (women and girls), and seeing who else is checking out the scene. The town square is beautiful. As I went strolling around it last night, I was amazed to find, of all things, a television in a store window with people standing in front watching it through the window.

CHINCHA ALTA - JUNE 25, 1972

This place is just darned difficult to leave. The Argentines and I have been sleeping-in until about 9 or 10 o'clock every day, and then we go sit around talking at the Europa Restaurant for most of the day. In the afternoons we usually go somewhere on the motorcycle. Two days ago, we went to the beach. That was fun, with the three of us tooling down the road on the motorcycle and the side car which is always a spectacle.

Yesterday we went to Inca or pre-Inca ruins which were nothing more than a huge hill of clay soil with many ancient adobe walls still standing after all these centuries. The huge mounds of earth appear to have been old vertical cities of adobe much like Taos Pueblo in New Mexico. All horizontal ceilings and floors have fallen in, but most of the vertical walls are still there. There are Native Inca people still living on some of these mounds. We went out to search for artifacts but found nothing but human bones: hip bones, skulls, leg bones and rib cages lying around. Grave robbers had dug up the graves, apparently looking for gold jewelry and pottery. They simply leave the remains in the sun to bleach. It was strange to stand on the top of that mound and look all around its base and see indentation after indentation all around where the artifact hunters disturbed the earth with their digging.

I was sifting the soil with my fingers in one of the pits and came upon a delicate skull of a child wrapped in cloth, partially exposed. The people who dug the hole probably already dug up the rest of the body and whatever was buried with it. I felt strange having pulled out that skull with the skin still on it. I quickly dropped it and felt like a grave robber.

We headed back to town, dusty, tired, and thirsty; and who should we run into in front of the Europa but three beautiful girls from Lima. Cutting it short, we wound up at a "fiesta" or party with a lot of young people dancing and having an enjoyable time. Before arriving at the fiesta, Roberto, one of the Argentinians, and I went to a bar where about fifteen local 30-to-40-year-olds were boozing it up as a preliminary to whatever might happen later. Two guys, a middle-aged man, and a young guy, were singing Spanish songs, and they were exceptionally talented. The older guy sang in a beautiful tenor voice. First he would sing, then the other would chime in. I don't see how they knew so many songs, but they kept it up for about two hours while we were putting down Chivas Regal whiskey that Roberto bought. Roberto is the guy who had picked me up while I was hitchhiking, the reason I'm still in Chincha Alta. We didn't get home until about 3:00 AM and slept till 11:00 AM.

Today Roberto and the Argentines went to Lima for a few days. I decided to wait here until they return before I leave.

Miguel took us to a practice exhibition of "cock fighting" without the razors. It's amazing to see those beautiful roosters raise their feathers and get after it like karate experts jumping at each other. I would hate to see it with razors.

Miguel won a wad of money this evening with one of his cocks, so he gave me a couple of dollars. I thought that was nice of him. I've hardly spent a nickel since I arrived here. The hospitality of these people astonishes me.

CHINCHA ALTA - JUNE 28, 1972

I'm still here in this friendly small town, and I'm still not sure when I will leave. I might go to the Sierras with a couple of the guys here to pick up a load of wood. Free food and lodging are hard to beat. It's just that they insist on helping me out. Damned good people!

Oscar and Carlos, the Argentines, returned today with Jorge, the guy who lived in the States for 10 years. Oscar was sick in Lima. He had a kidney stone which was blocking one of his kidneys. Using chemicals, he passed it. Wow, that must have hurt!. It was good to see those guys again.

They make a lot of wine around here, and tonight one can smell it in the air while driving down the sleepy, dusty roads under a full moon.

ON THE ROAD

I'm sitting in my little room
thinking about the days ahead

knife to orange, peeling the skin
listening to the river flowing in its bed

The museums of gold and Inca crafts
are only parts on a traveler's fife
learning the language and daily change
hearing and telling of places of life

Why are the sheets always so small
And the beds and blankets and pillowcases too?
These are questions I always ask
Where do you come from, what do you do?

It's never the same wherever one goes
to the beach or jungle or the city streets
it's the reason I'm on the road
for I know it's a life that can't be beat.

Hitchhiking a ride on a rattly truck
or sailing along in a Mercedes Benz
talking with people both rich and poor
learning of life till the very end

I think the indecisiveness I have been having on this trip is because I'm traveling alone across thousands of miles in foreign countries with no plans and no itinerary. I'm drifting and find it easy to settle in a comfortable place and difficult to move on traveling by myself.

CHINCHA ALTA - JULY 1, 1972

Last night turned out to be a remarkable experience, one of those kinds of things when one says, "What the hell, why not?" About 7:00 PM Roberto, the generous guy who likes to show his wealth by buying everything for everybody, said, "Come on Tomás [my nickname], change your clothes, and let's go to Lima. There is a big feast waiting." So, there were five of us packed in a little Toyota, engulfed in the blackness of night, speeding towards Lima. Roberto brought out a bottle of Chivas Regal, and three of us in the back seat went to work on it. Roberto was driving, so he only had a couple of nips. I was glad he had enough sense to not take more. I didn't want to get wiped out, but I knew I had to get loosened up for the journey to Lima because Roberto likes to drive fast. It's difficult to enjoy the ride in a speeding car, especially when I enjoy living.

Suddenly we were under the glimmering lights of Lima, the lights we had seen from a distance. I came to realize this big shindig was going to be quite a big event for the people in the chicken business. We were all the youngest people there and were much more informally dressed than all the others in dark-colored suits and evening gowns. I posed as a Dr. Brown, a representative of "Bacbuc Company" or something like that; and the other guys were posing as doctors, veterinarians, and such.

I think I must have drunk about every type of liquor in Peru: whiskey, pisco, champagne, wine, and beer. 3:00 AM came rolling around fast, especially after having to listen to such a dumpy band all night and most of the morning. We left to pick up the Argentines and headed back to Chincha Alta. I must have zonked out because I didn't remember anything until just before Chincha. Our car broke down on the final assent to town. The thermostat was haywire; so, there we were after a big binge, hitching the last five miles to Chincha. The first thing I did when I got there was hit the rack until 3:00 PM.

CHINCHA ALTA - JULY 2, 1972

Roberto just treated me to a big steak dinner; and this afternoon he has the Argentines, Oscar, and Carlos, and I over for a spaghetti dinner. Absolutely amazing! Miguel just gave me a belt which I mentioned earlier. He also gave me a book. These guys are the most generous and hospitable people I have ever known, and I'm a total stranger here. Incredible!

CHINCHA ALTA - JULY 3, 1972

Miguel fed me a good steak dinner and a Chinese meal tonight. These guys are really something. I will never forget them. Miguel and I share many of the same ideas and feelings.

Oscar and Carlos told me yesterday, before they left for Ecuador, that they only have $65.00 to travel from here to the States. I don't know how they will do it. On the other hand, I think they will. They started out with $100.00. I asked Oscar how they planned to return to Argentina. He said, "Maybe by deportation." I guess that's not too bad an idea and cheap if they don't ever want to go back to the States.

Tomorrow I'm leaving. I've got a ride 100 km to Ica, and from there I will hitch a ride to Arequipa.

ICA, PERU - JULY 4, 1972

I arrived here with Ricardo in his pickup truck. I've decided to make a day of it and only chalk up 100 kms today. Ricardo is traveling on an unlimited expense account, so we ate dinner beside the lake in a snazzy hotel and really did it up fine. Now we are in Ica, the Department capital; and we just checked into the ritziest hotel in town. Wow, I feel like a king. When Ricardo is finished in the bathroom, I'm going to take the first hot shower I've had in about a month.

Tomorrow I will be on the road again, back to the wilderness.

I just experienced my first oasis in a desert. It's called Huacachina and is a small lake, more like a pond, surrounded by high sand dunes. Around the edge of the lake are a small cluster of resort hotels and a handful of private houses. Ricardo says that this used to be an exclusive resort area for the rich; but, as with everything, it has changed. Now it is a very public area.

Ricardo just treated me to a Chinese dinner. It's going to be hard to go back to eating in the greasy spoons. Man, I've been eating good. I sure hope that if these people come to the USA I will be able to treat them as well.

ICA - JULY 5, 1972

My mind is getting strained. I've been hitchhiking for 3 hours with nothing to show for my effort except my dusty and tired face. I keep thinking I should have taken that last ride offer, but I thought it was too short. A short ride can leave you in a worse place to hitchhike. It's times like this when I begin to think I should take a ride from anybody who stops because moving, no matter how short, is better than nothing. However, it's better to get a good long haul if you can, but it seems like that's going to be difficult. I've been watching cars roll by for 3 hours now and can sense where they are going, whether they are going to stop, or if they are just collectors or private cars.

It's a down-and-out-feeling to not get rides. One flashy looking South American pulled up in his big Oldsmobile to fill up with gas. I asked him if he were going to Arequipa, my destination; and he said it would cost me $10.00. That floored me. The cars have really thinned out. I sure hope I get a ride.

George, a guy I met in Chincha who lives in Lima, gave me a nylon pullover jacket. That was genuinely nice of him. He got it when he was going to school in the States. He's another "Chincha" good guy.

CHINCHA ALTA - JULY 6, 1972

Yesterday, I had no idea what I was going to do, especially when nobody was stopping to pick me up; I was beginning to feel stranded and deserted. Then suddenly here comes two guys tooling up in a burgundy colored El Camino grinning from ear to ear. It was George and Ricardo. Wow, it was good to see them. When they dropped me off at this spot, I didn't know if I would ever see them again; but I thought they might return to the gas station to see if I was still there. They asked, "You want to go eat with us?" I said, "Sure, why not? I've put in a good day hitching." So, we were off to the Ica Country Club for drinks and dinner of Loma Saltado (stir-fried beef), my favorite.

I decided at that point to change my itinerary, go back to Chincha, and spend the weekend in Lima. On Monday or Tuesday, I will go with Miguel on our original trip to the mountains and Oxapampa in Eastern Peru.

Yesterday's events were a collection of odd occurrences. It is strange to be a hitchhiker, who, after trying for three hours to get a ride, is picked up by friends and "wined and dined" all in the same day. I felt like those three hours on the road were just a practice for the big event.

Last night I slept in my old bed at Miguel's. It felt like I was coming home; and I guess, in a way, I was.

LIMA (AGAIN) - JULY 9, 1972

I didn't think I would be returning to Lima, but I'm back. This time I'm not staying in a budget hotel. I'm staying with George and his family in a wealthy neighborhood. His family home is a multi-story Spanish mansion, one and a half blocks from the ocean. The interior is decorated with huge chandeliers, antique art, and exquisitely hand-carved arching old Spanish-style doorways. These people are living "high on the hog." In the States, they would be upper middle class. All the kids in the family are around 30 years old, have been in school in the States, and have college degrees. They all speak English and are living a fat life. All weigh over 200 lbs. so they are round. They are fine people.

Yesterday George and I had to drive out to their dairy farm. We drove in his father's Buick Electra convertible. I felt like I was in the Mafia tooling along in that mammoth huge, ritzy car. I've been involved in many of their family gatherings this weekend, eating delicious food, and drinking good alcohol. It's astounding to realize the unique situations I find myself in when I'm on the road. It's an experience to see all the different variations of life in these countries. I can think of no better way to know the people.

However, it's shocking to see the unpleasant dirty, dusty, squalid, conditions of poor people living on the margins of society on the outskirts of Lima. When all the rich people drive to the airport to fly all over the world, they must pass through this section of town. In fact, whenever anyone comes or goes in this city, they are forced to see how economically divided this country is.

LIMA - JULY 10, 1972

I had a good visit with George's father, Señor Corochano, while eating a very tasty steak. He talked about Peru's war with Colombia and about how senseless it is to kill humans over such a trivial matter as land. We talked about how ridiculous the war in Vietnam was, and he said he despises all military people. One time his father pointed to a donkey and a military man and said, "They are both one." He said he has never forgotten that.

He also feels that all South America will eventually be ruled by Brazil and Argentina and will morph in two large countries. I think I can see this coming.

Miguel didn't show up today for us to go to Oxapampa. If he doesn't show tomorrow morning, I will take a bus. It seems like Lima and Peru is holding on to me like a magnet.

Mr. Corochano just climbed into his big Buick, and his chauffer drove him off for business. George told me tonight that his father killed two policemen when he was young. The police officers thought they could use people for their own gain. One night while drunk, they stopped his father and ordered him to take them someplace. He said no and told them to get out of the way. They would not move, so he ran them over, clunk, clunk. He really hates the uniform.

Tomorrow for sure, I am going to Oxapampa. Tonight, I am trying to get a call through to my Army friend, Han L., in Charleston, South Carolina, to see if he is still interested in coming down here for his vacation. He mentioned he wanted to in a letter he sent earlier, so I thought he would enjoy seeing Machu Pichu with me.

LIMA - JULY 11, 1972

I didn't leave for Oxapampa today because the guy who was selling the wood is sick in the hospital here in Lima. Miguel and Alberto, who came up from Chincha, had to go back empty-handed or do some more negotiating here.

I just called my good friend Han L. in South Carolina collect to see what his plans were for coming to Peru. He said he wouldn't be able to because he was getting ready to change jobs and move to Georgia. The call was clear, and it was good to talk to him. He said he drove through Texas on his way to San Francisco and stopped to visit my brother and found out how much he resembled me. He was mystified to see how similar we looked. My plans now, I guess, are to head by train to Buenos Aires.

LIMA - JULY 12, 1972

George took off for Chincha again today; but before he left, he bought me a poster as a souvenir of Peru. It's one I've been wanting for a long time. It will be a good memory.

I just reorganized my "luggage" again. I always do before I hit the road. I like to see that everything is in its place. I look it over to see if I can get rid of anything to make my load lighter. I would like to get rid of my shaving brush and straight razor, but I will wait until I can find someone who needs them. I don't plan to do any shaving for a long time. I look at shaving as a very sadistic act one does to his face. If done every day, it tortures your face.

Tomorrow, with luck, I will be on the road again, this time for the Andes Mountains of Peru. I will be taking a 260-mile train ride which is said to be one of the wonders of Latin America. The train passes through sixty-six tunnels, over fifty-nine bridges and amazingly, climbs up the Andes with twenty-two zig zags. This railroad is one of the most important in the country. It offers unbelievable views during the assent. The train passes through Galera Railway Station which is only 98 miles from Lima and is the second highest station in the world (15,694 ft). The railroad was built between 1870 and 1893 by an American railroad engineer named Henry Meiggs.

I just finished taking a shower. When I returned to my room, the wonderful aroma of leather greeted me. It's nice to know that such a scent radiates from my large leather shoulder bag which I crafted in Guatemala. It holds my personal belongings and I carry it with a wide leather strap from my left shoulder. My rolled up sleeping bag hangs from my right shoulder.

I tried using the bidet for the first time, and what an experience that was. I turned the water on to let it run to get warm. When I turned the handle, it squirted me in the shoulder. When I jerked back, it squirted me in the face. About the time I was ready to give up, I decided to try it. It was a clever way to clean up. It was a little sloppy at first, but one gets used to it and learns to control the water pressure. With a little finesse, one can get very clean with that water squirter.

HUANCAYO, PERU - JULY 13, 1972

It's hard to believe that I finally made it out of Lima, and it looks like I might even make it to Cuzco this time. I bought a 1st class train ticket for $2.40 to Huancayo. The 2nd class ticket cost $1.40. The second class wasn't as comfortable and for a 9-hour ride, I thought it might be a little trying. The scenery as we traveled up into the snowcapped, weathered, craggy mountains was exceptionally beautiful.

While the train travels, passengers often begin to feel lightheaded from the lack of oxygen and, in some cases, faint during the assent. A guy in a white coat walks back and forth administering oxygen from a large bag to those who need it.

On the train I met a couple of college girls, named Sue and Sue, spending their summer vacation in the "wilds of South America." They are from New York and seem to be stable 22-year-olds. We have a room with 3 beds in it and are paying 80 cents apiece. The room even has a lavatory and a mirror; and would you believe, three light bulbs and no oil on the floors. This is really a "first-class joint."

I don't know how long I will stay here. Maybe until Sunday to experience the best Native Inca market in Peru. It's very cold in these mountains and I can tell the chilly temperatures of the Andes Mountains is going to take some getting used to.

I walked a short distance out of the village to see the countryside. The radiant sun is warming this fine-looking mountain valley. It reminds me of a mountain valley in Montana. The sweet smell of yellow flowers drifts across the valley lifting my spirit. I'm sitting in the brown grass of summer watching butterflies alight on the pretty yellow flowers. The sound of a train whistle floats back and forth from one side of the mountain to the other. Peru is truly a beautiful place. It's strange that Huancayo has such beautiful afternoon weather in the middle of the winter. However, when night falls, one has no trouble distinguishing it's winter. It's freezing.

I bought a $6.00 bus ticket tonight to travel to Cuzco. The ride is going to be an endurance test and will take over 30 hours on rough, dusty roads.

HUANCAYO - JULY 16, 1972

I spent about four hours today walking around an extensive exotic market where one can buy Native Inca articles of all types: ponchos, sweaters, blankets, rugs, carved gourds, and just about everything imaginable made from alpaca or llama wool. The Native Inca women are fine-looking in their colorful costumes wearing white hats that appear like sailor hats with round crowns and curving brims. Everyone wears hats. I was looking for a sweater but couldn't find anything less than $6.00, so I decided to make one myself. I bought a hand-woven, alpaca-wool blanket; and I'm now cutting out and sewing a pullover jacket. I paid $4.00 for the material. I'm enthused about making this coat. I've wanted to make one ever since I was a kid collecting "Red Ryder" shredded-wheat-cereal-box spacers that provided patterns for kids on how to make assorted items.

Sue and Sue suffer from the lack of experience traveling in countries other than the good ole USA. They have nothing to talk about except their boyfriends back home and gossip about all the friends they have ever had. They are very fussy with their food. They are nice people, but it will be good to split tomorrow. I'm glad they are finally getting some travel experience. They need it. They are planning to go down one of the tributaries to the Amazon River. I wish them all the luck.

CUZCO, PERU - JULY 19, 1972

Thirty-seven hours on a rattly, dusty bus driving through the Andes on a dirt and gravel road has left me drained: up and down, around the curves, and through little villages passing by. Along the way I could see Native Indian women in their flowing skirts driving cattle, sheep, llamas, goats, and pigs, all to their pastures for grazing. The ride was tiring but interesting. Heinz, an Austrian guy who was sitting beside me, kept telling me all about his travels around the world, having sex with prostitutes, and drinking 10 to 20 whiskies a night in the bars.

CUZCO - JULY 21, 1972

While on the bus from Huancayo I met a guy from California named Chuck E. We stayed the first night in Cuzco in the Grand Hotel Bolivar for 60 cents a night. A rooster began crowing when the sun came up, and I thought he was crowing next to my bed. It turns out he was. The wall between our room and the rooster was only made of chicken wire with large sheets of plastic hanging on it. I wanted to throttle him.

The next day Chuck and I changed rooms for one upstairs where its warmer and has less hassle with the roosters and turkeys in the courtyard below. Chuck and I have become particularly good friends. He is a remarkably interesting guy.

We met another young American in the hotel and the topic of the Vietnam war came up. He asked what we did regarding the war. I told him I attended four years of Reserve Officer Training Corps (ROTC) during college and was obliged to serve in the war. Chuck said he did not have to go due to his four-year stint in the US Peace Corps in Africa. The other guy surprisingly said he served time in prison for his decision to not serve in the war. All three of had to make monumental personal decisions about that war.

For the last few days, we have been exploring this ancient city. The Inca builders were true artists who had a special feel for space and detail. Their character still lives here in their ancient capital. Striking examples of Inca stonework line most of the streets. Their stone walls are so perfect the edges of huge boulders are so finely ground and fitted together. There is not a waiver or flaw visible in the joints.

I just found out that Chuck knows my Colombian travel friend, Jim S., from Quito. This was a surprise. They became good friends in fact. Surprisingly, in a small bakery last night, I met a guy named Jerry P., who was a Panama Peace Corps friend of Danelle's. Danelle had even given me his name, thinking I might be able to look him up while I was in Panama on my way south. I found out who he was after talking to him for a while. It's a small world.

I have nearly finished making my sweater. It looks like it's going to turn out better than expected, although I had underestimated the amount of time it would take to hand sew the pieces together with yarn.

CUZCO - JULY 24, 1972

I'm sitting at the train station waiting to lumber along the train tracks to the beginning of what promises to be another exotic journey. Chuck, an American named Roger, and his German wife Gotland, and I are going to hike the last 54 kms to Machu Picchu on an old Inca trail across the Andes. Roger found a hand-drawn map in the Cuzco visitor center, and we plan to follow it to the fabled Inca ruins named Machu Picchu. I packed a half kilo of cheese, thirteen candy bars, dehydrated soups, dried figs, three oranges, oatmeal, and thirty-six pieces of bread, enough for our six days trek. It's going to be a good journey and will feel good to be in the mountains again.

ON TO MACHU PICCHU - JULY 24, 1972

The second-class train to Estación (Station) 88, the drop off location for Incan Natives and hikers following the Inca Trail, was a 3-hour experience of Natives pushing and shoving with their big bundles of goods. Station 88 was nothing more than a flat spot near the Urubamba River on one side of the tracks at the base of steep Andes Mountains rising to the sky with sugar-white snow capping the peaks. Their height is overwhelming.

I'm sitting by our fire now after walking and climbing for 7 hours. The full moon just rose over the craggy mountain peak on the other side of the valley. It's a beautiful setting but is getting colder as night sets in. We are having a challenging time keeping the campfire going, but the water boils fast. Climbing to the top of that first mountain crest was excruciatingly difficult. I am still not acclimated to the altitude and that climb thoroughly exhausted me. I am suffering from a cold, and my back has been giving me a trouble. Now after this heavy packing, it's tense and sore and I am utterly exhausted.

There are two Uruguayans on the trail, but they are behind us. Other than them, the only people we've seen were Incan Natives walking or riding along with their horses. I sure would like to have had one of their horses at times, especially on the long climb to the first ridge. It's nice to have a full moon watching over us.

Terry lies exhausted, suffering from altitude sickness after a monstrous climb to the 13,795 ft Dead Woman's Pass on the trail to Machu Picchu. Photo by Charles Eilers.

Terry struggles to eat lunch while suffering from altitude sickness. Photo by Charles Eilers.

Feeling better, Terry and Godlind study a map for trail directions to Machu Picchu. Photo by Charles Eilers.

Terry, Godlind, and Roger enjoy morning tea while drying wet clothing and sleeping bags. Photo by Charles Eilers.

Terry, Roger, and Godlind sit high on a mountain ridge observing the ancient Inca ruins of Machu Picchu on a ridge below. Photo by Charles Eilers.

Roger, Terry, Godlind, and Charles Eilers pose in front of a craggy peak called Wayna Picchu. The Inca constructed temples and terraces on its crest. Photo by Charles Eilers.

Terry is photographing a pack of llamas. Photo by Charles Eilers.

World explorer, author, and photographer Charles Eilers.
Photo by Charles Eilers.

Argentinians Oscar and Carlos with their motorcycle with side car and author on the Pacific coast in Southern Peru. Photo by Terry Brown.

Chicken farmer friends from Chincha Alta, Peru who befriended the author and gave him a place to rest and recuperate at their farm. Terry is in the back row, far left. Photo by Terry Brown.

Portrait of Danelle and Terry in Buenos Aires, Argentina shortly before hitchhiking to Santiago, Chile. Photo by John Buster.

Portrait of Terry with beard and long hair in Buenos Aires, Argentina. Photo by John Buster.

Terry and Danelle at a Buenos Aires artisan fair selling their drawings and beadwork. Photo by Terry Brown.

Terry and Danelle with friends in a Buenos Aires park. Photo by Terry Brown.

Architects Hector Lacarra and Clorindo Testa on their studio balcony in Buenos Aires. Testa was a pioneer of the International style of architecture and hired Terry to work as a designer. Photo by Terry Brown.

Clorindo Testa's Bank of London in Buenos Aires recognizes Testa's bold geometric shapes and strong proportions called Brutalist architecture. Photo by Terry Brown.

Danelle and Terry hitchhiking from Buenos Aires, Argentina to Santiago, Chile. Photo by Terry Brown.

An elated Danelle and Terry celebrate their arrival at Bahia Lapataia National Park, Tierra del Fuego, south of Ushuaia, the "end of the world." Photo by Terry Brown.

Lyle, Mary, John, Robert (back row), Danelle and Terry (kneeling). All arrived about the same time by hitchhiking to Tierra del Fuego. The Quonset hut sheltered us from continuous wind. Photo by Terry Brown.

Summer and Winter post card images of Ushuaia, Tierra del Fuego. We arrived in the Summer, but it felt like Winter. Photo by Foto Santamaria, Ushuaia, Industrial Argentina.

Perito Moreno Glacier in southern Argentina. Terry and Danelle visited this glacier on their way up the Eastern side of the Andes. Photographer unknown.

After traveling for a year and a half, Terry returned to Antigua, Guatemala and thought it would be fun to pose beside a mural of Donald Duck.

Terry cutting his colleague's hair. Bob is one of the founders of the nonprofit linguistic center Proyecto Lingüístico Francisco Marroquín (PLFM) in Antigua.

Terry posing in the construction of a large ojo de buey (ox eye) window of his Mayan Cultural Center in Antigua.

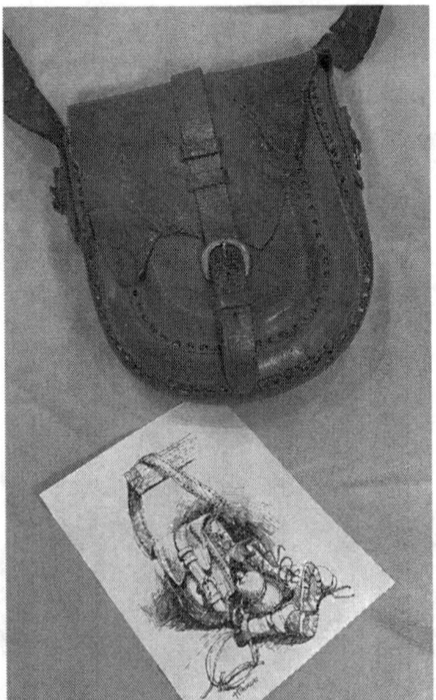

Cover drawing and photo of Terry's original leather bag he made to carry his possessions after his backpack was stolen in Mexico.

Copy of one of Danelle's journal pages displaying her miniscule style of writing.

Terry Brown's passport photo.

ON THE TRAIL - JULY 25, 1972

We got a late start this morning because we decided to wait until the sun came up to dry our damp sleeping bags. I slept well but was a little restless because I'm used to sleeping with a pillow and didn't have anything to raise my head. I did not get cold.

We climbed for about five hours today, much of which was along a clear stream flowing through a forest of moss-covered trees. I really love to put my face in a mountain stream and drink water from snowmelt. The views of the snow-tipped mountains high above and all around with steep grassy slopes falling away, was a sight that words can't describe. The grandeur of these Andes is overwhelming.

It was a good feeling to be on the trail with the sun blazing down on us and the meadows extending around us. From there we began another climb to the second pass. The climbing kept getting more difficult because the higher we went the less oxygen there was. We had to stop every few steps for a breath. It was an agonizing climb, but we didn't want to eat until we got to the pass. When we finally arrived, the wind was pushing clouds over the pass and around our heads. It was chilly and we had to bundle up again. I ate two sardine sandwiches and some figs and part of a chocolate bar.

From then on, it was easy because it was mostly downhill. We followed an old eight-foot-wide Inca roadway up and over the pass. The path is heavily worn; I can still see it wind its way across the mountains. It's said that Inca runners could travel about a mile in 6 minutes. It's hard to imagine a man going that fast on these steep roads. Those runners were no slouches.

We found a place in a small grassy area to camp for the night. I cut a lot of tall grass and made a soft bed which ought to help me sleep. I ate a cheese sandwich with my soup tonight and finished the candy bar and drank a cup of hot tea.

Alongside the camp is a huge flat boulder where we built our fire. The night was not cold. I am sitting here watching the huge blue-gray billowy clouds float up the valley and go right on by us. Chuck said he saw a cloud crawl into my sleeping bag.

I was amazed at the cleanliness of the trail, not a candy wrapper or piece of junk in sight. The Uruguayans passed us before we broke camp this morning, but we left them behind at the first saddle. They were stoned and just wanted to sit and dig the whole beautiful world around them.

I feel healthy, and my back didn't give me trouble today. I end the day feeling invigorated. We are in an area where no animals are seen; even cows don't graze here. The giant boulders are crumbling granite; and the towering Andes, silhouetted against the moonlit night, appear to be guarding us. There is no one around for miles, not even Native Inca; and we won't see anyone until we arrive at Machu Pichu.

This is one of those days that feels good to be alive. It's rewarding to watch a dancing campfire and think about all I've seen on this trip.

STILL GOING - JULY 26, 1972

I had a heck of a time getting to sleep and then woke up about 4:00 AM. My sleeping bag was wet from the night's moisture, and I had to take a leak. Roger and his wife were rustling around trying to set their tent up because it was starting to rain. I just pulled the rest of my plastic sheet over me and went to sleep until about 7:00 AM. Everything was wet, so we broke camp and went to the other side of the valley to dry our belongings in the sun, wash, and eat breakfast. It was a magnificent view of the soaring snowcapped mountains all around.

We started climbing to a pass which wasn't as difficult or as high as the first one. About halfway up, we came to an old Inca ruin. It looked like a fort guarding the pass. Nothing is left of it but a few walls. Near the ruins is a small cozy-looking cave where several travelers spent the night. The huge stone roof was covered with black smoke from fires built to keep its occupants warm.

Then we climbed steadily to the next windy pass and down into semi-jungle. Our entire journey today has been along the old Inca trail which connected various forts and out-posts. As we descended, we came upon ruins more impressive than the one we previously passed. It had a marvelous vista and protected vantage point due to its position on a ridge with a steep valley on both sides of the ridge. We rested there then descended into the jungle. After hiking through lush green tunnels of foliage, we came to a boggy lake which was a water supply for the Inca. Their earth and stone dam is still in place.

It's been a good day because the climbing hasn't been too difficult. Roger and Chuck are having a tough time getting the fire going because the wood is damp. Tomorrow we should be able to see Machu Pichu as we climb over the next pass. It looks like I'm going to sleep tonight with the chirping of frogs in the bog.

SITTING ON A PASS - JULY 27, 1972

Just before going to bed, I felt like some character in a foggy monster movie. The fog had completely closed around us, so we hit the rack about 8:00 PM. I woke up at 5:00 AM with a full moon shining in my face, and the sky was clear. It was beautiful to watch the sun come up and set the snow-capped mountains ablaze with the moon setting behind them.

There was frost on Roger's tent and pack and on the end of my plastic ground sheet. We packed up our gear while it was still damp and wet, drank some tea and ate breakfast and headed for the next pass. We figured to get an earlier start today and dry our equipment farther along the trail.

We continued along the Inca Road, which at times was completely covered with thick moss and mud, so our boots got soaking wet. After passing through an Inca tunnel and along a steep drop-off, we came to a saddle which drops steeply down to the Urubamba River.

We found a sunny area and are now soaking up the sun's warmth and drying our belongings. Down by the river winds the train track to Machu Picchu. Our equipment is nearly dry, including my socks, so we are going to pack up and push on for Huayna Picchu, which is a ruin near Machu Picchu.

LATER

The Inca Trail led us to this Inca ruin called Phuyupatamarca. We are about 11 km from Machu Picchu and due to its high altitude, it is known as La Ciudad entre la Niebla (The City inside the Mist). The ruin has five small, hand-crafted stone baths. The water is still flowing after centuries of use, so it was bath time. The water felt exceptionally refreshing.

My feet got wet again since our last drying spot; so, while we cook our noon soup, I'm vigorously trying to dry my boots and socks. Nowhere, since we started our journey, have we had to worry about potable water. It's everywhere; clear, and straight from the mountain snows and flavored with nature's beauty.

Following along the stone trail, we passed through more dense jungle, thick with all types of overgrowth. Moss and moist undergrowth is a foot or more deep, and the trees are completely covered with these plants, climbing, and dangling from their limbs.

Suddenly we rounded a ridge, and before us was the splendor of Machu Picchu far below us on a lower ridge. The surrounding mountain peaks, towering high over that ancient citadel, appeared to guard the ruin. I was a little disappointed to find it so low in altitude compared to the rest of the mountains around it. Seeing Machu Picchu with mountain peaks surrounding it reminded of a diamond setting. It was strange to receive the first glimpse of Machu Picchu from such a high angle because all I ever knew of the famous ruins was from closeup photos of the ruin.

From that vantage point we started down the mountain on a steep trail through thick jungle which we thought would take us to Wiñay Wayna, an Inca ruin along the Inca Trail to Machu Picchu. Our fears were that, if we missed the trail to Machu Picchu, we could be on one leading down to the Urubamba River far below and would have to climb back up. It was getting dark; and it sounded like we were getting closer to the river. We decided we had missed the trail and climbed back to where we started. We scaled a more direct but steeper route under the power line. It seemed like we were climbing straight up. In 45 minutes, we were at the top of the ridge again and extremely exhausted. We found a sheltered area to camp and set up tents before supper. It rained most of the night.

JUST ABOVE MACHU PICCHU - JULY 28, 1972

My cold has really been getting me down, and I feel weak after another damp night. In the middle of the night, I had to take some cough syrup and Dristan decongestant. It's 9:15 AM now, and we are completely enveloped in fog. It's a shame to be this close to Machu Picchu and not be able to see it.

Roger got up earlier and is out scouting for the trail. I really feel run down and am just lying here feeling blah.

LATER

Chuck, Roger, and Gotland took off in this morning's fog to look for the trail. I fell asleep and they returned about noon. The fog had lifted, and they discovered the trail we were on last night was correct and that we were too cautious and didn't go far enough down to meet the trail to Machu Picchu. So, we packed back down the trail the same way we went last night. We finally arrived at the ruins of Wiñay Wayna with its intricately constructed stone houses. This complex has terraces laid out in a lush steep valley, and a beautiful waterfall crashing against a rocky backdrop. This is a handsome ruin. I'm sitting here listening to a guy and his girlfriend playing music on flutes, which is appropriate for this setting. Ah yes, what a life!

Looking out through the front door of one of the buildings is a brutal drop of 8,000 feet to the Urubamba River. Beyond that, I see eight towering mountain peaks, each with their sides falling steeply to the river. The last and highest range is snowcapped.

One of the ancient buildings has a new thatched roof. We decided to camp in it tonight, so we won't have to put up the tents and dry them in the morning. That will save time for our hike to Machu Picchu. Our Uruguayan friend picked some flowers called Marsala, and we made tea out of it. It was tasty with honey.

MACHU PICCHU - JULY 29, 1972

We left Wiñay Wayna ruin shortly after sunup and hiked along the Inca trail towards Machu Picchu. After an hour hike, we came around a ridge and there it was, "The Lost City of the Inca" in the splendor of the morning sun. The stone buildings appear intact, except for the original roof beams and grass thatched roofs which are long gone. I appreciated that several of the historic structures had new grass roofs, which gave me a better idea of how this complex must have appeared. The roofs appear to be about the same angle as the mountain side.

As with most ancient Native American sites, this "city" has a commanding view of its area of the world. Although Machu Picchu is not situated as high above the river as I thought it would be, it holds its own against all other ruins like no other and is the most familiar icon of the Inca Empire. It was built around 1450 and abandoned a century later, about the time of the Spanish conquest. On the far end of this site is Huayna Picchu, a craggy rock outcropping towering high over Machu Picchu. It is lined with terraces and a ruin at the very top. It looks like something out of a Lord of the Rings story. We explored this ruin for the remainder of the day and were awed by the complexity and immense beauty of this site. Its terraced gardens and polished dry-stone buildings dazzled my senses. It is an honor to explore this magnificent site, a community set on the top of a mountain. It is said, the Spaniards never found it. I can see how difficult it would be to find looking up from the Urubamba River far below.

CUZCO - JULY 30, 1972

We trekked down the mountain to the train along the Urubamba River and bought a second-class ticket on the regular train back to Cuzco. This allowed us the privilege of sitting on the floor in the aisle of the first-class car. The only difference between the first and second-class seats is a small amount of padding was added on the first-class seats. Both cars have seat backs that are straight up. It was good to get back to Cuzco and have our reserved room waiting for us. My cold is on the rampage, and it's nice not to have to think about the effects of a cold breeze blowing on my head all night.

CUZCO - AUG. 1, 1972

The day after returning, we washed all our dirty cloths. The socks were the most difficult because there was so much dirt and mud imbedded in them. Chuck and I are leaving Peru and going to La Paz tomorrow by train and bus. I'm anxious to get to Tierra del Fuego, the end of South America.

PUNO, PERU - AUG. 2, 1972

We just arrived after a nine-and-a-half-hour train ride through some of the most handsome countryside in Peru. The scenery that passed by us and the clickety-clack of the train was my exact idea of what the Andes should look like. Golden brown grass, grazing llamas, and sheep and barren, snowy mountains in the background. Women with wide skirts and bowler hats tend their flocks, and adobe houses dot the vast countryside.

When we boarded the train this morning about 6:30 AM, there was a big French guy hollering and screaming that he was reserving or saving the seats of the entire second-class car for a tour group. He grabbed one guy, another Frenchman, by the collar and suddenly slugged him on the side of the head, breaking his glasses. I wanted to tear him apart, but he was too big. The guy he hit was a clean-cut, meek guy. The big guy, having a hot temper, as well as being disturbed that he wasn't going to be able to save enough seats for his group, said the small guy called him a drunkard. Come to find out, the big guy was the group leader. After the train was moving and everybody had their seat, he said he felt sorry for his actions. He and his unfortunate victim are going to settle for the damaged glasses later.

COPACABANA, BOLIVIA - AUG. 3, 1972

I have finally made it to another country which I had no idea I would ever see. Of all the countries I have seen or heard of, I have had mixed feelings about Bolivia. Part is due to the political turmoil and part to the poverty of many Native Inca people in this landlocked country. I was never sure if I should even come to Bolivia because of its problems, but I am glad I am able to visit the country and form my own opinions.

Chuck and I spent all afternoon and part of the morning riding in a rattly bus with worn out springs and shock absorbers traveling on a washboard road. The vibrations sure felt good on my back; but, after my whole body started to go limp, the vibrations got old.

Last night we checked into a room with one single bed, and I slept on the floor to cut expenses. We paid 40 cents apiece. Tonight, we have a room with two beds, and I'm paying 80 cents a night. There are several fiestas, celebrations, folk dances, and parades today and continuing tomorrow, so we are going to stay and watch some of it. This should give us an example of a portion of Bolivian life.

They sell delicious peanuts here as well as a flavorsome popped corn which tastes like sugar pops with kernels about an inch across. It seems like everyone is munching on them.

LA PAZ, BOLIVIA - AUG. 5, 1972

Today I'm 27 years old and am in La Paz. When I turned 21, I was in France and England. When I turned 26, I was in the Vietnam war. It's kind of nice to celebrate my birthday in extraordinary locations.

Yesterday I was doubled over in pain and cramps caused by a stomach ailment. I took Sulfasuxidine and Lomotil tablets and went to sleep. That did the job.

While still in Copacabana, we climbed one of the hills overlooking the town and witnessed some strange scenes. Native Incas, wearing their finest colorful clothing, were buying miniature plaster of Paris houses shaped like houses that wealthy people own, and small "tin" models of trucks or buses all painted and decorated in vivid colors. They would also buy plaster of Paris bulls and place these articles among the rocks with weeds, moss and pebbles forming some semblance of a model yard. The models are all wrapped with decorations. After drinking beer, people would pass the glass around. They pour beer on the models and wish luck on the things they wish they had or hope to have. It was strange.

The folk dancers and the pan flute players were exceptional. I had never heard pan music and greatly enjoyed watching the musicians in Inca dress play these exceptional handmade instruments. These guys really get it on. It was beautiful music.

LA PAZ - AUG. 6, 1972

The slow ride to this country's capital, La Paz, was climaxed by a shocking view of the city. It appeared to be a giant mountain bowl lined with shacks with the city center in the bottom of the bowl. The highest building in La Paz is 30 stories with a few other tall buildings huddled around it in the center. All other building are single-story adobe. Wealthy people live in the lower area of the basin near the center. The poorer a person is, the higher up the hillside he/she lives.

The best peanuts in the world are in Bolivia. Big and sweet! I just found another *Newsweek* magazine and devoured it from cover to cover. It's rare that I see one; and when I do, it's hard to stop reading. I enjoy catching up on the news. The same goes for *Time* magazine.

I went to see Tiahuanaco, the center of the pre-Inca Aymara civilization, which flourished between 600 and 900 AD. The ruins constructed around 1,200 AD pre-existed the Incas and are believed to be the oldest in the Western Hemisphere. Immense stone doorways, massive aqueducts, and temples form the center of this ancient civilization. These unknown people built huge stone obelisks and statues which remind me of the statues of Tula, Mexico. I particularly enjoyed the small, sculptured heads of people protruding from the lower part of the wall of a sunken courtyard.

VILLAZÓN, BOLIVIA - AUG. 11, 1972

I'm at the border of Bolivia and Argentina and will be in Argentina today. I have six days until my passport expires, so I should be able to make it to Buenos Aires in plenty of time to have it renewed. A French guy named Gad is going to travel with me. We are planning to hitchhike all the way, that is, if it's possible.

My last night in La Paz was a good one. Chuck and another friend name Bruce Allen and two girls, one Danish and one American, and I had a party with bread, wine, and some of the tastiest cheese I have ever eaten. The Danish girl, Marianne Kohn, was really a beautiful person; and we seemed to really hit it off during the few days we were together in La Paz. It's amazing, the experiences one gets while traveling, especially with people. I was heading for Argentina, and Chuck planned to go in another direction, so we parted ways in La Paz. I will miss him. He was a good travel friend.

While in La Paz, I was planning to go to the border riding second-class on the train for $6.00 US; but I found a bus company with a new, modern, "Greyhound" style dustproof bus going the same distance for $8.00. I took it because I really dreaded riding for two days and a night in a crowded train car with right-angle seats, stopping at every little station and sometimes in between.

Everything was going smoothly on that handsome new bus with padded interior and comfortable, adjustable seats until we got to the last major town before the border, a place called Potosi. There the driver pulled into a dusty yard, and we were directed to deboard and climb into a small, cramped, crowded, rattly old bus to ride the rest of the way to the border. I was told they don't drive the slick, padded bus on bumpy dirt roads. Everybody had their assigned seats, and the bus wasn't full when we took off. We stopped on the edge of town to pick up a lady and her daughter. She thought I had her seat, but the driver said the seat was mine and to stay put. She was determined to get my seat, so she and her daughter wedged in beside me; and before I knew it, she was stabbing me in my left thigh with a crochet hook. I pushed her hard and screamed with pain; and when I pushed her, the crochet hook spiked the soft part of her thumb and was sticking out the end. That calmed everything. Everybody in the bus wanted me to stay put, so I did until the first stop when she and her daughter took over the seat while I was eating breakfast at the bus stop.

I decided it wasn't worth the hassle to reclaim my seat, so I calmly went to the back of the bus where it was comfortable because I had the entire seat to myself. Unfortunately, it was a hard, hard ride and after twenty-six and a half hours we arrived at the border. It will be good to be in Argentina, the land of better buses and cheap steaks.

LA QUIACA, ARGENTINA - AUG. 11, 1972 (5,152 KMS TO TIERRA DEL FUEGO)

It's 3:00 PM, and I'm waiting with Gad and an Argentine lady named Rosario for the train to Jujuy. The hitchhiking out of this border town was not successful. This small frontier town reminds me of an American, old West town of the early 1900's with wide dusty streets situated along the railroad track. The weather feels like Spring. The sun warms the days, and the nights are cold. The trees have no leaves yet; but, because of the warm days, trees think it's Spring. I feel at home here. Gad and I will try to hitchhike from Jujuy where we hope we will have better luck. Border towns are always difficult to hitch out of.

JUJUY, AGENTINA - AUG. 12, 1972

We arrived last night about 10:00 PM after a tiring train ride and found a hotel for 40 cents a night. The first thing I noticed was that the trees were green, the air was warm, and the whole atmosphere was like that of a Caribbean town.

Gad and I hit the rack about 12:00 AM and were in a deep sleep until someone knocked on our door about 9:00 AM this morning. I woke up to the sweet smell of Spring weather with a cool flowery breeze. Birds were singing, and the sun was shining. I really feel revived and am excited about being in Argentina.

We met a couple of young Bolivian guys on the bus to the border. They are studying in the University in Cordoba, Argentina. They invited us to stay with them after we arrive. That should save expenses and give us a chance to visit Cordoba, one of the most attractive cities in Argentina.

ON A TRAIN FOR TUCUMÁN, ARGENTINA - AUG. 13, 1972

Yesterday wasn't too bad for hitching. Our second ride gave us a dollar and two cigarettes. Gad smoked them. We wound up in a small town called San Jose de Metán, where we befriended an old man selling grocery items out of a little clapboard, dusty kiosk beside the highway. He told us he was of Arabic decent and spent much of his youth in Arab lands. He cooked us a meal of fried eggs, a little meat, a lot of bread and tea for 20 cents apiece. Besides all that, he even put us up in his house for the night for three pesos. All this because he found Gad knew a few words of Arabic.

This morning after a refreshing sleep, we hit the road hitchhiking early but to no avail. We asked truck drivers, car drivers, and horse drivers for a ride; but all was in vain for we stood there for four and a half hours before deciding to pay 74 cents to go 100 miles to Tucuman by train. Then we will go on to Cordoba to visit our Bolivian friends.

ON A TRAIN GOING SOUTH

I wonder where I'm going
But then I wonder where I've gone
I know I can't go back
So, I must go on.

I'm riding on a train
Seeing the cows heading home
And the silhouettes of leafless trees
With an orange sun dipping down.

It's an enjoyable time to think about the day
As we rode along clackety clack
Hitching was bad but life is good
I made a friend of an old, old man.

As scenes pass by they're never the same
Through constant motion in changing times
I find a joy I once had known
But though a child I was before.

TUCUMAN, ARGENTINA - AUG. 14, 1972

As could be expected, we didn't make the connection. Our train arrived at 10:00 PM, and the train for Cordoba left at 9:00 PM from another station. As soon as our train arrived, we began walking with our gear to what we thought was the train station. We walked one and a half km; and as we neared the station, someone told us we were heading for the freight station. The passenger station is one and a half km in another direction. We walked and walked and walked and found out the train had already left. What to do? We decided to walk around the train yard and look for an open passenger car; we found one on a sidetrack and went to sleep on the seats. Luckily, it's warmer here than in Bolivia. This morning after a good sleep, Gad and I are taking the train six hundred km to Cordoba for $2.73. Incredible prices here! It is difficult to believe how inexpensive it is to live and travel here. Tonight, we should be sleeping in our friend's house.

CORDOBA, ARGENTINA - AUG. 15, 1972

It was a long, dusty, tiring day. The scenery was flat, dry desert; but luckily the second-class car we were riding in was comfortable and not crowded. When we arrived at Cordoba, we took a taxi across town to David and Alfonso's house for 35 cents. Everything seems to be so inexpensive here. Today we ate in a university cafeteria for an incredible 5 ¼ cents. We ate a T-bone steak, salad, goulash, bread, and an orange. It is no wonder there were hundreds of students standing in line waiting to eat.

Cordoba looks very European, like some place in Southern France or Italy. I guess Buenos Aires will even be more so. It was good to see David and Alfonso again, and it sure is nice of them to put us up.

CORDOBA - AUG. 16, 1972

My passport expired yesterday, but it doesn't matter unless the police throw me in jail or something weird like that happens. If the US Embassy in Lima didn't screw up, my extension should be waiting for me when I arrive in Buenos Aires. Before I left Lima, I asked the consulate to write for an extension and forward it to B.A. so I wouldn't have to wait a month in Argentina for it.

On our way to David and Alfonso's home, Gad and I bought two large pizzas for 20 cents each, and some bread and had a feast for the four of us. Alphonso bought several cokes and David bought more cheese. I also bought some Chubut cheese for 85 cents, the same as we had in La Paz for $2.00. It's some of the best cheese I've ever eaten.

It is strange to have traveled through poor parts of Peru and Bolivia and see the difference in life compared to this rich country and this metropolitan city. Everybody is all decked out in their finest outfits, walking along window shopping for more new clothing often seen in magazines. I guess the easier the life one has, the more conscious he must be about his appearance. At least that is the way it seems. Fashion parades and the rich are synonymous.

BUENOS AIRES - AUG. 18, 1972

Arriving in Buenos Aires is a milestone. I've traveled an estimated 7,500 miles to Buenos Aires and have 2,370 miles to go to Tierra del Fuego. Last night, Gad and I hopped on a train and rode the last 442 miles to Buenos Aires for $3.00. The train departed at 10:30 PM on the dot and arrived here at 10:30 AM. I had a sound sleep on a seat intended for three people. The weather is very dreadful. It's raining, the wind is blowing and it's cold. We are having no luck locating our friends. Later today we will know something. Right now, we are killing about two and a half hours in an ice cream shop drinking tea and waiting until 2:00 PM when Rosario, the girl we met in Bolivia, returns.

The countryside on the outskirts of B.A. is flat and appears to be mostly fertile farm and ranch land. It looks as if it gets regular moisture.

BUENOS AIRES - AUG. 19, 1972

It is a strange feeling to be on the other side of this continent from Lima. I've covered a lot of miles. On a map, the distance from Lima to here looks long in comparison to the distance from here to Tierra del Fuego.

When we went back to Rosario's house yesterday, her brother said she was not home and that we couldn't stay there because their mother doesn't like longhaired guys. So, we returned to the city center without seeing her. We rented a room in a hotel for 70 cents. Today we changed hotels to one costing 50 cents a night, but it has no hot water. That doesn't matter. Today I went to an address Eva gave me while in Lima and found her there. I ate a good lunch and a grand supper at the house of Eva's friends, Marta and Carlos. Carlos works with a theater group. They are good people. The weather was foul, but it was a good day because both Gad and I encountered our friends.

BUENOS AIRES – AUG. 20, 1972

It is amazing to be sitting at a drafting table in an architect's house completely at ease, listening to good music, drinking tea, reflecting on a botched day, and just feeling mellow. This young guy named Ernesto let us have his apartment, and he's not even living here. We have the place all to ourselves. The guy we've never even seen before turned his apartment over to us. It serves as an architectural office during the week.

I've been locked out most of the day and night because of a screwup with the key, but tomorrow we will get a couple duplicates made. I really don't know what I will do from here until I pick up my mail tomorrow. I will know what's happening back in the States with my family. Gad and I have a good setup here, so maybe I will hang around a while. One can rent an apartment here for as low as $10 a month. They are paying $50 a month for this place.

Gad received a letter today from his father saying there is a warrant out for his arrest in France and that he should be careful. He is evading their draft and must go to the French Embassy tomorrow to get his passport renewed, and he's not sure if they will arrest him or not. We will know tomorrow.

BUENOS AIRES - AUG. 22, 1972

As it turns out, the French Military Attaché told Gad that they cannot arrest him, but he must be careful what he does and where he goes, for he could even be deported back to France to face a military tribunal. They refused to extend his passport which expires in February, so he is now trying to plan where to go. Canada is his best bet because they have no military requirement. Australia was a thought, but it is too far away and sends its soldiers to the Vietnam war. Argentina is a safe bet, but they too require military duty. So, Gad is going tomorrow to the Canadian Embassy to see what the problems of entering as a landed immigrant are.

B.A. is a huge city of mostly high-rise buildings everywhere except downtown which bears heavily on historic European architectural influence. The people on the streets dress elegantly. I was told that until 1945 men were forbidden to go downtown without a necktie; and until about 5 years ago, one had to wear a tie to all functions in town whether it be a movie or ballet. There is no law now requiring ties, but the people still feel the need to wear formal attire.

Last night Ernesto, the guy who let us have the apartment, took Gad and me to hear the Buenos Aires Philharmonic Orchestra in one of the foremost theaters in the world. I wore a borrowed tie but entered wearing the only footwear I have, my combat boots. Can you believe it is expected to tip the guy ushering us to our seats?

BUENOS AIRES - AUG. 30, 1972

Gad left for Chile a couple of days ago. He took a train to the Argentine border and must fly to Santiago because the pass is blocked with snow. He has decided to immigrate to Canada and found it won't be much of a problem, especially since he has a college degree and speaks four languages.

While on the train in northern Argentina, I told an architectural student that I would like to get a job with an architect in Buenos Aires. He said, "Why not talk to the best architect in Argentina?"

Twelve days after arriving in Buenos Aires, I went job hunting and visited the office of Clorindo Testa, the most famous architect in Buenos Aires and is among the most renowned architects of modern architecture in Latin America. I located his office in an ornate historic, European-style building in the center of town and took the handsome, open-cage elevator to the sixth floor and knocked on the office door. The door had a small, engraved tag that read "Clorindo Testa Architect." A man cracked open the door and asked how he could help me. I told him I would like to speak with Arquitecto Testa about a job, and he asked if I had a business card. I said no, and he said wait a minute. When he returned he ushered me in and introduced me to Arquitecto Testa who surprisingly pushed his curved-back chair away from his drafting table and pulled up another chair in front of him and invited me to sit down. I told him I have an architectural degree and would like to work for him. We had an interesting talk and he asked me to come back in two days. I should know something next week.

Ernesto and I went to a concert a couple of nights ago to hear the music of Theodorakis which was directed by Theodorakis (Zorba the Greek and "Z") himself. His style of directing was completely unlike anything I have ever seen. He was completely liberated and used his entire body with wild, bold, arm movements to direct the musicians. If I were ever to conduct, I would do like Theodorakis. It was a beautiful experience. Besides being a great conductor, he was well received by the Argentines because of his political standing and troubles with the Greek government. He's a communist which therefore makes him a radical and an outcast in his country.

BUENOS AIRES - SEPT. 1, 1972

Today is Friday, the day I was asked to return to Arquitecto Testa's office. He told me he will hire me. He said to come to work Monday morning at 10:30 AM. In other words, I have just landed a job with the best architect in Argentina and one of the best in South America. This was exciting news. All the architecture students in Argentina would do anything to work for Arquitecto Testa. From judging the works I've seen of his, he is equal to the top Modernist architects in any part of the world. It's difficult to believe that a hard-traveled, bearded foreigner with worn-out clothes could walk into the office of Arquitecto Testa several days ago and expect anything of a reply, let alone, a job.

BUENOS AIRES - SEPT. 4, 1972

I began work today for the architectural firm of Clorindo Testa. His partner's name is Arquitecto Lacarra. Though I was told to show up at 10:30 AM, I wanted to make a good impression by arriving before 8:00 AM (per US standards) but found the office locked. I waited around for a half hour and the office was still locked, so I walked around the streets and returned before 10:30 AM. I learned quickly that Argentines work from 10:00 AM to 2:00 PM, then take a two-hour siesta or lunch and return at 4:00 PM and work until 8:00 PM.

I will be helping formulate design ideas to enlarge the size of a beach community called Pinamar, a resort town on the Atlantic Sea coast south of Buenos Aires. I will also help design the landscaping, street, and housing layout around the new golf course which is also being designed by this office. I began diligently working on a functionable design. This job is made difficult by the natural location of sand dunes and the edges of the new golf course. We must design around them.

I need dress clothes badly. My worn traveling clothes are not up to the Buenos Aires class. Anyway, I think I will wait until next week until I find out how long I can expect to stay with the firm. I didn't even ask him about money for it really doesn't matter. Getting this job is all that counts. Tomorrow I'm going with Ernesto to visit his university.

This last couple of weeks in Buenos Aires has been a fat, easy life. I wake up when I wake up. When I look at the time I lay back in the warmth of my sleeping bag and plug myself back into my dream machine. I can go on like that for hours with all kinds of scenes running through my mind.

I find my cooking skills very lacking. All I know how to cook is spaghetti. I boil spaghetti noodles and dump a jar of pre-made spaghetti sauce in a pan and heat it. I also eat toast with hot milk and dulce de leche. I really don't have much here for utensils, but it doesn't matter since I was never good at cooking except over a campfire where anything tastes good.

BUENOS AIRES - SEPT. 9, 1972

It's been a week on the job now, and I'm really enjoying it. I remember that on the day before I was hired, I was apprehensive of getting into something which would tie me down and take me off the road or loose the feeling of being able to leave whenever I feel like it. Now I feel good to be here working, learning, and replenishing my capital. I still don't know how much they will pay me; but I figure if they pay me $1.00 an hour, I will have more money in my pocket than I had last week. This feels great. That's enough money for a traveler to live for a month on a slack budget. It's a good feeling to know that when I leave, I will be able to travel without scrimping and cutting. Who knows, I might even go to South Africa.

In the morning, I catch bus #60 in front of the apartment. I found that, if I stand in the back of the bus, I usually always get a seat because the people in the back always get off first. After I ride for 20 minutes, the bus deposits me 3 blocks from the office. After work I catch good ole bus #60 two blocks from the office, going the other way, and usually ride standing (the return bus is always full by this time) 30 minutes home. The bus ride costs 4 cents.

BUENOS AIRES - SEPT. 14, 1972

It seems like I'm always on the go and never have time to just come home and hang loose for an evening. Working until 8:00 PM doesn't help. The half-hour bus ride home and the time for eating always leaves me with my evening beginning about 9:00 or 9:30 PM. It's not bad, for what else do I have to do. I enjoy my work, especially now that I am designing the layout for the properties around the golf course of the Pinamar community. I will be paid $100 a month. If I don't spend it all on expenses, whatever I save will greatly help pay for the rest of my journey.

I have met many people so far, so I am rarely alone. I enjoy being totally submerged in this Latin society where I must speak, read, and think Spanish all day long. I met several girls, one named Marita del Carmen P. who I have been seeing regularly; and another named Alicia P., who has invited me to a party she is throwing tomorrow night. I met her through an associate in the office. One thing about her is she has an apartment and is living by herself instead of with her parents as most single girls here.

I'm glad she called because I wanted to see her again. She works in the USIS office and speaks perfect English. From Marita I found out a strange custom here. If a guy invites a girl to his apartment by herself, by her accepting the offer she can be expected to sleep with the guy.

I must hand it to Clorindo for being able to put together a good crew. He's got three beautiful young female architects, four young guys, and one middle-aged gay guy, who tried to put the make on me when I first started work, and another middle-aged guy who is turning out to be a good friend. There is also the daughter of another big-named architect in B.A., the two bosses and a secretary.

A contributor in a book I am reading said of Saharan mud structures, "Those are not round forms, they are tender forms. This is the shape of clay, and this is the shape of the hand, and hand follows the shape of clay, and clay follows the shape of the hand. Hands can't follow the shape of a rectangle." He is so right. This also respects the centuries-old adobe structures built by pueblo Native Americans in America.

BUENOS AIRES - OCT. 2, 1972

It seems strange after keeping this journal for the past ten months and writing on a regular basis, that I could let this past month slip by, especially when this city life is as much an adventure as the mountains of Bolivia and Peru. When I think about it, this city life is an adventure

of hassle. It's a different kind of adventure, especially because these people look like me and I enjoy this place. On the other hand, I don't relate to this place at all: 24-hour noise, smog, crowds, constantly dodging people as I walk, and losing consciousness of anything else outside of one small area of this city, the part I live, travel, and work in.

The trees are starting to spring into life with new leaves sprouting on the branches, but it's difficult to be aware of this miraculous change when all trees are dwarfed by huge buildings, traffic, noise, people, and city life. Most of the streets are lined with trees; but they don't seem important, and even I don't really notice them. Part of this is because most of the new leaves haven't started sprouting; but even so, it's unenjoyable to touch a tender new branch of a tree and see dirt and grime all over it and on your hands as well.

I'm still going to work every day in my combat boots. They almost seem a part of me now that I've been wearing them daily for two years, but they can't last forever. The soles are split in half and the sides are pulling away from the soles. I get paid my first check tomorrow so I will be able to add to my meager wardrobe and buy some new boots. I've also been wearing the same pair of pants every day for the past month. I wash them on weekends of course. My other two pairs of pants have patches all over them.

Ernesto is still trapped in Chile and can't get back to Argentina because the mountain passes are still covered with snow. He and his friends have been there over a month.

Buenos Aires is a lively place. This accounts for the 24-hour noise which I guess every big city must put up with. The "Paris of the South" is a city where one can buy beautiful flowers from vendors on the streets as well as magazines, newspapers, coffee, and a shoeshine. There are only a few polite, blind beggars and a handful of shoeshine men; all are old. They don't hassle people like all the little shoeshine boys in other Latin American cities. They just wait patiently for someone to walk up and put his shoe on his box. Taxis are everywhere day and night, and they are cheap. It's incredible. The subway costs 2.5 cents. Walking down the street here is like strolling through a fashion show. All the very latest in trends are being paraded by the young girls, young guys, and everybody walking along looking at the latest styles in the ubiquitous clothing stores. Everywhere I go, there are clothing stores.

This city, the largest in the Southern Hemisphere right now, is the seventh largest in the world. It's 6.7 million inhabitants are quite a wonder. They have been able to retain the neighborhood grocery store, drugstore and every other type of neighborhood store needed to serve the needs of the people. There are also neighborhood meat markets and bakeries. It's a great system and cuts down on the necessity of the automobile. They also have a good public transportation system which uses buses called "colectivos" [collectives]. The bus I travel on back to work was designed by the Argentines and is a unique style of bus. The driver not only drives, which is a feat in this city; but he must stop and start, shift gears, make change, and count money of all the odd sizes due to the various size of bills and shapes of the coins. He answers questions, opens the doors, and keeps asking people to move to the back of the bus. Those drivers are amazing.

Last night I was cooking creamed carrots and cabbage; but after putting flour in the pot, I quickly realized I needed milk, which I did not have, so it all turned to paste. I ate the carrots but couldn't save the cabbage.

BUENOS AIRES - OCT. 12, 1972

It is still difficult to find time to write while living in B.A. What little time I have after work is usually spent with young ladies and other friends.

Clorindo, my boss, had a painting exhibition titled "Pesos y Medidas" (Weights and Measures). All his paintings were done with spray paint and demonstrated the distance of a shout or other sounds. It was interesting to see the spray can used in the art world.

John B. and I have moved to a room in a beautiful old Victorian mansion named Hotel Victoria, which is now a hotel or pension. It is complete with stained-glass windows, wood paneling, historic toilet fixtures, and the works. We have a small balcony with two old wooden doors and two tall windows which allow us to look out and touch the tops of three-story-tall Maple trees. I can hear the birds chirping and singing, and the sun is shining through the open windows. As John said, "This is the best room I have ever had in my life."

BUENOS AIRES - OCT. 13, 1972

When I walked back to the office after lunch, I found, to my great surprise, Danelle ringing the office doorbell. I hadn't expected her until November or December. It was certainly good to see her. Luckily, we didn't have much work; so, I took off the rest of the day to get her and her Peace Corps friend settled in a room for the night. Unfortunately, one cannot have the opposite sex in hotel rooms during the night or day. This is only allowed in Alojamientos (motels) where couples can rent a room and have sex for two hours. I sure would like to have had a place to put them up; but instead, I had to get them a hotel down by the train station. It sure is good to see old friends, especially one as good as Danelle. I gave her $10 to help her get settled and give her a financial break which she really needs.

I started to find myself back in the same old rut of acquiring a string of young ladies with whom I seem to always be spending my time, instead of devoting myself to something creative. I really enjoy being with people, and I feel lonely and left to my wandering mind if I am alone. I function better with people. One time last week, when I really had nobody to be with after work, I wound up hanging around the office hesitating to come back here to be by myself. It's a strange feeling.

Last week, I found out that Oscar and Carlos, my two Argentine friends whom I met in Peru, had returned from their motorcycle journey a month ago. I spent last Sunday with them. It was a wonderful reunion and so good to see them again and hear their stories of crossing South America on their motorcycle with a side car. They said the Mexican border guards would not let them in. They were turned back because they did not have enough money.

People are a-buzz today about the report of a Uruguayan plane crash carrying a Uruguayan rugby team. The plane with 45 passengers and 5 crew members, flying from Montevideo, Uruguay to Santiago, Chile crashed high in the snow-covered Andes Mountains. People who have seen the Andes know this is a serious event.

BUENOS AIRES - OCT. 22, 1972

It doesn't look like I'm going to be saving any money this month because at the first of last month's pay period I had to have a $20 advancement. Paying for a couple new pairs of pants, $10 for Danelle, good eating, numerous movies, and dates have about drained me of last month's pay, not to mention having to pay $20 a month rent.

I've been spending a lot of time with Danelle and Jan, who are still staying in an old hotel near the train station. Last night, George,

Maria, Danelle, Jan, and I went to an old restaurant near the port to eat German food.

We are now sitting beside a beautiful man-made lake in a spacious park. People of all types are strolling along the water's edge. Gypsies in their flowing robes reading palms, people in love holding hands and hugging in the setting sun, little boys fishing, and strolling vendors selling coffee and grapefruit juice complete the scene. It's a beautiful day with happy people all around.

BUENOS AIRES - OCT. 25, 1972

Instead of standing up in a crowded bus all the way to work and back, I take the commuter train for 9 cents round trip to the main train station and back. From there I take the subway to Station 9 de Julio and change to the other line which lets me off 3 blocks from my office. They have just raised the price of the subway from 2½ cents to 3½ cents which ordinarily wouldn't make the least dent in my finances; but now that I'm living on Argentine wages, I feel it.

My combat boots are really falling apart. It is about time when I won't be able to put it off anymore and break down and buy something else. I am still living with three shirts and two pairs of pants. It is not difficult, especially when it's been a year since I've had any more than two or three changes of clothes. It is nice not to be materialistic.

Sometimes my work really gets me down, but then there are days like today when my mind is really running with designs. It is a nice feeling.

BUENOS AIRES - OCT. 31. 1972

This past week has been a very warm and lovely week. I met a friend of Rosario's named Marta V., and I haven't spent the night in my apartment since I met her. She is a very warm, appreciative, and open person. I have really enjoyed being able to spend the nights sleeping with her instead of having to spend an hour waiting in the early morning for trains and buses to get home, only to wake up within a few hours and head for the city again. Being with her is like watching a new leaf grow on Spring days. Unfortunately, she has a great fear that I will, in time, leave. She is afraid that she will be very hurt when I leave because this happened to her once before. She has a very lovely body which I love to hold and caress.

BUENOS AIRES - NOV. 9, 1972

It seems that no sooner do I get involved with a woman, then it's over. Last night Marta told me crying, that she was falling in love with me, but she couldn't be happy with our relationship because she knows I will be leaving. She wants someone more stable now, and she needs him. I was surprised and found myself for the first time looking at the situation through her eyes. I really don't blame her. The way she was talking, I almost felt guilty for being a traveler. It's best to not get involved while I am on the road. Hell, I don't know. I'd just as soon live day by day and worry about the future when it comes. After a short, fast two weeks with her, I feel kind of bad about having to cut off this beautiful relationship.

BUENOS AIRES - NOV. 13, 1972

Last weekend turned out to be a very full and rewarding one. An Argentine friend named Andy invited John and me to go sailing on his family yacht. It was a beautiful boat about 35' long with two masts. After pulling away from the mooring at the yacht club, we motored out to a larger river and dropped anchor right in the middle and soaked up the sun the rest of the afternoon. When I'm on a boat like this one, it sure makes me want to have money. What a beautiful way to enjoy wealth!

Andy's father is a big man in the carton [cardboard] industry, and I guess has done well. He sends his kids to school all over the world, has an expensive house and a boat, and even must have a detective or guard standing in front of the house to keep would be kidnappers out.

Nevertheless, it was a beautiful day which ended up with a 2-to-3-hour discussion with Andy's father on world economics and politics. One of the most interesting observations of the day was the thousands of boats, large and small, sail or motor, on the water's edge. Never during my year in the Army while stationed along the Potomac River in Washington, DC, did I see so many luxury boats.

Sunday, Danelle, and I and many of the people in my office went to San Antonio de Areco in the heart of the Pampa to watch a Gaucho rodeo. There is a Gaucho Museum here with exhibits on gaucho life. The highways and rodeo grounds were crowded, but seeing the gauchos and their beautiful horses again was worth the trip.

I have not seen Marta since she decided to call it off, but she called me yesterday wondering why I haven't called her since our last talk a week ago. It was good to hear from her.

BUENOS AIRES - NOV. 17, 1972

Today General Juan Peron, ex-dictator of Argentina exiled for the past 17 years, returned at the age of seventy-seven years. The entire country has been excited, motivated, or people saddened by his return. General Lanusse, the current president, must do all he can to halt any mass gatherings by restricting the number of people greeting Peron at the airport to three hundred. Their names had to be submitted beforehand. Also, today Lanusse made the day a national holiday so the schools and factories would be closed as well as most all businesses. The Army and police are everywhere with their machine guns and helmets. Also, by making today, Friday, a holiday, all the workers would tend to use the three-day weekend for a vacation with their families and not listen to the labor leaders who are Peronistas (Peron supporters). A life saver was the wind and the driving rain all morning which appears to have dampened the hearts of the protestors. Did President Lanusse order the rain as well? I wonder how Peron felt coming home for the first time in 17 years to such a terribly wet and miserable day.

BUENOS AIRES - NOV. 18, 1972

I put Danelle's pack on my back and felt like a king of the road. And what is more, I wanted to be on the go again. That must be how the hobo before my time felt. Light, free, and ready to shove on at a thought! When he got lonesome and tired, he just hung his hat somewhere and called it home wherever need be. Woody Guthrie, Danelle Crowley, and Terrance J. Brown are old hands of the road. It takes a special person to keep moving on, and I guess I will keep roaming for the rest of my life.

For me it is a great feeling to go anywhere in the world with nothing more than a sleeping bag, a sharp knife, two changes of clothes, a good pair of boots, toilet articles and books. Often I feel I have too much stuff. I feel mellow with a pack on my back. Those are good sensations that I remember even as a Boy Scout packing in the mountains or hiking along the Big Horn River. I am being drawn more to the simple life of the old Prairie Indians such as the Sioux, Cheyenne, and the Crows, who I had the pleasure of going to school with.

The girl upstairs came down about three hours ago. We got to talking, and amazingly we wound up making love in so many ways. What is strange, I was sitting here feeling like I would like to be with a girl instead of being solo, but I did not think I would be with her. Anyway, it was an on-the-spot reaction which turned out to be a lovely evening.

BUENOS AIRES - NOV. 21, 1972

I spent the weekend with Oscar and Carlos. They fed me and entertained me, so it was a very full weekend. Sunday night I went to a cabaret show staring Nelida Lobato who is a statedly limber girl. She had the best body and form of all the other chorus members. It was a very professional, but relatively tame performance with uncovered breasts.

BUENOS AIRES - NOV. 25, 1972

Today being Saturday has been lazy and hazy. It rained part of the morning, but the late afternoon has turned out to be exceptionally beautiful with the afternoon sun setting everything ablaze and reminding us that tomorrow is going to be a beautiful day.

Yesterday one of the bosses told me that the end of the month will be my last day. So now my feet have been getting more itchy, ready to hit the road again. I felt it coming weeks back, when all work including mine, was being completed and nothing new coming in. I am genuinely hoping that Danelle will be able to leave with me. She will if her job does not come through during the first few days of December.

It seems strange that, after being gone for a year now, I might be heading back to the USA in four or five months. It is scary because I know that once I get home, I will want to be on the road again. I have felt that way before.

I saw a great flick last night called *Slaughterhouse 5* about a guy whose mind is bouncing back and forth in time from his experiences in World War II to the future, and he may even have always been in the future.

BUENOS AIRES - NOV. 27, 1972

This day marks a year of being on the road; a spectacular, long, and interesting journey that few accomplish, or even think about beginning. I have been on the road with nothing more than my common sense, a sleeping bag, few clothes, and other possessions. Being robbed, depressed at times, meeting wonderful people including other travelers, having feelings of fear or happiness, and being cold or in sweating jungles are only fragments of this Latin American adventure.

I started out a year ago with the goal of seeing Mexico and South America. Traveling to the southern tip of South America was just an idea. Now it is a reality. I can remember wanting to see Tierra de Fuego when I was in high school. I even had trouble remembering the name of that part of the world.

In Mexico especially, and in other Latin American countries, there are hundreds and thousands of travelers; but the farther south one goes, especially south of Panama, the viajeros (travelers) become fewer. I hardly see one in B.A. coming though. South America is getting to be the must-see location for travelers as was Europe ten years ago. I remember three years ago I wanted to travel here but decided not to because Mexico and South America were said to be dangerous places. I really was not thinking because I cannot think of any place more dangerous than Chicago or New York City. Traveling with no responsibilities and few articles of clothing and possessions on my back is a wonderful way to travel.

At this point of my travels, I needed this rest in Buenos Aires. My Spanish has improved, and I am now ready to move on. I am eager to head to Tierra del Fuego, and I even look forward to returning home although that will be some time yet. Since Marta and I stopped seeing each other, I feel adrift again. Therefore, I am eager to complete my journey.

I started authoring this journal after my Mexican adventures. It is sad that I did not start writing when I began this trip, but it does not really matter because I will never forget that part of the trip. These travels are an adventure and a liberation from ten months in the Vietnam war and two years in the military.

I learned that I will never be able to work for someone unless I have the responsibility and freedom to make or help make decisions. If I cannot add to my work or profession, I feel stymied and cut at the roots. However, here under Clorindo I make suggestions and they are listened to and often accepted. I feel strong and know what I am talking about, and I have design sense. I am going to have to set up my own design studio with a friend or friends who I respect and who respect my judgement. If that is not possible, I will go it alone.

Last night I had a beautiful time with a girl who is a good friend. We rented a rowboat and went boating on a warm summer night with the scent of flowers drifting in the breeze. The handsome trees and arching bridges all added to the pleasant atmosphere. Live tango music from the stage in the cupola set the exotic tone of the day. The park is called Paseo El Rosedale Garden and is noted for statues of famous poets. Gypsies stroll the walks reading people's palms. The entire scene is enchanting.

I am at work for another day with nothing to do except sit and pass the time. It is sad when the greatest architect in South America does not have any work on the tables. The last big project has been the final stages to the Provincial Capitol building in La Pampa.

Yesterday John Buster and I were walking around in an area extraordinarily rich with artfully designed houses. One entire city block is called "La Manzana de los Arquitectos" (Architects' Block) because the houses in this area are designed by the architects who live in them. We were invited into one of the houses and given a tour through the house. We wound up talking and passing the afternoon in this beautiful atmosphere. What a life! The architect's name is Jorge Aslan, and his house is most impressive. The life of a traveler exposes one to all sides of culture and class; rich, poor, and middle.

The most exciting thing that has happened around the office lately is the newly installed water tank hanging on the wall high above the old toilet. This tank uses old technology and has a pull chain like its predecessor but takes no effort at all to flush. Previously we thought the chain would break pulling on it. It's good to know I will be around this office a few more days so I can use this new water tank.

BUENOS AIRES - NOV. 28, 1972

Danelle came to the office today saying she needed a hernia operation. She has had a pain in her groin for months. She knows a woman from the Hippie Fair who says her father is a surgeon and that he will operate on her for free. The only thing she will have to pay for is anesthesia. Danelle, dejectedly, said, "All travelers come down with ordinary run of the mill illnesses; but I get the weird, serious ones such as hepatitis, typhoid fever, amebiasis and now a hernia." She will have to rest at least a week after the operation, so we will not be leaving for a couple of weeks. Her operation is scheduled for tomorrow.

John is an excellent roommate, a likeable guy, and quite interesting to talk to. He is intelligent and I found I can trust him.

I am getting very tired. Julie, the young lady upstairs, came down; and we were amorous again. She just left, and I think I will hit the rack and watch our freaked-out, neon light bulb pulsating over my head. It is a strange neon light. When the switch is turned on, it is, as I described, an effervescent, pulsating demon.

BUENOS AIRES - NOV. 29, 1972

I am still at the office, and I should be doing perspective drawings of the street scenes for the urbanization project around the golf course at Pinamar; but, emotionally, I must stop for a while. I just received letters from people I love very much. My mind is full of thoughts, things they say, and things I want to say. My brother says I might be able to teach in the architecture department at Texas Tech starting the 15th of January; but I still have too far to travel and much to see here before I return to the States. I would like to take the offer if I could. Mom is beautiful. She is doing all she can to take care of my personal affairs and is appreciated.

Danelle's operation was today. I cannot visit her this evening, but tomorrow I plan to go out and see how she is doing.

BUENOS AIRES - 30 NOV. 30, 1972

I put the final additions on my work today. Before leaving the Testa-Lacarra office to complete my South American journey, I discussed with the staff on what I thought needed to be done to complete my design drawings.

BUENOS AIRES - DEC. 5, 1972

It seems like everyday things are changing. It is a good thing that my mind is accustomed to being flexible. My job is going to end sooner than I planned. However, I understood the job was temporary, so I never really let myself get settled to the point of total acceptance. I had three exceptionally good months of stimulating work. I am proud of the work I did designing a new addition to the existing resort community along the Atlantic Ocean south of Buenos Aires called Pinamar. One of the best parts of my design was the fifty to one hundred meter-wide, continuous park system curving through the entire new city. This green parkway offers inter-neighborhood connections and public playgrounds for hiking and horseback riding with trails leading from the polo fields to the ocean. There are also other amenities and services often lost by the advancement of an urban development. I also studied the city and its surroundings to help determine future areas of expansion to include traffic plans for interconnecting new roads to provide for a smooth transition between new urban areas and the existing community. We studied the placement of high, medium, and low-density housing as well as commercial centers and public parks.

Danelle's hernia/appendix operation went well but left her knowing she never wants another operation under only local anesthetic. She could feel them pulling, cutting, pushing, and sewing, not to mention the surgeon's roaming fingers inside her, dragging out her intestines to have a look to see what else may be a problem. She walks slow and carefully and will be laid up for a couple of weeks before we can hit the road.

BUENOS AIRES - DEC. 9, 1972

I just cleaned out the gooseneck under the lavatory. Something was plugging the drain, so I took my spoon, opened the drainpipe cleanout, and found a gob of hair, bobby pins, and a long kitchen knife which I wrestled out after a little struggle. It felt good to solve that problem. Then Danelle and I went to the "Hippy Fair" to see what we could sell. This is an open-air artisans' market where artisans sell their crafts: leather bags, shoes, beadwork, jewelry, drawings, books, and about anything. People enjoy strolling through the crowd looking at crafts or simply relaxing on the cool shady grass. Some people are sunning themselves and snoozing.

We displayed Danelle's beadwork, and my pen and ink drawn Christmas cards on Danelle's poncho. We had an enjoyable time. I sold three cards for 50 cents each, and Danelle sold a few beaded items. We both left feeling satisfied with our small monetary gains.

Gift Card Designs

By Terrance Brown
Buenos Aires, Argentina

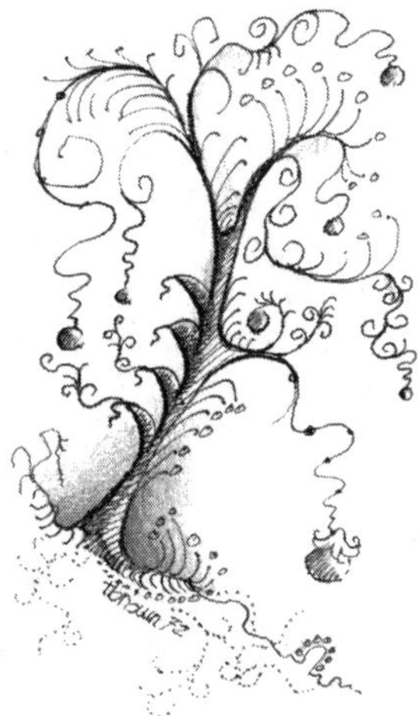

BUENOS AIRES - DEC. 13, 1972

Danelle and I are planning to leave next Monday. I am chomping at the bit. Mom tried to send my other pair of Vietnam combat boots, but there was a screwup in the mail. The boots only got to Washington, DC, and were returned to her. There was a problem with using John's name, c/o Sgt. V., because the name was not authorized for military mailing privileges. Since I cannot find boots that fit I will eventually have to have mine repaired.

Carlos and Oscar, the guys I met in Peru, work in a camping goods store, so today they let me borrow (sneak) a puptent to use on our trip to Tierra del Fuego. Camping in the tent will save us money.

BUENOS AIRES - DEC. 18, 1972

Let me tell you about last night. But first I must tell you about the entire day leading up to the night. Danelle and I went to set up our stand in Plaza Francia (Hippie Fair) to sell Danelle's beadwork and my stylish Christmas cards. Danelle sold a considerable number of items, including a beaded belt she made in Colombia. She brought it with her to sell and made $9.00 from that sale alone. The funny thing is, she sold it to an American girl.

I got off to a bad start. After setting up our stand, I found I had left my drawings back in our room. I quickly made a telephone call to John who brought them. I sold all but one at 50 cents apiece, so I came out with well over $15.00.

The sun was blazing ferociously; but the sound of guitars, flutes and bongo drums drifted through the sticky air. The entire place was alive. I bought a bamboo flute made from the "flute man." He tried to get $2.00 out of me, but I have been traveling long enough in Latin America to know one does not always have to pay the first price the vendor asks.

At 6:30 PM, Santiago and Ana Maria come by the Fair to take us to Jorge's house for an asada (Gaucho's typical meal) consisting of chorizo (sausages), meat around the ribs of beef, salad, "mucho vino y soda" (lots of wine and soft drinks), budin de pan (bread pudding) and rolled cake. It was a satisfying meal cooked over charcoal.

I am thoroughly wiped out. We left about 12:30 AM and arrived about 1:30 AM at the La Pay Confitería (pastry and candy store) where Danelle was supposed to meet a friend of hers named Ricky. Soon after we met him, he suggested we get a bottle of wine and have a party at his place. So off we went: Ricky, Danelle, two gorgeous girls and I. Ricky's apartment turned out to be a small room with a double bed, leaving about three feet on three sides of the bed, and a balcony looking over the Botanical Garden and the Zoo. After downing a bottle of wine, everybody began getting zonked. Karina R. hit the rack first. I jumped in the middle of the bed and Christina L. crawled in on my other side. Danelle and Ricky curled up on the balcony under blankets.

So, there I was, in the middle of the bed with an almost naked young lady on each side of me. I really didn't want to sleep because it was steaming hot. The sun was coming up, and we needed the blinds down to darken the room. Being between those girls did not help. I began to caress Christina who was on my right but got no response. Later, still not being able to sleep, I turned towards Karina. What a lovely young lady with a beautiful face, sensuous full lips, and deep brown eyes! It was an intense feeling when she crossed her leg over mine to let me know she wanted to be intimate under the steaming sheets. Ricky and Danelle were on the floor beside us and Christina on the other side of us on the bed. Karina is a hauntingly beautiful young lady, and I will never be able to forget her.

We parted after an early morning stroll through the Botanical Garden across the street. Karina and Christina hitched a ride to the Center. Karina is intriguing and I would like to see her again. Laying in that steamy bed listening to the lions roar and the elephants trumpeting in the zoo added strange background music to the beautiful, open evening.

When we had walked upstairs to Ricky's apt., Danelle had turned to me and said, "Be ready for anything, anything."

RIO CUARTO, ARGENTINA - DEC. 21, 1972

We did it! Danelle and I finally departed Buenos Aires. We left items we don't need for this trip south, like books, extra clothes, etc., at Don and Margo's house and hopped a train to a suburb near the beginning of the Pan American Highway. A taxi driver drove us to the highway and didn't charge us. A heck of a nice guy! Danelle stuck her thumb out and snagged a ride with a big truck which took us 135 kms to a place called Pergamino. As we were tooling across the Pampa (flat, green, rich ranch country), I saw a flock of ostriches for the first time. That was a remarkable sight, not to mention the vast numbers of livestock and horse herds grazing on endless green grass. After a long way, we stopped for a rest under the welcome shade of a tree row. With our truck driver we drank mate, an Argentine tea drunk from a gourd with a metal straw which is passed around. He heated the water with a small alcohol burning stove.

No sooner did he drop us off in Pergamino than a 39-year-old man and his son picked us up in his Peugeot and sped us along 608 kms across infinite green pasture, past a setting ball of orange sun and warm sunset, along a slow-moving river, to the campsite in Rio Cuarto. We ate a cheese sandwich, yogurt, and a few yellow plums. We got the tent set up and draped the mosquito net inside it. I'm writing this entry by candlelight in the warm pup tent environs. Outside, there are guys playing guitars and singing to their girls. I'm thinking about how boundless this day has been. We've had one of the best hitching days of this trip. Good night!

[THIS IS DANELLE'S FIRST JOURNAL ENTRY.]

DEC. 21, 1972—**D.C.**

In Buenos Aires last-minute preparations and farewells. Brown answers the knife sharpener's shrill, distinctive whistle tones with his new flute; they converse a moment that way. We took a train ride to bustling General San Martin and free taxi to Highway 8 where we hitched and watched drivers stare at us. Truck driver says he's going 30 kilometers but takes us 100 where we see green pampa, tree-lined roads leading to ranch houses, windmills, combines, cars, and pickups very old and new, trucks signaling company companions and resting in shade, a herd of ostriches, loading chutes by railroad tracks, horse-drawn carts of many shapes, towns with English names, farms with Italian looks, beautiful horses, mowed hay, harvested wheat and more and more windmills.

Beside the highway in the shade of an evergreen we feel the breeze, hear it in the pine needles, and drink the truck driver's ever-present maté. In a small wooden box, he has his stove, sugar, and tea in open containers; metal cup with metal straw, and kettle for heating water (never to boiling point). We pass the cup as is the custom. Upon departing, he asks us to write him a card from Santiago since he'll never be able to go there himself.

Before putting down our packs, we caught a very fast ride to Rio Cuarto where we put up our tent for the first time beside the river where there are free and very convenient camping facilities, even clean. Bread, cheese, fruit, and yogurt are our supper. Around us are other campers, cook-outs, and small parties. Music of diverse kinds from Santana and Aretha Franklin to Argentine country violin reaches from the bars and restaurants across the river. My predominant feeling of today was that of being brought back to life, revived, strengthened, ecstatic.

DEC. 22, 1972—**D.C.**

It was tempting to stay beside the Rio Cuarto, but we went on and enjoyed views of countryside like Texas Panhandle and the US Midwest, then like New Mexico and Arizona, then Italy with Mendoza grape vineyards, people on bicycles, square brick houses, poplar trees. Even though it only went 10 kilometers, we took the ride in the 1926 Chevrolet, red with red wheels, black convertible top. The driver, friendly, with dark glasses, khakis, and a straw hat, puts my backpack on front seat and sits on it. He has to bend down a little to see road which he scarcely looks at since he is talking to Terry who's in the back seat on old worn-out, black leather upholstery. In 1926 the car cost 2,600 escudos or rather Argentine pesos, about 2 dollars' worth of pesos now. We were so happy for the ride since we had gone crazy with admiration for this old car, as we sat beside the road hitching, and watched it pull up to nearby "Nafta" (gasoline) station.

White and yellow butterflies, Herefords, and Gertrudis cattle, and traveling wheat harvesters with square wooden, brightly painted trailer houses pulled behind old combines, all pass us by. I wanted a lift from them but instead got a wine-tanker truck. Blistering sun and then black storm of wind, dirt, rain which was exciting to see coming but disappointing to miss its center. Dog riding on running board of old car! Here and there along the roads are shrines to La Difunta [deceased] Correa with bottles of water around. Pobre Campesina [poor peasant woman] died of thirst while looking for her husband in the hills near San Juan, but her baby lived on by sucking her dead but milk-filled breasts for several days until he was found. Now she is as miraculous as the Virgin Mary and ordained saints. Truck drivers especially pay her homage. As with other miraculous figures in Latin America she is given gifts of all types, visited in pilgrimages, made promises, etc.

Brown naps in truck driver's bed while I become hypnotized by slowly changing scenery. We are left to camp 40 miles from Mendoza in San Martín behind a gas station. I'm too tired to be kept awake by noises of vehicles, machines, people.

SAN MARTIN, (NEAR MENDOZA) ARGENTINA - DEC. 23, 1972

After a restful night we found it difficult getting out of our sleeping bags and on the road. We were taking our time, packed up, took a bus to the other side of town, and stuck our thumbs out. We caught a 50 km ride; and then, after we stood a half hour in the blazing sun, a guy in a 1926 Chevrolet stopped. He said he was only going 10 kms but would take us. Even if it had not been blazing hot, we would have jumped at the chance to ride in that funky old car and go any distance. We were slowly cruising down the highway with the driver who talked endlessly, seeming not to look at the road. He fit the car perfectly with a funny straw hat and sunglasses and appeared to be a plain country boy. He enjoyed telling me words in English and French but didn't know what language they belonged to. It was fun listening to him.

There are so many old cars still being driven in the "campo" (countryside) that, at times, I am in the time of the "Carpetbaggers" or "Bonnie and Clyde." We saw a guy driving by in a 1920s Ford pickup with his little white dog riding on the running board. It was an amazing sight.

We then caught a slow-moving trucker who crawled our way to San Martin, a town near Mendoza. We arrived at 9:30 PM last night and pitched our tent behind a gas station. A huge wind woke us up at 3:30 AM. There was a widespread storm rolling in. After thinking about getting thoroughly drenched in a Texas-type storm, we got our things packed up and are now waiting in the gas station listening to "rock and roll" music blaring on the radio. I think I will try to catch a few more winks before the sun comes up. It has stopped raining.

We were excited to learn two survivors of the Uruguayan plane crash in the Andes, more than two months ago, made their way to safety and were rescued. They directed helicopters to the crash site to rescue the remaining survivors. It was a surprise to learn that sixteen out of the original twenty-five passengers survived the rigors of 72 days on the top of the frigid mountain. The survivors suffered unimaginable hardship including exposure to brutal elements, two avalanches, and starvation. They were forced to resort to cannibalism to survive, which must have been a very difficult decision.

SANTIAGO, CHILE - DEC. 23, 1972 (17 HOURS LATER)

Shortly after I wrote this morning, we were kicked out of the gas station. The caretaker said the owner would be coming shortly. Later in a pickup truck a guy, who looked like my uncle Sheridan, and his wife stopped and took us to Mendoza where we had to pay 60 cents apiece for a bus to take us out of the city. We were picked up by people who just took us down the road a short distance and dropped us off in the middle of nowhere. Danelle got out on the road and flagged down a rich Chilean in a new 1973 Fiat, or something like that, who took us to the tunnel where a landslide had blocked the mouth of the tunnel. We arrived just in time to watch another slide almost hit the caterpillar being used to open the tunnel for us.

There I met a freaky-looking guy named Sergio, who, even though loaded to the gills with luggage, decided to take us and our gear over the pass to Santiago. What a time that was! I knew the minute he shifted gears that he was a hotrodder pushing the car to the limit when the car would run right! We often had get out and push the car up to the pass because the engine timing was bad. He was tearing that poor car to pieces nearly scraping the bottom out. The exhaust heads were disconnected or broken, and exhaust was rolling into the cab. The entire scene seemed to be a freakish dream, especially when he misjudged a tight curve with a bridge and nearly drove off a cliff into the surging river 30 feet below. A small mound of dirt was the only thing that stopped the car, keeping us from dropping off the cliff.

We had a little hassle getting into Chile because we told the border patrol we only had Argentine pesos. Unfortunately, they did not think we had enough money; but, after some persuasion, they let us have a one-day visa until we could get to the bank. However, the bank won't be open until after Christmas.

A few fast hours later we were over the mountains and across beautiful Chile and finally to Santiago, not bad for two and a half days of hitching. Danelle called a friend she had met in Guatemala. We are staying with his family who live in a small, but efficient, house in a posh neighborhood three houses away from President Allende's house.

DEC. 23, 1972—**D.C.**

The storm I was disappointed to miss yesterday reoccurred at 3:00 AM this morning with us in the middle. We had to grab our tent and run since it can't endure the fierce winds. I slept sitting in chair in gas station a while. The bus ride out of Mendoza (where 2 Brazilians told us to say at the border that we were going to a pilgrimage at Coquimba for the Virgen de Andacollo, on Dec.26) left us at Potrerillos, beautiful site near river in barren mountains. Tunnels were being dug. We got a ride with ex-factory owner from Chile and a woman from San Juan talking about the degeneration of Buenos Aires, another lift with hot-rodding photographer Sergio, long curly hair and mod-looking guy, and his sister Carmen. Cassettes blasted American music and baggage was crammed in. It seemed we were pushing car to start it every few minutes, much trouble climbing mountain roads. In the pass at the border much of the winter's heavy snow remained, melting, dusty yet impressive.

The Argentine border station Las Cuevas of steep-roofed wooden Alpine-like buildings, wood-burning stoves, and snow all around was very surprising. We passed from Argentina to Chile through long, eerie, wet, and slushy, cold tunnel with train tracks. We crossed the border halfway thru the tunnel. We had to change $10 worth of pesos at a very bad rate, even after much discussion and insistence that we had no money, that we were to stay with Sergio, etc. We must go to Central Bank later to arrange all. Very frightening ride down and to Santiago, it was the closest I've come to an accident in Andes when Sergio missed a very sharp curve with a bridge in it. Only a small bank of dirt and brakes kept us from plunging to rapids of a rocky mountain river. Terry was already screeching "cuidado, cuidado" (careful, careful) long before we'd reached the curve at absurd downhill speed. For the roughest, wettest places in the road Sergio speeded up. Once we were out of the mountains, he pushed the speed to 170 clicks, much for a small car on narrow roads full of Saturday evening strollers, bicycles, horses, carts, old cars, and trucks. Los Andes is a beautiful town, a mixture of what we'd seen, plants of Argentina and house forms of Perú but in bright colors, horse and buggy taxies around the plaza, and many red houses. We were going too fast to see the details of the small wooden country houses and people. Terry and I exchanged expressions of relief upon leaving Sergio's car still alive.

While Terry waited near Plaza Italia with backpacks, I went looking for place to stay, located Steve G.'s place but not him, then got Edgardo T.'s father on phone. He immediately invited us to stay sight-unseen without even asking Edgardo about us first. On a small bus (liebre) crammed with people, we jammed on with our packs. With much offer of help from very nice people, we arrived easily at Edgardo's and were greeted as old friends by his parents Guillermo, son of Bethlehem Palestinians, and Sara. Immediately we were offered a bath, fed, spoken to with extreme hospitality, and finally given spots on floor to sleep after a short, intimate conversation between Sara and me about Terry's and my sleeping arrangements. She loaned me a 20-year-old, long, pink satin gown for sleeping, very strange for crawling into dirty, travel-worn, sleeping bag stretched out on Sara's bedroom floor. Edgardo comes in later; he seems not to know what to think about my being here.

DEC. 24, 1972—**D.C.**

After breakfast and conversation with Edgardo about "old times" at Hotel León in Guatemala and our travels, we go to Feria del Forestal but find nothing that Edgardo wants to buy for Christmas: toys, plastic, clothes, all inferior quality, Christmas trees made of brushes, mesquite wood lamps, end-tables of diseased tree trunks, booths beside the river along pine tree lane. Then we went to the Casa Cultural (UNTAC) of very modern architecture. The sculpture in front is abstract and surrealistic with much female-male representation, chairs, and bed with body-shaped indentions, etc. A cheap restaurant and book shop are inside. Cerro Lucía is a beautiful park nearby. On Providencia Street, where hippie types sell artesanías [handicrafts], friendly people keep saying they hope to see me there again. I rapidly sell all my beadwork and have my ego boosted by all the admiration for it. I explain to a few how I made different things, and last-minute purchases are made before nightfall.

We ate much Arabic food for both lunch and supper, stuffed squashes (with rice and hamburger), grape leaf roll (same stuffing), and Italian squash puree (from squash insides) with homemade wine almost as strong as whisky and a Kool-Aid type drink. The T.s have meat for the first time in a month and complain about food and cigarette shortages, prices, how life isn't as nice as it used to be. House is nice middle-class with lawn; but furnishings, lack of car, etc. show that their economic situation isn't so good. Less than a block away lives President Allende in house surrounded by white stucco walls and guards, another half block away is Drive-in Oasis, a red-light type, almost tropical style, bar/brothel. Next is a new, small, unplanted Martin Luther King Plaza with black metal, abstract sculpture.

Back to Christmas Eve, it's treeless in this house with only practical gifts since times are bad as the señora (lady) says; nonetheless she gives me a woven Native belt.

Big news here is the survival of Uruguayan soccer players lost for 70 days in Andes after plane crash. Sensationalism here emphasizes their eating flesh of dead companions for food. We had heard guards talking about it at the border crossing.

SANTIAGO, CHILE - DEC. 25, 1972

Yesterday we went to the city center to look around. It's Christmas Eve and people were buying and selling anything for Christmas. Most of the items for sale on tables lining the streets were just cheap plastic junk.

Late in the afternoon Edgardo's brother told me there were two girls living across the street. I said I'd like to meet them, so he introduced us. A few minutes later their father came and invited me to spend Christmas Eve at a fiesta with the girls and the rest of the family. The two girls had lived in the USA for a year and a half. The oldest girl, Marisa, and I hit it off; and I wound up spending most of the night with her. About 5:00 AM, I finally crossed the street to crawl into my sleeping bag for a few hours of sleep. I'm getting used to sleeping on the floor.

DEC. 25, 1972—**D.C.**

Another dead Christmas day! However, I did find the house of Erica's sister Manuela and met her. We talked about Erica, my problems with the bank, etc.

DEC. 28, 1972—**D.C.**

I haven't felt like writing for the last few days since time has passed mostly in our trying to deal with the bank and their money exchange rules. We went 3 days, one with Manuela, the next to tell that we'd been signed up to work as Voluntarios de Verano [summer volunteers] with Federación de Estudiantes [the Student Federation], and finally the last when we'd returned with the necessary stamped letters. After a final hassle and demand to see Sr. Villalobos (a higher-up), we were exempted from the exchange. We spent much time walking up and down the very dingy, old halls and wards of San Borja Hospital looking for Edgardo, Angela F., and others we needed to sign our letters. We had to explain over and over our problem and listen to many useless suggestions from people who knew someone in the bank, or the Foreign Affairs Office, or Embassy, or Police or even the President.

In between hassles we managed to get to the very pleasant Plaza de Armas and Central Post Office where it cost more than a bank-exchange dollar to buy and send 3 post cards. We walked up Santa Lucía Hill with its stone steps and lookouts, flowers, trees, and memorials (McKenna); observed the Gypsies [Romanies] (much poorer looking than the ones we saw in Argentina); went to the Market La Vega (one of the bridges on river covered with fruit vendors' stands) and walked thru the Parque Forestal. There were peaches, apricots, and plums downtown, bananas, nectarines, oranges at the marketplace. Signs in shops and kioscos read "No hay cigarillos y PUNTO." [There are no cigarettes, PERIOD!] Smog!

So here we are in Santiago with old gray buildings against high rise glass, amazingly over-crowded buses, people getting on who won't wait for you to get off first, very busy streets, and more lines. We learn by seeing others, then trying ourselves, that hitching inside the city is best transportation and easy. We learn very quickly that bank-exchange rate for dollars would force us to leave or to stay in extreme poverty if we had nowhere to sleep. Forty escudos for half a dozen peaches is almost a bank dollar while on black-market 15¢ or less. We can't afford anything if we use the official rate! Meanwhile my friend Steve uses black market exchange, buys farms and horses in the South, keeps Santiago apartment, travels by air, skis (and has practically free medical care for his broken leg), drinks wine and eats in restaurants. I did finally find him at home after several days of trying. He offers nothing of the hospitality he promised in Cuzco. Even two other American friends have gotten a hotel room. I'm very uneasy in his apartment with blaring tape cassettes of American music and everyone's lack of friendliness. I slept every chance I got these few days and have been about as depressed and limited as anywhere I've been.

It was a difficult decision to sign with the volunteers since the training, beginning the 8th of Jan. and work 20 Jan. to 20 Feb., will take our best time for being in Tierra del Fuego. However, working with the health department and medical students for a month seemed a fabulous opportunity to learn something about Southern Chile. We'll suffer rain and cold later. Next decision was what to do between now and the 8th, so we decided to try seeing the lake district.

DEC. 29, 1972—**D.C.**

We got out of the house around noon, headed south with packs on back. Bad start when bus refused to take us with our packs to hitching spot, but we thumbed. Alicia, Chilean woman from Canadian Embassy, and her boyfriend, John S., Canadian high commission for Jamaica, gave us lift, not only to highway but also an hour further. We passed thru an old, poor, very interesting section of city we hadn't seen. I called Manuela who says she'll leave key with neighbor.

Our next truck ride was with Germany-educated driver along mountain-valley orchards, always snow-capped range to the west; brush; many bathers in streams, ponds, rivers, and puddles; willows; poplars;, corn; and dairy cattle; and adobe houses with colorful blooming flower gardens, carts, horses. There were asentamientos [settlements] where houses are the same, yard plots same size, and communal farming. One town had much straw weaving, baskets, frames, furniture of all types, toys, etc. Many hosterías (inns or restaurants) sat along highway. One boy was selling crayfish by the road; others had baskets or chickens. As we go south, rivers look bluer and clearer (and colder). Another well-educated, well-traveled truck driver takes us to change of scenery: Salta de la Laja and pine woods and rolling hills with roadsides and fields of Bluebonnet-like flowers.

It's the 30th now; we slept in the bed of the parked truck and early enter Collipulli, very picturesque town of wooden houses with smoking stove-pipe chimneys and dirt streets. Road, or rather detour, curves down with a pleasant view of a railroad bridge designed by Eiffel, same man who designed the Tower. There's such steep grade out that large trucks must be pulled by tractors. Ox carts in groups brought in wood, the men in dark clothes, ponchos, black hats. (Our truck driver is one of those types who likes to bring up the conversation of sex whenever possible but is reasonably delicate.) Old Mapuche Indian women in kerchiefs were wearing big, fringed shawls of two colors. Mist covered a small pass, and drizzle began. More wooden houses, some steep-roofed, some painted, some with flowers in front, some condemned and deserted-looking, but people came and went from them. Very gray sky, mist, the pines, and steamrollers, steam engines and steam-engine sawmills, all look very old. All blends to make an atmosphere in which I am calm, happy, somehow very at home.

In Loncoche we walk seeing run-down wooden hotels, fences of railroad ties, people too shy to stare or speak and some even seem hostile, much rain, tractors pass loaded with passengers as are trucks carrying milk cans. Sounds were of train whistles, goats bleating, and distant radio. Many people with huge (5 liter?) wine jugs were all around the area, plus hills, pastures, pine trees and beauty.

In Villarrica, with much rain and not-so-friendly people, we took refuge in a new, light but ugly church where we wrote until the rain stopped. Bread, cheese, and peaches were our meal; we had hardly eaten since Santiago. We set up tent beside a lake that's still with a few slow-moving row boats, frogs, distant voices, clover, eucalyptus, and cloud-covered hilltops on the other side. Many noisy teen-agers further down the beach enjoy themselves. I was in such a good mood that I walked down to lakeside with Brown. Together we brushed our teeth! Nearby one well-dressed drunk, after crying on another's shoulder, stripped nude and took a dip. We sat at end of rocks in water and watched a crayfish.

(Mustn't forget Alicia's story about how she wasn't allowed inside a certain copper mine near Rancagua. The mine is a jealous woman. If another woman is allowed inside, she will become furious and collapse in parts. Even a priest cannot wear his dress-like vestments in the mine since she might mistake him for a woman. He's only allowed to enter in slacks.)

There was an orderly slogan-sign painting on building, red-lined with black, re copper nationalization support, others anti-imperialist, pro-Nazi, etc.

SANTIAGO, CHILE - DEC. 29, 1972

Two nights ago, Marisa and I were in each other's arms. It is strange how things work. Yesterday I went with her and her sister and two of their friends to visit the nationalized Anaconda Copper Mine. It was picturesque sitting on the side of a hill looking over Santiago. The buildings were, of course, built in true American Colonial style, much like the historic American National Park buildings. Santiago's International Airport is very small but new, nothing great architecturally.

Everywhere we go there seems to be a line of people waiting for something: cigarettes, a bottle of cooking oil, salt, sugar, etc. They have not had any meat here for 2 months. This is a challenging time for these people of Peru, Argentina, and Chile who have eaten meat all their lives and don't know how or even care to learn to cook fish. Most of the women don't even know how to select fish in the market.

VILLARRICA, CHILE - DEC. 30, 1972

With a little hassle we got the Central Bank to allow us to be in this country for three months without changing the $10-a-day as is normally required. We had official letters from the public health department and the medical school confirming the fact that we were going to be doing volunteer work in the south for a month and a half with the Department of Public Health.

Danelle and I don't have to begin our classes until the 8th of January, so we decided to see the Southern Lake District instead of getting bored in Santiago.

We started out yesterday at noon trying to take a bus to the Pan American Highway, but they wouldn't take us with our gear; so, as usual, we hitchhiked. In no time at all, we not only got a ride to the highway, but they took us to the next town 40 kms south. The guy was a Canadian working for his embassy in Jamaica. He had flown to visit his fiancé who is a Chilean living in Santiago.

After waiting a while, a young guy named Peter stopped and picked us up in the cab of a new Fiat truck. He took us 300 bumpy, hot, and jostling kms. No sooner did we put our stuff down than we got picked up by a couple of truck drivers who took us 300 kms farther down the road to Puerto Montt. The snow-capped Andes mountains were rushing past as we bounced along. The driver just couldn't stop talking and was well-informed.

Late in the night the two truck drivers wanted to stop and sleep, so Danelle and I hunkered down in the huge truck bed filled with light bulbs and dozed off for a warm comfortable sleep in our sleeping bags. I had a dream about them coming and robbing us but that passed easily. They let us off in the rain at the intersection that went to the lake. As soon as we stepped off that truck, we entered an old-world community of black, steaming train engines; shabby wooden buildings; oxen pulling carts along dirt streets; and flocks of geese scurrying across the roads. The men with felt hats and ponchos were riding horses, wagons, bicycles, or walking. Many people were riding on tractors pulling anything from horse trailers to nothing.

We are sitting in a newly built Catholic Church waiting out the rain. It is a miserable day, especially since there is no warm fireplace to sit in front of.

It looks like it's clearing up, so we'll be looking for a place to camp soon. We had a couple of cheese sandwiches this noon. I know for sure now that we can't live in this country without changing money on the black market. The value of the government money is too high.

I just found the blue pen I thought I had lost. We left the church and set up our tent on the edge of a clear blue lake with the mountains and Villarrica Volcano rising high in the background. The sky has cleared. Danelle and I, for the first time, have been able to set up our tent up easily without the hassle of wind or rain. It is simply a small pup tent for two people and is composed of two sides that snap together. Danelle and I each carry one of the sides with our gear, and each has a tent post. I have enjoyed the afternoon with her. She feels like my sister. I've missed having her as my traveling companion across South America. It's incredible to realize how much money I have saved traveling with her. What little we've had to spend since we left Buenos Aires has been for food, and that hasn't been much.

It's going to be another good night, but this time in our well-set-up pup tent. We've had to push the ill-fitting poles into the ground about eight inches to get the sides of the tent to touch the ground.

I'm still wondering what to do with my life. Good question!

It seems like whenever I need something essential to travel with, like a good pair of boots, I don't have them. Today while walking in the rain, I felt like I'd felt before, I was dressed inadequately. My rain poncho and hat were stolen in Mexico with all my other possessions. My Vietnam combat boots are falling apart. The soles are broken across the balls of my feet and "eat" water, dirt, and rocks. The leather boot tops over my feet are pulling away from the rubber soles. They are of little more use than sandals. The problem is, they don't make shoes or boots big enough for me in these countries.

Thinking back over our journey south of Santiago, it's difficult to remember all the details I saw along the way. Well-fed cattle were standing among immense fields of blue flowers appearing as if they were in a lake. People were swimming in all the rivers we crossed; and because of the heat, I would have liked to jump in with them.

Just out of Collipulli we crossed the Malleco River that runs at the bottom of a deep gorge which has a handsome railroad bridge called Puente (Bridge) Malleco built for train access only. It was strange to see this magnificent steel bridge built in 1890 in the "middle of nowhere." Oddly, there was no bridge across the chasm for vehicles. They had to carefully drive to the bottom of the canyon and struggle up the other side. On the rim on the other side of the river, trucks were lined up waiting for a tractor to pull them up the steep canyon slope.

It was early morning and old men with teams of oxen by the two's were hauling wood towards town. These huge animals were connected to a yoke by the horns and were guided with a bamboo pole. The men seemed to be giving signals to the oxen by tapping them with the ends of the long poles.

Danelle just reminded me of Alicia's story of how women are not allowed in the mines. The miners believe the mine is a woman; and if another woman enters, the "woman" gets jealous and falls apart. A priest cannot enter with his robe for the same reason. He may be mistaken as a woman in a dress, so he enters in pants and shirt.

VILLARRICA - DEC. 31, 1972

We woke up this morning to a thick overcast sky that never thinned the entire day. All it did was drizzle. So, there we were, lying in our pup tent (that's all we can do because the tent is so small), sleeping, reading, and writing. I'm reading *The Portrait of an Artist as a Young Man* by James Joyce. He's done such an excellent job of writing that it gives me a feeling of glowing warmth, like it's all there, nothing was left out. His descriptions are infinitely detailed.

The opening of our tent faces the lake which stretches flat and blue to the rising mountains on the far side. Somewhere beyond is the Villarrica Volcano, but the clouds have kept it obscured since we've been here.

Danelle and I are thinking about trying to cross the border to Argentina for a few days before returning to Santiago. That way we will be able to see the famous ski resort town of San Carlos de Bariloche, Argentina, and the beauty of the Andes.

I would not trade this past year of travel for anything. Camping here sure beats whooping it up in a bar in Montana. Last New Year's Eve we were on the beach of Pie de la Cuesta, just north of Acapulco.

DEC. 31, 1972—D.C.

We spent much of the day reading and sleeping inside the tent while the sprinkles and drizzles from the heavy overcast threatened a downpour, like yesterday's, which never came. In one of his trips to the toilet Terry was called over by a large group of campers who invited us to celebrate New Year's Eve with them, so we decided to stay around for that. They had also offered him wine, bread, and traditional dish of spiced coagulated goat's blood. Fortunately, they were out of it by the time I was called over, offered punch, and asked many questions as everyone crowded around me. Recurring question from every side for that day and the next concerned my relationship with Terry. Whatever we told them, they didn't seem to believe. The group was all one family, old and young married couples, singles, children of all ages, and a deaf-mute who was constantly the butt of jokes and object of teasing. There was a fire and folks dancing waltzes to accordions and guitar.

Because of the characters we had seen who walked back and forth examining our tent and me, we finally decided around dark (10:00 P.M.) that we would take turns watching the tent. We figured that there would be less drunks wandering around before 12 and less risk for me to stay alone, so Terry went to the party first and came back a couple of hours later all happy. Then I walked down the pine tree-lined lane since it is well lit, but I had only gone about halfway when a young man came up from the beach and thru the trees. I walked faster and was tempted to run, but he also went faster and easily overtook me. He tried to talk and immediately became aggressive, stopping me with an arm clasp. I walked on. He separated when 2 men were coming toward us, (I was afraid to ask them for help since they might be worse) and was soon grabbing me again by both hands throwing me on the ground, landing on top of me, trying to kiss me, etc., all of which happened very fast. At once I screamed "ayúdame" [help me] and to my surprise he jumped up and ran away hollering back at me "estúpida" [stupid!] .

I was very glad to arrive at the party where there were many more questions, much drink, roasted goat, records of Spanish waltzes, Colombian cumbias, American soul, and dancing on pine needles, and at midnight (announced by the city siren) hugs, handshakes, and best wishes like "que se cumplan todos tus deseos" [may all your wishes be fulfilled]. All evening the deaf-mute made signs that we should slip away, that Terry wouldn't know. The women were afraid that Terry would be jealous because I stayed so late. Thankfully, I was accompanied back to the tent by 3 people. The wine, combined with a secure-feeling rain to drive away maleantes [bad guys]), put me to sleep.

PUCÓN, CHILE - 1 JAN. 1973

The first words Danelle said today were "What an ugly number, 73." She was suffering from a wine hangover and referred to the date.

The entire group of people camped down the lake from us invited us to their New Year's Eve celebration which turned out to be the only excitement of the day. It never stopped raining, a constant drizzle all day. We spent most all day lying horizontal in our cramped pup tent.

I went to the neighbor's fiesta first, so Danelle could feel more at ease about guarding the tent alone. She figured there would be more drunks and people straggling around after midnight then earlier in the evening. So, while at the party around a fire, I ate the best roast beef I ever tasted, along with sliced tomatoes soaked in olive oil and dusted with parsley, bread and punch made of white wine and pineapple chunks. It was beautiful. Those people just kept firing questions at me about nationalization of their copper mine and my relationship with Danelle, which they never could figure out. I'd tell them we were brother and sister and don't sleep together, but they wouldn't believe it and would start in on quizzing Danelle when she arrived. They just kept poring wine in my glass; and after a few hours of dancing to records and playing the guitar, a couple of guys got out their accordions and played a Chilean song written for President John F. Kennedy.

I left the party "light on my feet," giving many thanks saying, "Viva El Chile." Strolling along the lighted, arching trees to our tent really felt good; but I had in my mind "what a good place to get mugged."

Well, it was my turn to guard the tent, so Danelle then strolled along the same arching tree way to the party. When she returned, she had a harrowing tale. She told me that, while on her way to the party, a young guy had jumped her and thrown her to the ground. When she started screaming (I didn't hear her), the guy ran off yelling *"estúpida, estúpida"* (stupid). That's another one to chalk up in her book. At the party they filled her full of wine and danced her legs off. A guy and his wife accompanied her back to the tent. Danelle just said, "I better get my karate back in shape or pay heed to what the people say around Latin America, 'Don't walk alone at night.'"

Those fine people fed us breakfast and dinner with a juicy vegetable and meat soup and even gave us three tomatoes, salami, and cake for the road.

I noticed that Danelle has begun writing a journal. She writes ridiculously small, so, mimicking her, my writing is beginning to get smaller, and I'm putting more words on the page. In fact, her writing is so tiny that it's difficult to read.

It took us three hours to hitch 20 kms to the next town of Pucón where we are now. It's another handsome, old-wooden-house town on the other side of the lake. We tried to hitch to Argentina, but after an hour, decided to find a place to camp beside the lake. We pitched our tent under a willow tree on the black-sand beach with the tent opening overlooking the gently curving beach lined with multicolored fishing boats. High, green, craggy mountains, much like those in Colombia, rise all around the bay, poking their heads into the evening's gray clouds. Watching the fishermen ride the waves, as they lined up their approach with flapping oars, was quite a sight.

The only thing that could dampen our spirits is if all those millions of tiny crawling bugs around the base of the willow tree somehow invade the inner sanctum of our mosquito net. When you squish them, they are filled with a red-orange juice. We will just have to see. I think we will be here until we return to Santiago.

JAN. 1, 1973—D.C.

Seventy-three seems like such an ugly number; perhaps the year will make up for it. Breakfast was with our New Year Chilean friends and much of their sweet maté (tea). I tried a good liver and onion soup. Police came and told us we had to leave our campsite. They say it's private property. We were leaving anyway. We pass to say good-bye to our friends and are invited to a lunch of stew and given food to take along as we leave. The road to Pucón along the side of the lake is strangely paved (strange since the one from Loncoche to Villarrica isn't). Summer homes and camping businesses line it, castaña (hazel nut) trees, blackberry bushes in flower, flowers both wild and domestic. Main streets of Pucón lined with flowers, geraniums, and roses. We decided to try to go to Bariloche but couldn't get a lift. It was late so we went to Pucón's public beach. It is very beautiful with the mountains (ones we saw from Villarrica) here, the waves like an ocean bay, black sand, rocks, trees, row boats of bright colors and a white pier. When we first arrived, there were many people who soon left. A Chilean woman gave us "pan de Pascua" (Easter cake), Blitz soft drinks, and "cola de mono" [monkey tail], a drink of milk, coffee, and aguardiente. She talked a while, mostly about shortages. She said that one reason for meat shortage is the killing of female cattle, even pregnant ones. As nightfall neared, rowers brought in the rent-paying, tourist fishermen; then rowers stood around kiosco (kiosk) drinking, listening to music, and telling day's events. By night, when lights on pier went on, beach was completely deserted; and we settled down in our tent with the edges held down with rocks, under a tree by the lakeside. Orange-blooded bugs crawled over.

JAN. 2, 1973—D.C.

So much sunshine today that I washed my jeans (which are rapidly falling apart) and sunburned my legs. Terry found out from a fisherman in straw hat and rolled-up slacks, who was painting his boat bright red, orange and white, that each rowboat owner was trying to paint his boat the prettiest, thus the bright array of colors we could see from our tent door. Boats are sometimes taken to a point upriver and rowed down to lake while tourist fishes for salmon and rainbow trout. My walk was on very hot, gravelly sand; icy lake water was only a shock, not relief. I saw summer vacationers sun-bathing, campers among the trees, private homes, dairy cattle grazing, then a sign warning of quicksand.

We could see the top of Villarrica volcano, pouring volumes of smoke, much snow except around the top where it's melted. It had been a year since it last erupted. It's beautiful to see it through the trees which stand around a big red-topped, gray wooden house. We made a fire, our first on this trip. Terry practiced on his flute, and I enjoyed the warmth. I was so awake by the time I crawled into the tent and wrapped up in my sleeping bag that I couldn't go to sleep all night.

PUCÓN, CHILE - JAN. 3, 1973

Yesterday we were able to see Villarrica Volcano for the first time. It is one of Chile's most active volcanos and a marvelous sight with its snow-covered sides climbing to its craggy crater. Puffy white smoke was rolling out its mouth and floating with the breeze. I climbed to the top of the peninsula which rises behind the tent to a lush lawn-covered

forest where fat geese were feeding in the meadow. An unforgettable view of the volcano can be seen from here.

This is a rich morning with a cool breeze floating across the bluish-green lake. The sky is clear, and the air is sweet. It is a good life. We are going to boil six eggs in a bucket on our fire tonight. Danelle blew her mind when she saw I had a bucket, instead of a little can, to do this job.

JAN. 3, 1973—D.C.

Forced myself to bathe today; water wasn't so cold as yesterday, but the breeze was colder. I soon dried in sun and was warm again after changing clothes. Terrance paid 70 escudos for 1/2 kilo of tomatoes today, $1.40 on our exchange. Then he bought some eggs but got nothing to cook them in until our newly made fisherman friend loaned him a bucket! This man I'm speaking of told us more of the volcano; it has been predicted that the next big eruption will destroy all this town Pucón where we are now. "If death comes, it comes," he says. When the volcano stops smoking it is studied, and the prediction is made as to when the eruption will be. However, the people don't evacuate. They can move out to the Park Peninsula Hill he says. Eruptions occur about every 4 years. Then the guy took Terrance rowing in his boat.

Later Terry talked to some Danes who mentioned a rodeo. The boatman told me later that it would take place the 6th and 7th and that huasos [cowboys] with four or so well-cared, beautiful horses from all over the country would come for the event. There are different events like roping (on foot), bronc and steer riding, horse showing, wild horse flag race. I forgot that he told us also that they were considering trying to deactivate the volcano by putting a bomb in it.

JAN. 4, 1973—D.C.

Another rainy day, squawking birds and rain blowing from the tree onto the tent woke us, but we couldn't pull ourselves from our sleeping bags to face the cold wet grayness for another four hours. Instead, we crowded each other around the tent trying to keep from touching the sides and turned our heads to the door so we could get some light to read. I kept putting off going to town for food but when I finally got out, the rain was pouring even more than earlier. Still there was movement in the town, people riding horseback, a kissing couple leaning against a tree trunk in the large plaza, people buying in the stores and leaning against shop doors and walls, carpenters hammering, children playing. A few were dressed as gauchos in short black jacket and bloomer pants, black Andalucian hats. Most people were men, probably campesinos in felt hats, rubber boots with pants legs stuffed in tops, vests, old suit-type jackets, and dark colored ponchos. Saw intricately carved wooden stirrups, kind shaped as boot toes, saddles of sheep hide and blankets and leather cover as I saw in Paraguay and Argentina.

Food stores look badly stocked. We continue eating cheese and bread and some cherries for today's special. Young American traveler-student types sat in cafe talking about the exchange rate,

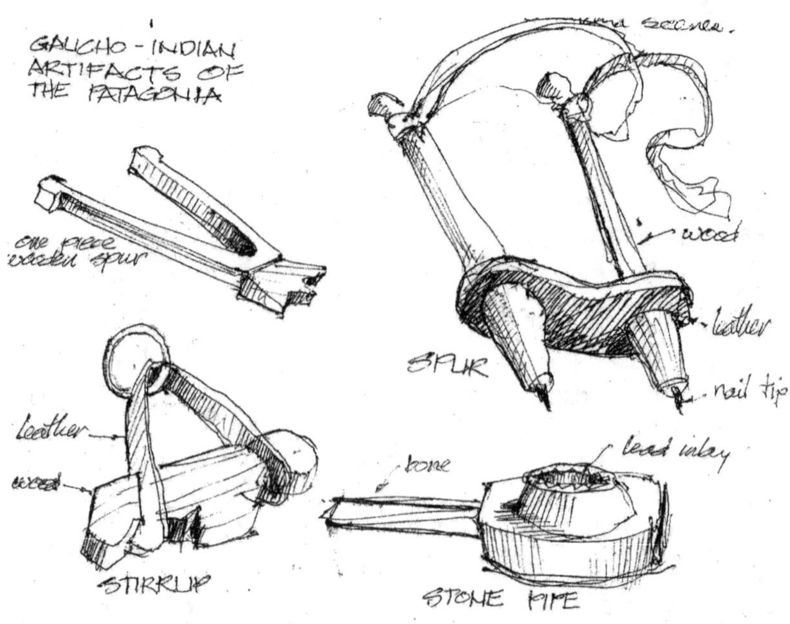

visas, plans for traveling around Chile, etc. After going to town Terry later returns with two of them, a couple, says he met them in Embassy in Quito. They go off down the beach to camp. No work for the boat rowers so they gather for a game of coin tossing. We toasted cheese sandwiches over the fire tonight.

PUCÓN - JAN. 4, 1973

It just occurred to me I could a get a cobbler to fix my boots. I knew that I could repair them if I had the tools and material; so, when I was in town buying a few things to eat, I started asking. The first cobbler said he'd do it, but it would cost 80 cents. The second cobbler wouldn't even look at the boots, and he had a sewing machine. The third cobbler said he'd do it for 65 cents and would have them repaired today in the late afternoon. So, the job was his. He did an outstanding job. First he attached the leather sides of the boots to the soles, then he cut off the boot tread, glued a half-sole of old automobile tire to the bottom of the boots, and stitched all around by hand. I sure feel more secure with these boots. They are in running shape again. They are beautiful. It has been raining all day with a heavy wind. I felt like a mummy lying in that tent all morning, so it is good to be out running errands.

JAN. 5, 1973—D.C.

Went walking thru the peninsula park today. Very beautiful views of the beach and mountains behind, of various parts of the lakeside farms shaded by fruit trees, campgrounds hidden on lake peninsula shore opposite the town, Pucón, wooden shingle or corrugated iron rooftops dispersed among treetops, the volcano slowly being unveiled of its blanket of thick clouds, pastures and fields dotted with small trees or surrounded by tall poplars, distant hills, and forests. Fresh smells of trees and grass. Meadows and brush inviting rest, fantasy, and childhood memories of dreams and story books, wooden benches here and there, songs of birds, crickets, cicadas, and breeze.

On my way to visit John and Mary whom I didn't find, I had to pass thru the section of bathers from the luxury beach hotel. Drew the looks of bikinied tanned young women who seemed curious, disgusted and/or threatened perhaps, by my somewhat masculine appearance, worn-out Wrangler denim shirt, brown patch-print Lees with holes, boots, pouch hanging from belt. In the evening Mary came to our campfire to talk and eat coal-baked onions and toasted cheese sandwiches with us. Find out she is a belly dancer who learned from working with performances, also studies dance at UCLA. Exchange of usual travel stories. Two high school boy "mochileros" [backpackers] also join us. They and many like them come from all over Chile, often with only a blanket or sleeping bag to lie on the beaches of the lakes. They later leave blankets with me and go off with Terry to the hotel "discoteque."

JAN. 6, 1973—**D.C.**

We had decided to stay for the rodeo but the morning looked cloudy, threatening, and drizzly so we stalled our decision. When things were looking better we decided to pack up and start out. We were barely finished when the rain began to fall and did so for several hours steadily. First we waited under a kiosk roof with two other mochileros, became tired of that so got even wetter walking to the ice cream parlor on main street where we sat until the rain stopped. Despite the very late start we were lucky. A woman and her daughters who turned out to be the family of a diputado [senator] and nieces of a former president picked us up because we were foreigners and complained about material conditions in the country.

Next a diputado (deputy) René García, who happened to be friends and of same party Partido Nacional as the ride before, gave us a lift and shouted as in a public rally his opinions and accompanying statistics, examples, anecdotes. He was in the area campaigning for another party member. He had had several farms confiscated, spoke of human selfish interest as the reason socialism doesn't work, etc.

In the back of a truck, we went the rest of the way to Victoria with a stop to see an over-turned car that was attracting much attention from passers-by. We were let off in Victoria's neighborhood Club Hípico. At first small crowded unpainted wooden houses with women sweeping bare dirt yard, a few houses with small flower or fruit gardens. A few soccer fields, from one game someone hollered "Tomás" a few times; it was Edwardo, youngest son of the O. family, we were looking for.

We didn't realize how many of the people at the fiesta would be here, most of the young people, the deaf-mute (a neighbor?). The trucks also belonged here. All the family was very surprised to see us. Apparently they hadn't been aware that their daughter had given me their address and invited us. At any rate they were hospitable, asked us to stay for supper of pea soup, hot bread and butter, the popular Instant Nescafe. Then the boys begin to drill Terry full of questions about Vietnam and later took him to drink and tried to get him to go to the brothel. I soon discovered that I was supposed to remain in the women's role.

When the Vietnam talk began, I was called away to the living room and television set by the two females and a child. A televised dance contest was taking place. There was tango then rock-n-roll and then soul. These latter two were extremely exaggerated and acrobatic and sometimes off-beat. Even the typical, traditional Cueca with huaso (cowboy) costumes of huge spurs, fringed boots were somehow exaggerated and ungraceful. But it was an interesting program. When the 15-year-old daughter went to bed I was called to do the same. There were more questions about my relationship with Terry which showed a lack of comprehension of what I'd said before, like I wouldn't trade Terry for another ever, would I? Could they ever understand that a man and woman could be together, be friends, not belong to each other in a play of threats, jealousy, sexual desire, romance? What do I do when I'm ill? I didn't understand the question but finally it was explained that enferma (ill) meant menstruating. Was Spain near the U.S.? Sleeping in a bed for the first time since leaving Buenos Aires wasn't so easy. I could hardly get to sleep.

JAN. 7, 1973—D.C.

I never investigate the rooms of this wooden house because I feel easy and cozy in the kitchen where the wood stove is lit and covered with pots and pans (as is the gas stove). I watch the cooking and shop for food with Isabél who expresses her boredom with her neighborhood, the housework which is constant and her obvious lack of freedom. Even the señora complains about having to be always in the kitchen cooking for the five men (who are busy working on the truck outside). The women make bread every day. There is much work for lunch and little waste, a sharp fresh salad of cabbage, parsley, and lemon juice; the lemon peel is saved. Extra egg white is thrown in a soup of potatoes, onions, whatever is around. The little meat they have is cooked with onions and tomato sauce to put on spaghetti. The men don't come when called and when they do they have to be served. When dishes are done, bread must be made, even for a Sunday like today. These women get no rest. They tell us good-bye, take us to the highway in the old Buick.

We later get a ride with a forester. We see a huge fire, a sawmill is burning, the buildings, the finished lumber piles, the residences which are being evacuated of all within. Many cars are stopped, fire engines are there but it is out of control. We are so tired from the questioning in Victoria that we decide not to stop by in Collipulli and go on to Salto de La Laja where beautiful water falls in a river cutting a deep gorge and strange formations in the clay rock. I walked very near the falls and was soaked by the blowing mist. The rocks were slick, and algae covered. The powerful fall and agitation of the water was exciting. When I joined Terry, a crowd of very drunk young men who called themselves socialists, and poor men had begun slobbering out politics and raining questions on us to see whose side we were on. As usual we try to appear to be on everyone's side, as much as possible. One was especially pushing up close to talk to me, but we were in a good mood with the beauty around us and didn't become disturbed about this situation.

A long hitch on the bridge finally got us a lift into the night and even at 1:00 AM we were later able to catch another lift at a gas station which took us on to Santiago and gave us a cheese sandwich and coffee. This man had never talked to a foreigner, he said, except for Argentines. He talked of his wife whom he had married at an early age. He's 33 and married for 15 years. He was clean and neatly dressed as a dandy, down to his cologne as Terry noted, and he had been making his living driving the lumber truck for years. Along the highway somewhere we saw the candles burning in a group of small, blackened shrines where 15 or so years ago a drunk truckdriver hit a single file of schoolgirls walking back from a class picnic and killed about 21. We were then told that the sentence for stealing a chicken (about three years) was longer than that for attempted homicide.

From I Ching: K'uei-Disunion (Mutual Alienation) In the symbol "harmonious satisfaction is attached to bright intelligence... Heaven and earth are separate and apart, but the work which they do is the same. Male and female are separate and apart, but with a common will they seek the same object. There is diversity between the myriad classes of beings, but there is an analogy between their several operations. Great indeed are the phenomena and the results of this condition of disunion and separation."

JAN. 8, 1973—D.C.

Early morning back in smoggy crowded Santiago. At least we can enter Manuela's house easily; young caretaker is here, also neighbor gave us key. We slept at once waking up hungry at 2:00 PM and anxious to see how our first day of summer volunteer training would go. All well on schedule we found out that the meeting would be at 5:00 PM and had lunch at UNTAC, rested in snack bar after. At once, Terry and Belgian traveler who he met before in Quito recognize each other. We meet several French people with him, who happen to know Nito, who have been in Santiago for some time. The woman, Martine, took us to the apartment of a Venezuelan student with whom Nito and friends had been staying but they had already gone, and for good, about three hours before. Quite a disappointment for us but also common! It is doubtful that we will see them since they seem to be headed in opposite directions. Even if they were still in Viña del Mar when we got there in a few days we could never find them.

Then we go to San Borja hospital where the meeting is to be held and are very soon told that they have decided that the work will be too specialized for us so we can't go with them to Chiloe, that we should check FECH for another place. We were so let down by that after having hitched so hard to get back here (only to have to return the same route again) that we quickly decided not to go to FECH at all but to split the country as soon as we see what we want.

After hanging around the UNTAC a while with the French people we decide to visit Steve G. but catch *Romeo and Juliet* at the movies first, a movie I've been wanting to see but haven't had a chance for years. At Steve's we talk a short while, meet his partners Patty, plus an American fellow, and a Swiss guy. We are invited to return the next day with vegetables to pitch in for supper.

We hitched a ride home with a university professor of chemical engineering who plans soon to receive his doctorate at the University of Texas. (His name Juan? Guzmán.) He picked us up because he had mistaken us for friends of his.

SANTIAGO - JAN. 9, 1973

After a couple of days of our hard hitching, a Senator campaigning for office, who knew all the details of Chilean politics, picked us up because we were Americans. Then a truck driver drove us to Victoria.

There we visited the family who had invited us to their New Year's Eve party at Villarrica. They are a big family living in the lower middle class. They have an indoor toilet, but they treat it as if it were an outhouse. They are a good family who fed us well and gave us beds to sleep in, the first beds we've slept in in three weeks. We were constantly bombarded with questions of all types. The night we arrived, the boys took me out for a beer and then tried to get me to go to the house of ill repute to get laid. That's all part of their macho trip, and they couldn't believe I didn't want to go. Typical of Latin customs, while I was out with the boys, Danelle was in the kitchen with the mother and daughter. She said they never wasted a bit of that food. They used everything, including the lemon rinds.

We hitched all night and arrived about 8:00 AM here yesterday, dog-tired, took a city bus part way, and hitched to Manuela's house where we are staying. She's on vacation but left the keys with the neighbor for us.

After hitching our asses off to get back here from the South, the bummer of all bummers was when we went to the hospital for the meeting and found out we couldn't work in the medical program. Before we had left, they didn't seem to think there would be any problem. Anyway, that's the way it goes; we are still going to see Chile.

Met French travelers in the UNTAC building yesterday who told us they have been to Tierra del Fuego. They took a boat from the Straights of Magellan to Puerto Montt for 200 escudos or 70 cents. Said the conditions weren't too good though and had a lot of rain.

I learned that Chile is extremely long; 2,653 miles from one end to the other and only 110 miles wide. When you look at the country on a map scaled large enough to see details, it is usually cut in three narrow pieces that are placed side by side. The Pacific Ocean and the Andes Mountains squeeze this country to an extremely long and isolated coastal area.

JAN. 9, 1973—**D.C.**

A day passed in washing filthy clothes, bathing, etc. In the evening, we bought vegetables and hitched to Steve's place. We devoured their new *Time* magazines, drank wine, ate, conversed, relaxed, were invited to visit their farm on our way south.

JAN. 10, 1973—**D.C.**

We wanted to mail some letters, Terry wanted to look for a book, buy film, etc. so we went to town. We passed through a beautiful old area of town at the foot of Cerro Cristobal, along the edge of the river, then looked around several bookstores. Decided to separate and meet later so I went off looking for Librería Orientalista [Orientalist Bookstore], passing the Justice Department or Courts and the pleasant white Congress Hall with its enclosed yard of flowers, grass, classical style sculptures supporting globe lights and adorning fountains. The oriental bookstore was located at a door along a passageway between two building facing the Congress (on Catedrál Street). I knocked at the closed door, but no one answered. (Right now I'm reminded that I must look for the "answers" myself, letting the necessary or rather accepting that the necessary procedures will come to me of themselves.) The sign on the brick wall beside the door read: LIBRERIA ORIENTALISTA/Sabiduría oriental/Filosofía y espiritualismo cristianos / Obras de naturismo y de Cultura física, emocional y mental (1145A Catedrál).

At the post office I finished a postcard to Mother mentioning that I had read in the papers today that the government had decided to start rationing food here in Chile. I thought it might just be for those foods which are scarce, but Mrs. T. says later that it will probably be of all foods.

From post and Plaza de Armas, I walked toward the UNTAC and once again encountered Gypsy [Romany] women at the foot of Cerro Santa Lucía. A pale and malnourished-looking baby dressed only in a cotton shirt sat on a brightly designed and colored nylon apron which was spread on the grass. The women mostly barefoot, whose once-elegant, long, full nylon skirts looked worn and dingy, aggressively approached passers-by asking to tell their fortunes (decir la suerte) for only 1,000 pesos (1 escudo). "And that's all I'll charge you," she said. "And if what I tell you isn't certain, I'll give you back the money." I had heard stories (like the one Ricki told me) about how these people would trick out more money some way or another, but since I have been looking for an opportunity to have a Gypsy tell my fortune at a reasonable price, I decided to take the risk of a small loss just to see how it was done.

We sat on the ground in the shade. Her weathered but active features examined me briefly and she asked a friendly question of my nationality, how long I'd been in Chile, and I answered correctly assuming that it would guide the fortune she told which it didn't very much. Then she took my palm and began by saying that I would live a long life. "You are hot-tempered and become very angry, but your anger doesn't last long. You appear calm and happy but in fact you are disturbed and unhappy especially in respect to love and affection. He loves you very much but there is another woman. Be very careful of other women. They envy you very much; they want to do you harm. They make the world laugh at you. Two women have taken your loved ones from you. Care that women do not do this just to spite you. You need a home, marriage, happiness." She hesitates a few seconds after. "Do this. Let me see your handkerchief. Touch it here, here, and here while saying these words 'For home, love and happiness I ask God the Father, the Holy Virgin, all the Saints.' Now give me a bill--no, I'm not charging you, it's just so you'll have fortune, live well, never have money problems. No, this isn't worth anything. It won't work. You have more money there; how much are you carrying there? You must make a cross on the handkerchief with all your money or your bad luck with money will do you great harm. You need this charm because money has caused you many problems."

Another Gypsy comes over with a metal cross and tries to talk me into pulling out the money. "Listen to what she is telling you. She is the most powerful of the Gypsy women and can help you very much. She knows secrets and charms that no one else knows. She has healed many curses and brought much wealth to those who do as she says. Take out the money and make a cross over this cross of our dear Lord." They both spoke and looked completely serious never smiling or glancing away. I was surprised at their seriousness and certainly couldn't keep mine. When I said I was going and tried to take my handkerchief and 10-escudo bill, she held tight and continued, "And without letting me cure you?" (That one did jolt me a bit.) We argued back and forth as she kept pointing to my abdomen and genitals talking about the "maldad" [evil] there until I thought she would put a curse on me. I got the handkerchief, but she kept the 10 saying it wouldn't buy anything, to leave it for good luck. Then she turned away seeming almost angry and sat tucking under her lace skirt. "Don't trust people like that," she said about a long-haired boy who stopped to talk a few minutes. I talked with him (Conde) and Doris later in the snack bar at UNTAC. They just came from Buenos Aires where they had seen me at Plaza Francia selling beads. They now have a 37-day old baby boy. Conde talked about Brazil where he gave me addresses and encouraged me to do my work with beads there since they sell very well and are easy to obtain. Later Martine came by saying that she was going to Viña del Mar also.

We visited Mrs. T. to tell her good-bye. As usual talk went to politics and inflation with her commenting that the Chilean had developed into a race who wouldn't work unless someone told them what to do. Repeatedly we hear that "we Chileans are too lazy" from the usually middle-class people we have met.

Then we go to the house across the street to say good-bye to Terry's women friends. I am like a creature from Mars landed among these young people who are darkly tanned, fashionably dressed, and harshly made up with dark red lipstick and nails and black lined eyes. The one who is Terry's lover draws near him while I sit with the other three and try to involve myself in their play of words which could hardly be called a conversation. When young men begin to arrive, there is very much grass smoking with negligible effect. The social signals change with strange passages across the room, some romantic or evasive schemes are taking place it appears. One handsome young man is perhaps the object of all this, or maybe the only real occurrences are in my mind as it tries to recall past life and way of thinking. I know that I struggle with my ego; I don't want the expression of a certain feeling to reveal itself, a feeling that I and my experiences (and Terry's) are more exciting, more interesting, more worthwhile than what these people in their settled lives have. It isn't true. We don't understand each other's worlds or are afraid of them. I feel the power of the Gypsy's suggestions. Before I have not thought that other women considered me with envy, only perhaps with pity or a fear and repulsion of the different unknown. It occurs to me that Terry, like a brother for whom I have no attraction, is very attractive for many others. They can't seem to comprehend our relationship. Perhaps some of these women would like to be with Terry as often as I am.

I began talking with one of the women sitting near me about the Gypsies. I asked her what she thought of them. "They are bad people because they rob. Also, they are dirty." This conversation led to my telling her fortune, imitating the Gypsy, all much to everyone's surprise including mine. I began thinking again of how I might get some Tarot cards. On went the evening, one interesting event being that, after much questioning of us, the young man said, "Now ask us some questions." (I was made fun of somewhat. Clever Gypsy!)

JAN. 11, 1973—D.C.

Day of rest, patching, eating, reading *Time* magazine (very depressing), some yoga, and even trying to catch up with this writing.

SANTIAGO - JAN. 11, 1973

This city is still as much of a hassle as before, even though I know my way around better. I decided to get all my shopping done on one day so I would not have to hassle with it more than once. Danelle and I left the house in the afternoon early and caught the lift all the way to the Center where I bought an architecture drawing book called *Dibujos de los Arquitectos* (Drawings by Architects) for $2.00 (black market price) and found an old cardboard box to wrap it in and sent it home for about 40 cents. Not a bad deal! Then I bought a couple of rolls of film and a pair of socks for 25 cents and even changed some more money on the black market for 300 to 1.

After that prosperous afternoon we went to visit Mrs. T., the lady we first stayed with, and then went across the street to visit the girls, Marisa, and Anita R. When we arrived, there were already two other girls visiting, and a little later two guys came. Danelle was doing a beautiful imitation act of a Gypsy telling fortunes, and it was hilarious. I don't know when everyone got around to leaving, but it was late. I do know that the birds were signaling the coming daylight when Marisa and I fell into an exhausted slumber after an amorous night. I was one tired man.

I am starting to enjoy living and buying things here in Chile now that I'm spending black market escudos. They sure go a long way. Chilenos use their paper money like it was an old rag, or a piece of wastepaper, stuffing their bills unfolded in their pockets or purses. When they hand the bus driver a bill, it's usually just a sick looking wad of paper. I guess that's just about what the Chilenos think of their money. One could carry a coin for months before he could spend it. The coins are almost worthless.

JAN. 12, 1973—**D.C.**

One of the three rides and much walking it took us to get out of Santiago on the road to Viña del Mar was with María Luisa C., a jolly woman of 45 or so, dressed in a brightly colored maxi-robe.

She spoke English with an English accent and told us how she had landed in Miami with 50 dollars and had hitchhiked around the States for over a year and was raped once (forced with a knife) in downtown Washington, D.C., 10 pm. She spent three months in jail in Laredo, Texas, for possession of marijuana (wasn't hers, she said). She only recently returned from this trip. She gave us the address of Sonia and Alfredo in Viña.

We went hitching the Pan American Highway north, only to find out that it was not route to Viña, that we would be going out of our way. But we saw the Aconcagua in the distance, highest mountain in the Americas. The foreground reminded me of riding with Francisco from San Francisco to Los Angeles. The high hills are covered with tall golden dried grass, small cedar and mesquite-like trees, and occasional eucalyptus scattered around. In watered valleys grow vegetables, peaches, chirimoyas, avocados, etc.

At Calera we see a Gypsy [Romany] camp of high tent-like structures, with canvas-colored roof, four supporting poles, brightly colored with huge stripes are the four sides. Outside campfires, a few cars, children playing, women in bright red clothes stroll over to chat with neighbor. Inside are piled belongings of pillows, mattresses, etc. The camp stretches out for three-quarters of a mile. Driver says there are always many here; they even plant crops sometimes. Huge avocados grow in this region.

Hard hitching finally brings us to the sea at Con Con and along a beautiful beach drive with small beaches between rocks, blue water, big white waves, expensive summer homes on hills and then views of Viña and Valparaiso stretched along the bay. Victor, who gives us our last lift into the interesting town invites us for tea at his family's new wooden house in a crowded almost slum-like neighborhood. Since they have recently moved in, the place is somewhat cluttered; and they apologize for it. Victor's mother is extremely affectionate; they talk of another American friend, a newspaper reporter. We devour toasted bread, cheese, apricot jam since morning we hadn't eaten. Victor will very soon go to

Germany to work, thanks to the help of a German pen pal. He was once in the navy on a huge ship with sails.

We have Victor leave us at the house of Alfredo (an eccentric-looking professor) and young adventurous wife Sonia. Paintings on the wall give it the look of an artist's house. Several teenagers arrive, making themselves at home; and soon rock music is blaring from the stereo. Someone arrives with a homemade waterpipe and begins experimenting. Obviously no one feels paranoid; door is left open, people walk in and out, grass and joints and roaches are everywhere, and all to no avail since the grass is probably not even half pure. The night goes on with much movement, sounds and flirtations of the adolescents who act quite adult most of the time. One girl, who draws well, has her starry eyes in Terry's direction; but she is 15 and appears to have younger boys more interested in her. Another girl with curly hair is 14, another 13. They all come in and out mixing, going for all-night walks, eating what they wish in the kitchen. We were amazed to see all this going on. We feel uneasy about where we'll go to put up our tent and finally get the courage to ask to sleep on the floor.

JAN. 13, 1973—**D.C.**

After a breakfast of bread, butter, and tea we say good-bye (are invited to drop by later) and look over the beaches. Others are camped there but we don't like the crowds of people, the trash, etc. so walk on to the main street, Ave. Valparaiso, and get a bus to Valparaiso where we get a glimpse of the crowded bustling city built on the port and hillsides. The part we see looks quite poor, with its zinc and board shacks compared to Viña with tree-lined streets, flowers and grass, and old wooden mansions, and new apartment buildings. In a section called Colón, near the highway to Santiago there is an extremely crowded marketplace stretched along the avenue. Again, hitching was bad to Algarrobo; we finally ended up taking a bus from the silent, one-storied town of Casablanca. We had to stand all the way and the ticket vendor tried to cheat us dearly. Fortunately, we had asked the price in Valparaiso. The bumpy dirt road led to the tourist-filled town on the hillside above the sea.

The beach was beautiful, long, and wide, stretching around the small bay. Waves were crashing dangerously on the steep shore throwing mist with the cool wind. Soon fishermen were arriving and so there were many sea birds. As the sun began to set there were more people than earlier casting flies into the surf with both poles and lasso-like swinging of weighted lines. Fires were built here and there. I looked out occasionally to see the sunset, but the frigid wind didn't invite one to linger and soon I was inside sleeping bag.

JAN. 14, 1973—**D.C.**

The walk on the beach was long but pleasant. Further down were less people, more birds fishing, big waves with foam, and seaweed on beach. Around canal-like lagoon are many campers with tents. The small town Mirasól is above cliffs. Sea-worn granite rocks with pink, orange, purple and light green spots, and thick leaves, moss-like, flowing purple red on long stalks all give many colors to gray rock cliffs. Past this point another small beach is framed from above by rocks. Even there it is crowded with people. Still, I felt I could walk forever and not find anyone I knew. Streams of people have shade-covers, but hardly anyone goes into the chilly water. Instead, there are soccer games, picnics, and sand-castle building.

Our ride goes all the way to Santiago but has a flat and a stuck gear shift, finally burning brake fluid. The driver must change cars. He shows us his lumber yard. It seems we'll never get home, but we see streets with beautiful houses and lower streets like Ave. Portugal with much atmosphere. With the sunset on snow-covered peaks, I start to think that Santiago isn't so bad after all. I'm sunburned though.

ALGARROBO, CHILI (A BEAUTIFUL BEACH TOWN) - JAN. 14, 1973

How can I ever remember all the excellent details, which I do not write down as I experience them, three days later? It's absurd and my past is broken into broad generalizations. Nevertheless, I keep writing.

It's strange to think of all the rides it took us to get here, and the experiences gathered in such a short span of time. First, a lady speaking English picked us up near our house and took us closer to town. She said that she and her husband were going to Viña del Mar (where we were headed about 1:00 PM) and that, if we were still there, they would pick us up.

After about half an hour of hitching on busy Avenida Kennedy, a freaky middle-aged woman with young twin sons pulled up in front of us and told us to hop in. During the short ride with her in her Jeep, she proudly proclaimed the fact that she has just returned from a hitchhiking journey in the States where she had been in jail in Laredo, Texas, for marijuana, and robbed and raped in Washington, DC. Amongst her stories she said she was glad to be back in Chile where she felt free. She left us nearer to the exit out of Santiago and with an address in Viña del Mar.

Because we were near the market, we bought a dozen beautiful peaches to add to our meager foodstuff for the journey. We had boiled eggs, a few plumbs, half kilo of cheese, some left-over lettuce from the party, which I buried on the beach (too wilted), and our peaches. Oh yah, we also had tomatoes. We then walked past an eloquently decorated train station and put our thumbs out full of hope. We were passed by beer hauling trucks with huge casks and brawny laborers with paper-sack hats. Also passing us were taxis with black and pale-yellow tops and vehicles of varying sizes and shapes.

We decided to ask if this were the best way to get out of Viña and were informed by a guy in the kiosk selling peaches, etc., that we would have to take the road on the other side of the train station to get to the Pan American Highway. So, we walked and walked and walked until we came to what we thought was the Pan American Highway. A plump guy stopped and took us down the highway a short distance, never getting out of residential areas. When he turned off, there we were hitching our asses off and still not out of the city. Danelle said she felt like she was hitching on a Los Angeles, CA, freeway, passing though one of its suburbs.

I really don't know how long we waited for a ride in that dusty place; but finally, after more than an hour, a young guy stopped; and we were on the road, oh heavenly road, going where I'd never been before. The guy spoke English and said he was working for an agricultural chemical company and began naming all the benefits he gets from his job while living in a country where most people must do without. His clients give him freshly picked fruit; he buys, at decent prices far away from Santiago, avocados for as many as eight of his friends while he is on trips. While with him, we stopped to load the trunk full of this buttery vegetable. He paid 55 escudos for two pounds (20 cents per kilo).

While cruising along the road, we passed rolling yellow hills with short green trees speckling the broad layers of yellow. It reminded me of Arizona or New Mexico and photos of Africa. We passed a Gypsy camp with their colorful, stripped, boxy tents. They are everywhere in South America.

Finally, our cordial driver dropped us off, and we caught another ride to a small village along the ocean near Viña del Mar. After about an hour of hitching to get to Viña, we landed a ride with a guy our age named Victor, who invited us to have an "Once" (eleven o'clock tea and bread with jam and cheese) at his house with his mother. As we were riding in his old Ford, I could not help but be refreshed by the ocean and its rocky environs. Sun, surf, sand, and beautiful people! What a spiritual place this is along the ocean! I was beginning to wonder if it was worth it. It was. I had almost forgotten how wonderful the ocean can be.

After eating a pile of bread, jam, and cheese, Victor took us to the address Calle 10 ½ which the freaky lady gave us while in Santiago. I couldn't help but notice how beautiful this seaside resort city was with its well-designed high-rise apartments and hotels, clean avenues, and it holiday feel. Once we arrived at the house a new, or not so new, but strange environment opened to us. After talking with the mother and many teenage kids, most of them not hers, some young guy brought a newly fashioned marijuana water pipe made from chemical lab equipment, tubes, jars, etc. He soon found that the pipe didn't work well and needed more work, so someone began rolling joints and I don't think they ever stopped. Everyone from the 12-year-old boy and up, was smoking both inside and outside the house with the front door wide open. I was paranoid at first, but they assured me that this was Chile, and it doesn't matter. Wild music blaring into the street and young "freaks" everywhere! Anywhere else in the world and everybody in the house would have been arrested. After about 2:00 AM, most of the 13-to-15-year olds left to continue their party at another house. They were up on acid and could not sleep. Danelle and I put our heads on our rolled-up pants and, snug in our sleeping bags, dozed off. I woke up when Danelle got up to investigate a rustling noise in our food bags. She came back and said there was a big frog sitting on our stuff. I got up to see him. It was a big toad which I put out the door.

We could not believe the massive quantity of "roaches" (remains of a marijuana joints) lying all over the floor when we got up. We checked out the beach in the morning and decided to split for Algarrobo because it probably wouldn't be so dangerous or crowded. A big hassle to get here with a lot of hitching time! We went through Valparaiso, a port town with a curving beach, and hitched our asses off again and finally, towards the end of the day, made it here. This is a beautiful beach, not too many people, where we pitched out tent and watched an orange sunset and the black silhouettes of surf fishers.

JAN. 15, 1973—**D.C.**

Another day of rest in which the main activity is the making of a bean soup, porotos granada is the base like one we've had before on several occasions. The ingredients cost us dearly, but soup lasts us 2 meals. It requires boiling shelled, fresh beans until soft; then adding fresh chopped corn and squash and albahaca [basil] leaf spice. Onions, garlic, peppers, tomatoes are fried separately then added when squash is done. Later I discover in Manuela's bookshelves *Living on the Earth* by Alicia Bay Laurel. While reading thru its how-to's, Terry got enthusiastic again about writing and illustrating a book on South American travels. I set to copying a few things like how to make falafel and caught up with this writing today.

JAN. 16 AND 17, 1973—**D.C.**

Both days we went to town to the UNTAC building and sat around, just watching the people, always hoping that Nito would appear but no sign of him. We did finally get to see Edgardo who seemed to feel rather guilty about our not getting the job at FECH. After a chat we said our farewells. All around us, talk was of politics. Terry says that even the writing on the toilet is not pornographic but political. A group of Communist youths had a rally. All dressed in maroon shirts they went out waving flags, chanting, and blocking the street in front of UNTAC and the Catholic University, supposedly a reactionary school. In the UNTAC and other places in Santiago we have seen much interest in Russia. We saw a very nice display of photographs of several distinct aspects of Russia, and on another day an exhibition of Russian handicrafts. We have seen many worn-out, patched jeans on youths everywhere in the city, combined with high platform shoes and braless knit blouses which tie in back. Always there are the anti-war billboards and much talk of humanitarianism. An exemplary contradiction is Edgardo's telling us how the patients with medical problems at the psychiatric hospital where he's working this summer have not been examined in three years. Why? Because doctors don't feel they are paid enough to work there and don't like tending to chronic patients.

We are very restless now and are preparing to leave early tomorrow, hopefully for good. The smog was terrible today, matching our general impressions of the city. The people have been so kind that we would like to find their city beautiful also, but despite finding certain beautiful areas, our over-all opinion of it has been pretty bad. I have rarely ever experienced this feeling about a place.

SANTIAGO (ONCE AGAIN REVISITED) - JAN. 16, 1973

Here we are again for the third time. We hitched for one and a half hours to get out of Algarrobo and caught a funky ride all the way to our front door. Had a flat tire, had to fix the stuck gear-shift lever, and the brake tube broke spewing brake fluid over the exhaust pipe and smoked up a storm. It was good to get back and know that, when we leave for Tierra del Fuego, we won't be coming back.

SANTIAGO (FOR THE LAST TIME) - JAN. 17, 1973

We are sitting in the coffee shop of the UNCTAD (United Nations Conference on Trade and Development) building, waiting for Edgardo. The place is swarming with students, all wearing maroon shirts with epaulets, both men and women. They are communists, but Danelle thought at first they were all in a singing group. They are just like everybody else here, sitting around drinking their Coca Colas. Not only now but always is there political talk in the air. Even the graffiti on the toilet stall walls is political writing in lieu of pornography.

JAN. 18, 1973—D.C.

We had an unusually easy time hitching out of Santiago although our second ride, a lumbermill owner in a rickety old red pickup, had to screech to a braking halt about three times in order to avoid hitting someone. Terry was being thrown around the back quite a bit. We were glad to see the heavy smog of Santiago behind us.

After a mile, our rides came easy. An architect from Viña gave us his address and asked us to visit him if we returned.

When we got down at Rengo, immediately a pickup driver offered to take us when he returned from town. There were already four other hitchers at the spot, so we sat back and waited. There was only room and weight allowance for two, so we were a bit harassed by the others who felt they should have the ride before us. Fortunately, we rode in the back where we didn't have to listen to the constant, loud, misinformed ravings, mostly anti-communistic, of the driver. He was very friendly to say the least. He was showing around a 12-year-old, overly mature, sad-eyed Peruvian niece who was in Chile for an operation. He entered every main town along the route and drove around it: San Fernando (where he treated us all to a delicious lunch of porotos granada), Curico, Talca, San Javier, Linares.

At Talca we were shown a museum where O'Higgins signed the declaration of independence in his elegant handwriting. It was a beautiful old house around several patios. The exhibited Chilean paintings were delicate and accurate expressions of the Chilean atmosphere. I liked them very much; they were very human, romantic realism. We had "once" (comes from the eleven letters of the word aguardiente, we were told) beside the river Claro. There was very tasty, deep-fried frog; and "chancho en piedra" (pig on rock), a tomato sauce made and served in the mortar, with garlic, pepper, cumin, and onion in it, eaten with a heavy brown bread. Very tall trees shaded the banks of this river. Talca was very commercial.

Often the driver stopped right in the road to get out and tell us something. He was such an indefatigable talker. Outside San Fernando he pointed out the sierras where the recently found Uruguayan plane crash survivors had crossed 70 kilometers back, he said. High, rugged snow-covered, these mountains seemed hardly crossable. He showed us the river they had used to guide them to a settlement, the one they had thrown across the written message with a rock. At one stop he showed us an old horse-drawn type coach which in his youth was used only by the very wealthy. It had fine glass windows and rich black leather upholstery and was completely enclosed for the passengers who were protected by leather roll-up shades. Very elegant! We stopped at a roadside town where we found baskets woven with mimbre, a willow-like material, for sale.

As in other South American countries, I saw on a farm beside the highway, horses being driven around and around to trample the grain (wheat) stalks to separate the grains from the stalks. I disagreed with Terry when he observed that a West Texan would feel completely at home in Curico. The cultured contrasts of the meeting of town and country would daze us. At its entrance beneath a sparsely pined hill is a small park with a decorative brick fence. There are slums of wooden shacks and even brightly colored Gypsy [Romany] tents in the open spaces. The squared, uniform, one-story buildings are distinctly Spanish American, and the quite unadvertised humility of its businesses is like an Andean open-air market. The shady bench-lined walks of its central plaza are peaceful like the impression of the town. Here and there small parks contain sculptures. Taxies are the many horse-drawn carriages which pass up and down the streets looking for passengers. Cowboys in flat-brimmed Andalusian type black hats, short jackets, woven belts, pants gathered at bottom walk or stand at corners talking among passers-by in miniskirts, slacks, and braless blouses, longhaired young men and other types between the latest mod and the most traditional campesinos chilenos. Two Gypsy women color the comparatively subtle tones of the town and people. This ride took all day.

By the time we reached the road to Bullileo and Steve's farm (feeling glad we had not had to listen in the cab to the anti-Allende senseless rantings), the sun was setting, and there was no possibility of finding public transportation for the 30 kilometers we would have to go toward the Cordillera. We waited anyway to try our luck at catching a lift. We were fortunate to catch a lift way after dark for a 10-kilometer ride which left us in a small village with a carabinero (highway police) station. We were told as usual to ask the carabinero for help, but he said it was "strictly prohibited" both to stop us a ride or give us a place in the yard to lay our sleeping bags.

After waiting a few hours, we decided to sleep in the nearby, bus-stop shelter. I rested well but didn't sleep for a long time. The full moon shown very brightly right in front of us; the strong wind blew the poplar trees which lined the road. Crickets and dogs spoke. Fine dust came in from the road. After the moon passed the door, I slept a little; but dawn came soon.

JAN. 19, 1973—D.C.

No one would pick us up this morning, so it appeared we were going to have to wait half or all day for the bus. We considered walking but the already bright sun and the size of our packs discouraged us. Eventually we got a lucky lift with a construction crew in a dump truck which was going to the mountains to work on a road to Argentina. If we had walked, we would have seen nothing but an occasional farmhouse and miles of poplar trees and thick 10-ft. high bushes blocking the view. On the road to Patti's house there was a cool pine-tree lined entrance, then a down-hill curve which gave us a beautiful view of a huge tree-filled valley with snow-capped mountains behind. Soon a car came; it was Patti on her way to buy food with a male neighbor.

We walked on wooden plank bridges over clear water canals past a couple of small wooden houses with many little children out front. At the gate of a wide yard an old man with few teeth introduced himself and let us in. He told us he had been here 16 years, had cleared this place and planted the trees and flowers "with his own hands". He showed us first the garden he planted in halves with the owner, then his own which stood next to his small adobe house with the grape arbor shade in front and benches to sit on which he had also proudly made. The garden sadly reminded me of so many I had seen before among the poor Latin farmers. Poor soil, insects, disease, and rodents made the work of hoeing, planting, watering, staking, pruning, spraying, etc., almost worth nothing. Like some healthy and flourishing plant one day would dry up and die from a plague just as it was beginning to produce. We got to know several tobacco and grass plants. When I told Armides I was 27 and unmarried, he began to tell me how lonely he was without a family, how bored he was of living alone. Later while we slept he walked for miles thru brush pastures looking for three missing sheep.

Patti's neighbor friend Tito took us to his hired-hand's place, a new adobe, tiled house with glass windows. There were twelve children in this household. Tito bought this land with money he made driving, then selling a truck. In the evening, he returned with his wife María Olga, a quiet woman with distinct features who had married him when she was 15.

Days here on the farm blend together. The 21st has almost passed now. I have slept a great deal, waking only a short while in the mornings when the maid comes with one of her numerous children. She came yesterday without being sent for because she heard Patti had company. Even in the humble furnishings of the farmhouse we feel like aristocrats with the maid cooking, serving us, and refusing to sit with us. Armides is the same. They feel they must eat in the kitchen, not at the table with us. They work away while we read and sleep. Repeatedly, we see this very humble, servile attitude. Armides won't do anything without asking the owner for fear of losing his confidence. The maid only cooks exactly what we tell her and refuses if we say, "cook whatever you want." We have eaten extremely well here.

Association with Tito gives us an even sharper sensation of the elite. The families of both he and his wife are nine generations almost unmixed Spanish aristocracy, especially hers. They speak of their family pride in having no Indian blood. Yesterday we were taken to María Olga's father's farm where the clan lives in a 100-year-old, tile-roofed house with pinkish red walls and glassed-in furnished verandas. It is a large house but country and modest, quite lived in. Antique photographs and delicately designed, colonial-style sofa somehow blend with TV set, the more modern but worn furniture, and puma hides. One wall of the kitchen is covered with old fashioned wooden, screened cabinets with upward-opening bend doors and a mixture of miscellaneous items of dishes in the shelves. This family lost a great deal of land recently; but even with the pain of this, they maintain the image and atmosphere of a wealthy, landed family who loves their place enough to live on it.

Tito's daughter is twelve but exceptionally mature and beautiful. Unless she continues to isolate herself with her drawings and paintings (of landscape she tells me), she will surely be the victim of the desires of many others. Her mother wants to bring her out to be more sociable, while her father treats her like a child and bosses her around in a way he is apparently unable to do with his wife. What kind of chance will she have to continue to develop her interests and abilities?

We crossed beautiful pastures of tall, seeding grass surrounded by trees and hills with snow-covered peaks in the distance to get to the clear rocky river where we were going swimming. I mistakenly didn't bring my bathing suit bottoms, but my dark blue bikini panties seemed to serve without causing too much (if any) disturbance! (Remember the drunk cowboys walking along the road trying for a lift.)

Maria Olga's father reminds me somewhat of Granddad, his dignified carriage, his need to talk. "Choma," he demands to be called, not "don" or señor.

I spend a great deal of time listening to the silence here as I alternate between breeding restlessness and calming desires. Steve has an *I Ching* which I began reading for the first time after many times of seeing it and wanting to. With coins I asked it the first question, the answer centering around retreat quite appropriate for my character I would say. One line moving denoted a retiring tail which I thought cynically funny considering my question. Hours pass, but truly little seems to stimulate me to activity aside from a few yoga exercises and this writing. I barely scan the *Time* magazine news, something I once devoured word for word.

PARRAL, CHILE - JAN. 2, 1973

I was sitting in the back of a pickup truck with only the rubber of the spare tire to soften the jostling bumps as we sped away from the ever-smaller growing Santiago and its smoggy valley. It was a good feeling indeed as the green countryside began passing beside us. Santiago is one city I do not care to visit again. If it were not for its fantastically friendly people, the city could be death in itself. Its general impression did not excite me. I did not believe I would feel that way about a city.

The UNCTAD building is, I think, the most impressive and best example of modern architecture in Chile. Its spaces are designed so well for human use that humans enjoy spending hours there. Every inch of space is a joy to be in with it varied vistas, textures, and its fine integration with the arts. This combination is the spirit of the entire building. The exterior air ducts become a powerful red sculpture standing like a guardian at one corner. Concrete sculptures break the hard edge of a high supporting wall, and brightly colored tapestries reveal the times of today. The building's structure is a space frame of rusting steel which gives a warm feeling of use. The building cafeteria always has people waiting in line for up to an hour to eat the 12-cent, three-course meal, served at noon.

The youth of Santiago take pride in their jeans and repair them with flower designs and unique patches. All the pants seen there have had the bottoms of the pant legs opened and a triangular piece of cloth added to make bell bottoms.

People waiting in lines is a common sight in Chile. Walking through a grocery store is a strange experience. Three rows of shelving along the aisles are bare, and the other twenty rows have general household goods. Chileans will either starve to death or get used to very bland diets.

The day before we left, I met a wonderful, tall, attractive young lady at the bus stop. She caught my eye and I caught hers, and a conversation began to grow, as did our feelings for each other. We were together mentally. Her name is Carmen F., and she has a hauntingly beautiful face, a long slender body, light in spirit, and a personality as open and warm as anyone could ever want. She said, "Let's walk," and we did, nearly all the way to her house two miles away. What we did not walk, we hitched. She prepared an "once" for me which included a boiled egg, jam, bread, and tea with milk. We played dominos. The entire time I was with her was wonderful. I loved to touch her, smell her wonderful fragrance, and hold her. She gave me affection, and I reciprocated. I cannot believe that such a relationship, newly born, was over when I parted on a passing bus five hours after I had met her, knowing I would never see her again. The next morning, Danelle and I left Santiago.

We are now at a farm four Americans our age rented for $30 a month, with the cost split between them. The owner let them choose the price, and they did not know what to say. So, they are paying $7.50 apiece per month to live in this beautiful valley with snowy mountains rising in the background. They have three horses, of which the newest one cost them $80.

There is a grizzled, 65-year-old man who built this place and takes care of it. He said he smoked marijuana with everybody here for the first time on Christmas Eve but did not feel anything. It must not have been good grass.

PARRAL, CHILE, RANCH - JAN. 21, 1973

Now we are on the "Rancho donde viven los gringos" (where Americans live). This place and this country life is magnificent. It is difficult for me to fathom, in this beautiful area of Chile, that farmers

Rio Longavi   Fundo Santa Filomena
Parral, Chile

in their 20s want to leave the farms and ranches for the big city. Life is disturbingly short to be wasting in crowded conditions in large Latin American cities and seems antithetical. What we need is preservation of self, a growth of spirit, and a strong, relentless respect for nature and the natural process.

We went swimming in the Longavi River which flows by the house, and it is impressive. It is clear, drinkable, and not too cold to swim in. In fact, it was just downright refreshing. Chica, the little dog, was the first one in and looked like a weasel swimming around. This little dog is something else. She was a street hound in Santiago, scrounging for food and sleeping on the concrete, homeless as a waif when two little kids decided to take her home. They soon found they could not keep her, so Patricia took her. She brought Chica to the ranch, and she is really a joy to watch discover this wonderful new world. She is just having the time of her life chasing around the horses and people, playing with tufts of wool from the freshly skinned lamb, and in general acting like a little city kid who just came to the country. A couple of days ago, she was on the bed across from me when I took out my flute and played several notes. She cocked her black fuzzy head, first to one side, then to the other, in the most curious way. She is a beautiful, little, happy, incredibly lucky dog.

I rode horseback for the first time in about twelve years. Quite a joy! Got to gallop and enjoyed it immensely. The speed, the air blowing through my hair, the grace of such a huge animal was breathtaking. I will have to do that again. I was thrilled but was hanging on for my life. Oh, what a great feeling it must be to be rider and horse as one! Someday I will have that chance.

As the sun was going down, I was out helping Almendaz, the 65-year-old man, chase down the sheep. He is a tough, toothless man. I could not believe how well he could run chasing fifteen head of sheep. Every evening, he herds them into his yard surrounded by high barbed wire fence to protect the flock from wild dogs or people. Times are bad in Chile for both wild dogs and people, and a young sheep would be a nice prize for either.

PARRAL, CHILE, RANCH - JAN. 22, 1973

The maid, a snaggle-toothed lady, made bread this morning forming the dough in six-inch long circular forms. She then let them rise and built a fire outside and placed a home-made oven over the fire. This oven was constructed of a 55-gallon drum cut in half with both

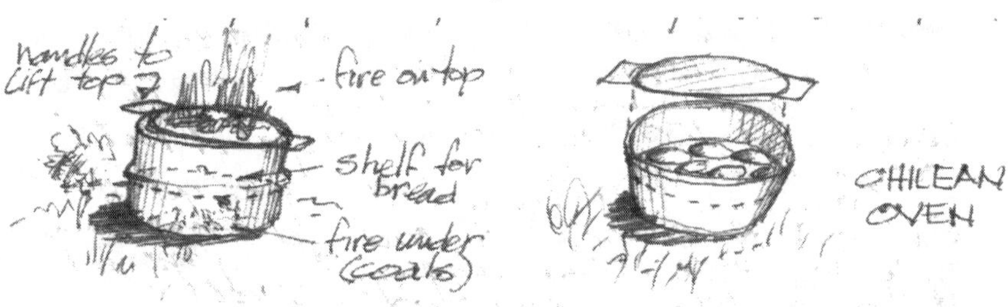

top and bottom removed. One of the ends was placed in the middle of the half drum (sitting on wire). The other end is used as a lid and a fire is kept going on top of it. Un pan muy sabroso! (A very delicious bread!)

COLLIPULLI, CHILE - JAN. 24, 1973

We stuck our thumbs out again about noon. Waited for two hours, about average, caught a ride to here with a guy our age in his little Austin. He lives in Puerto Montt and gave us his address which will be a significant help.

We are visiting a family that we met while camping in Villarica. They are beautiful. We arrived about 5:00 PM. The mother was in town, so the three kids hustled around to make us feel at home. The oldest little girl, thirteen, got the fire in the woodstove going and heated up the milk. The boys were all doing something to help by shaking the crumbs off the tablecloth, setting the table, and sweeping the floor. All had exquisite manners, "perdoneme" (pardon me), "con permiso" (with your permission), etc. and came out with their hair slicked down with water and freshly combed. All this without mom around!

JAN. 24, 1973—D.C.

We all got up comparatively early and spent the morning waiting (I have been reading Chinese thought from *Confucius to Modern Times* by Herrlee Creel, an interesting but superficial overview) for Tito to come to take us to the highway so we could hitch south. He was supposed to be there at 9:30 and finally made it at 12 :00. We were still hitching when he returned from Parral, so we were able to send back money we had forgotten to give to Patti for the food we had heartily consumed while at the farm.

After the long wait we felt very happy for our fast car ride that took us all the way to Collipulli. The driver gave us his address in Puerto Montt.

The C.s' house, which sits very near the Pan American Highway, is typical of Collipulli. A wooden gate opens to a yard of flowers and trees. The wooden house has a plain, painted-blue front and zinc roof. Inside the walls are wood also and the ceiling quite low. A friend let us in and called the children who came running. While still panting heavily, they all worked hurriedly to lay out the table for tea. Bread in bread box, honey in bowl, wood in stove, meat in oven, cups on table, each one was doing something. Then they invited us to watch on the T.V. "Música Libre" in which bikinied females and fully dressed males did completely ungraceful, choreographed interpretations of mostly foreign rock music on the edges of an elaborate swimming pool.

Emilia came very surprised to see us. Her husband hustled Terry off to see his shop while she laid out another hot milk and bread for me. Our conversation went from the death of Aristotle Onassis' only son and the signing of a cease-fire agreement in Vietnam to a personal conversation in which Emilia talked of her aging and her regret over her looks, quite beautiful in my eyes. She certainly doesn't look older than her husband. Then she practically apologized for her family's having questioned Terry and me so much about our relationship and not accepting that we could be only friends. We discussed the common belief here that a girl should be a virgin when she marries. She also told me that when foreigners are trying to learn Spanish here, the people play jokes on them by teaching them dirty words in place of the correct ones. By the time the men came, we were given "once;" I was already so full I could hardly eat. Before bed I watched a political TV program with Emilia. Senators from each political party had a given amount of time to speak, but usually they were so drowned out by interruptions from each other that the M.C. had to constantly plead that they do not interrupt, or he would stop the program. They were all fanatical, and their rhetoric was trite, emotional, and mostly aimed at the election in March.

VALDIVIA - JAN. 25, 1973

PEACE AT LAST – I HOPE! I just heard a news broadcast on TV that the USA and North Vietnam have come to an agreement, and the war is over. I never thought they'd ever want to stop. What a wonderful feeling!

The family put us in the kids' beds, and the kids slept doubled up. We had a good breakfast of bread and cheese and were off. Caught a ride almost immediately to Camuco; but, halfway there, the driver asked me to help load 150 sheets of corrugated metal roofing. That was a lot of work.

We spent three hot hours trying to get a ride out of there and picked up one 27-km ride; and there we were, stuck again. A guy named Antonio stopped and took us all the way to Valdivia and even five miles beyond where we camped for the night. He was an easy-going guy who works for a bank up in the desert and said he was transferred there as punishment. I didn't ask for what. Three days ago, he rolled his car and just had it fixed. He said the other driver was at fault and paid for all expenses including a total paint job.

We camped on the land of a little person named Raul. He is a typical campesino but about three feet shorter than the rest. He watched in amazement as we pitched our tent and took me to the well where beautiful crystal water trickles from deep inside the hill. He's a good man and did not hesitate to help us.

Chile is a beautiful country with great forests and rich pastureland! The golden wheat is being harvested, and the songbirds are in abundance. Harmony with nature!

JAN. 25, 1973—**D.C.**

We had to do a lot of waiting today; but once we got a lift, we traveled fast. We noticed many other hitchhikers along the road. While waiting in Temuco we saw a white wooden hearse drawn by two old black horses. Only ten people walked behind. We also saw a cart break down, throwing out some of the people and goods. The poor horse hardly even acted surprised. One place where we waited was by a stream where many little boys were swimming. They would warm themselves by lying on the highway. They constantly harassed us in Spanish and play-like French and English. When we got a ride after several hours, they mobbed the car saying "Chio."

As before there are many wildflowers along the roadside, but they are a distinct species now. The bluebonnet-shades of color have been replaced by a different purple flower, by yellow and light shades of pink and rich gold and brown grass on the hills. The weather permits clear views of the volcanoes and valleys especially over the pass which was mist-covered when we last crossed. For several miles at one place the air was filled with smoke from burning off cleared land, common in the dry months in many countries. The driver Antonio treated us to eggs cooked and served in a "paila," a small frying pan without a long handle.

We saw many miles of marshes which were formed when an earthquake caused the land to sink and fill with water. Most of the valuable, valley's cultivatable land was lost it seems. Tops of fences are seen. We passed thru Valdivia, a town built around the union of two rivers. It looked beautiful with its huge wooden houses with shingled walls.

We were left some distance out of town near a carabinero's station. While asking the police where we might camp, we were offered and directed to a place by a midget campesino with a very mature, weather-worn face. He watched us put up our tent in the designated place just inside the fence of his property. Behind us was a gentle grass-covered hill from which there was a sunset-hour view of the long sunken water-filled valley, the surrounding tree-covered hills, distant houses, and the filled-in highway to Valdivia with its few headlights moving. The dark-shadowed marsh grass formed patterns like canals in the water. The wind in the pines, the soft-singing crickets, and birds whose song I'd never heard, sounded in the background.

JAN. 26, 1973—**D.C.**

We were very happy when a bearded man with hat and dark glasses motioned us to come and go with him to Puerto Montt, then to Chiloe. We sat in the back of the pickup parked on the Central Plaza of Osorno while the driver and company had lunch.

Later we passed a spot on the highway where the large Lake Llanquihue could be seen stretched out at the foot of snow-covered volcanoes, one Osorno with a near-perfect cone, like Fuji the Chileans say. We could also see the roof-tops and streets of the village Llanquihue, all this forming a very beautiful view. As Hernán's companions got out here and there, we replaced them in the cab.

He drove us around Puerto Montt and the port market Angelmo where hand woven wool rugs and sweaters, baskets, foods, etc. hung near booths of strung, dried sea food, seaweed, dried, fresh, live, smoked, all types of fish and fruit and vegetable stands too. There was much movement here, with the buying and selling, horse-drawn carts mingling with cars, trucks, buses, and grounded boats. Across the water a nearby island bustled with bathers on its sandy beaches contrasting with the warmly jacketed, rubber-booted, capped men on the market side. A few women selling fish had long skirts with fringe which looked like woolen blankets wrapped around them. The sea mud and moss, the fishy smells, the peeling paint or aged natural wood of the boats and vendor shacks and booths, the cold breeze, and a view of the volcano across the bay all combined to form a classic, stimulating atmosphere of excitement.

I was so impressed by the town, its varnished wooden church of rectangles, the hilly streets, and all the earthy mixture of wood, dirt, moist decay, fading paint, crisp breezes. I hope chance will have it that we spend time here later. Southwest to the Chiloe ferry the highway crosses through low, rough, almost uncultivated brush and through places where forests have long been cleared, leaving blackened stumps and logs between where cattle graze.

The gray farmhouses sit isolated, alone. Small fruit trees grow in the gardens, and the cleared pastures are near.

To us Hernán is a very interesting man, very humane, and very rational, even in political conversation (a rare Chilean for that). He works with the government in a leadership training program with the principles of group dynamics as its basis. "Capacitating organizations," as he calls it. Representatives from various groups of community organizations meet. Each person talks about the problems which have appeared in the organization, etc. Someone writes these in a list on the blackboard. Then after everyone has spoken, they together eliminate the less important points and discuss solutions to the rest. They have group projects that relate to these problems like making posters, etc.

Hernán studies theater and drama in school and was working in Cuba when the Chinese invited him to their country to work. He was there for 4 years, learned very much. He told us about the importance of drama there where even the market, factories, etc. have plays of their history. Their pajama-like garments are only outer-protection for the clothing which is sometimes scarce. Although there are factional disagreements as to how socialism should be established, there is a general agreement that socialism is best among most people according to Hernán. He has traveled in several other countries also. We figured him at about 35 years old. He has three living children of an ex-wife. One child died from drinking pesticide at 1 yr. 9 months. He has very mature and open-minded opinions concerning poverty and the possibilities of socialism. His experiences even include two years of weaving for a living since he couldn't get a job in Chile after returning from China. All this and much more we were able to learn from him since we had to wait in line over 5 hours to get on the ferry to cross to Chiloe. He treated us to wine and a plate of erizos—raw, sea urchin flesh--cold, soft, mushy-like tongues of porous flesh spiced with lemon, chopped onions and parsley. We said it was very different and pretended to like it. Because of this rare snack we lost our place in line. The guy behind us was in front and the last to fit on the launch, so we waited for the ferry. The call Hernán was trying to make finally came thru about then, and he found out that he had to return urgently to Valdivia.

We had to walk onto the ferry, an experience which reminded me of a European ferry crossing in the detail of the stairway to the second floor. The top was different with its plain bar and wooden benches unlike the large, fancy, cafeteria-style restaurant and pullman type seats I saw in Scandinavia (I think. Or was it the British Isles?) We got a lift in a truck hauling hay to Ancud where we were let off in a vacant lot behind a big, barn-like community hall where a teen-age record dance blared all types of music, rock, soul, cumbia, merengue, sentimental pop. We set up our tents behind it in the dark to the sounds of Santana. In the middle of the night the silence by contrast was so profound that it scared and woke us.

DALCAHUE, CHILE (CHILOÉ ISLAND) - JAN. 17, 1973

After about three or four wasted hours waiting for cars or trucks that never even slowed down, a bearded guy in a pickup stopped to let someone out and motioned for us to come on. Not only was he going to Chiloe, the island, but to Castro where we wanted to catch a boat to Tierra del Fuego. We passed by a perfect snow-covered volcano named Osorno. It was so majestic and perfectly formed it reminded me of Mount Fujiyama in Japan.

We arrived at the ferry crossing and waited for six hours for the ferry to launch. What an inefficient system!

I was surprised to see a little penguin swimming in the water by the loading ramps. Seeing this penguin made me finally realize how far south we are.

Hernán, our bearded driver, turned out to be an interesting and intelligent man of about 35 years old. He spent two years living in Cuba and four years in China, and his stories and events were of great interest to us. Here was a man with a deep knowledge of socialism and communism, and a world traveler who told about his experiences but did not preach them like so many of the young students we meet who are constantly screaming and ranting and raving about this and that and nothing. Hernán is a social worker now, but in his travels he was working in theater. He says the Chinese even put on plays in their factories.

He treated us to his favorite sea food, sea urchin, which looked like a bowl full of little pink tongues. They had a very sharp taste which I had to season with half a lemon to make them palatable. A bottle of wine with bread and butter and we had a meal. But, while eating, we

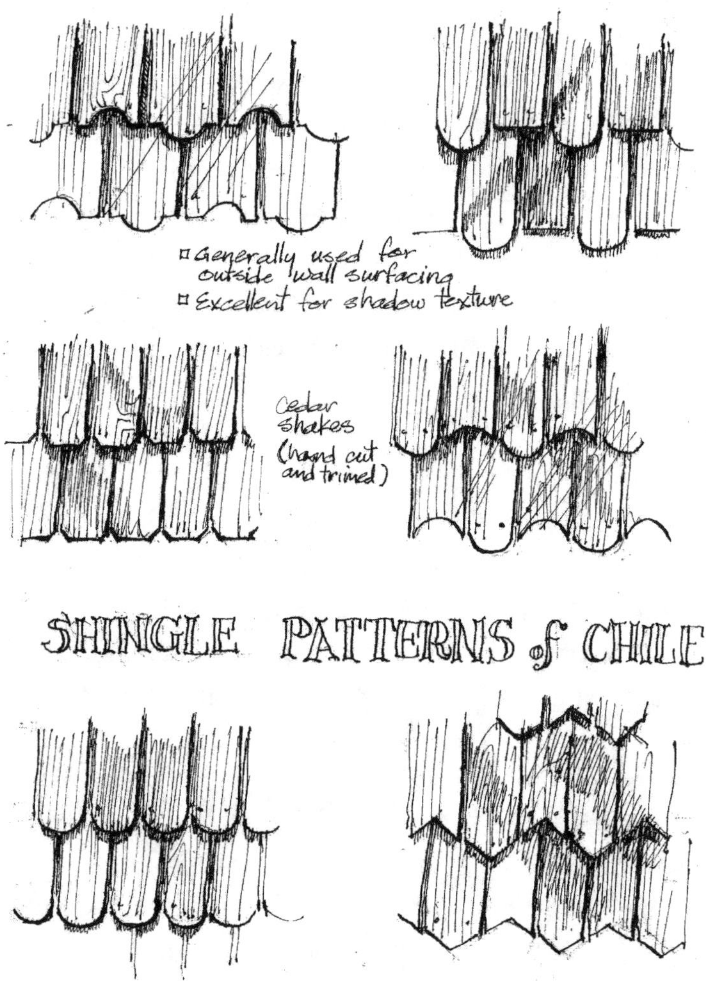

also missed the incoming launch, for which we had waited six hours. Hernan called his office to report in and check on things and found he had to return immediately to Valdivia, three hours back. So, Danelle and I decided to cross on the ferry and head on down the road. We never were much for going back, especially when it means more of a hassle the next day.

A twenty-five-year-old truck driver on the ferry took us through the early night to Ancud where we pitched our tent behind a huge dance hall blaring out music of all types. I went to sleep easily but woke up at 4:00 AM thinking I heard people outside. It turns out to have been a pig on the other side of the fence.

We were lucky hitching out of Ancud this sunny morning. The people in the truck behind us in the line for the ferry, who were the last to board, invited us to ride with them and took us to this little coastal town. We camped on a grassy meadow overlooking the bay. The sun is still warming the day.

This a handsome, rugged island with tree-lined hills and shingle clad houses, typical of this part of Chile. It feels like we could be in Europe or Canada.

JAN. 27, 1973—**D.C.**

It was a long walk from the center of Ancud to the Castro intersection, but it passed quickly with such beautiful and interesting surroundings. Fortunately for us, the people in the small truck, which had kept us off the launch, saw us hitching and loaded us in the back in their make-shift bedroom and took off a part of the door so we could see out. We told them we were going to Dalcahue to see the market tomorrow, so they decided to go also, very lucky for us since the town wasn't as close to the main road as we had thought. We rattled across the roads, sometimes dusty gravel. We peeked out at almost uncultivated (except for a few potato patches) countryside of grazing land, brush and

JAN. 29, 1973—**D.C.**

This morning we loaded all in the truck for the short drive to Castro. Quite a commotion was caused when Carmen's children gave all their comic books to the several little boys who had befriended them and had hung around camp quite a bit. The sidewalks of Castro were busy but almost every shop, all with big "importaciones" [imports] signs had practically empty display windows. There is almost nothing to sell these days. The rusting, corrugated tin church also had dilapidating steeples.

I went boat-hunting down at the harbor. A Danish girl was also waiting at the door of the Empresa (boat company), and we were told that there was no possibility of our getting a boat to Puntarenas from Castro. We asked about some smaller boats, but all we learned was that I got to see the medical boat, the one which travels along the southern canals attending campesinos. It was clean and well-painted and attended, but I couldn't find out if it allowed passengers.

We decided to try to hitch back to Puerto Montt. We sat down at a spot near a filled-in bridge. On one side a water-front street followed the edge of the bay. The back parts of the big wooden houses were supported by many stilts in the low tide mud. The outhouses were overhanging too. Drying clothes and the green-pastured hill in front of the houses gave bits of color to this dark murky scene. On the other side of the bridge was more low tide mud. There a woman in rubber boots, dress and big- brimmed hat, chopped holes in the mud with an axe and occasionally bent down to pick up shellfish, which she threw in her basket. A few black-tarred boats also lay in the mud. Across the water was a peninsula like we see so much in this area with scattered farmhouses and small green pastures enclosed by bushes and trees.

Along with some campesinas [country women] we finally got a ride in the back of a politician's pickup. He was driving around handing out his propaganda. He picked up Chilean hitchhikers too. They had been going to towns and villages talking to people, begging food, trying to get to know as much as possible.

At Ancud, Terry and I walked across the long bridge over a bay inlet. When we were tired of hitchhiking, we went to camp right there beside the inlet. Other campers were there also; it appeared at least to be a public picnic spot. At any rate it was a very pleasant place with grass, trees, bushes of raspberry, and red wildflowers. There was narrow sandy beach along the edge of the clear, icy water. We had a view of the water, the bridge, the town Ancud sitting on the hills across the bay inlet. The bay was nearby thru the trees; we could hear the sound of waves. We were invited to have tea around the campfire with the other campers. Terry went but I was already undressed and inside my sleeping bag. (Is a palote bug poisonous?)

JAN. 30, 1973—**D.C.**

It rained during the night (and the tent didn't leak!) so we took some time to let the tent dry out before rolling it up. It was almost dry when, as we were speculating how these black clouds should blow over, another short rain came and wet the tent again. We got on a launch this time to cross to the mainland. Both cars and pedestrians loaded on the platform with the rickety wooden side rails. The steerer had his place in a small toilet-house-like cabin raised above the level of the vehicle tops. These types of ferries make one wonder how they can cross all day, year after year without ever losing a car. Two of the vehicles on the launch were pick-ups belonging to Gypsies [Romanies]. The cabs were crowded with persons of different ages with dark eyes and brows and curly black hair. The women jumped out to direct the driver as he backed the pickup down the narrow concrete loading ramp. The back was piled with poles, canvases, and cloth, etc., and on all this were a couple of tricycles and some pigs. These people had the type of faces which had always been very attractive to me since I was a child. I felt somewhat embarrassed by staring at them so much. The children sat on the platform with their mother. Their dirty, ragged, make-shift clothes only made their physical beauty more acute. The mother sat cross-legged with her skirts tucked under. When asked for the fare later after the trip was half-over, she asked the money collector, "What would you do to me now if I didn't have the money?" I don't usually recognize Gypsies unless I see the women in their typical dress, so it was a new experience for me to be able to observe one of the young men with them. And this one was wildly exciting with wide smile which permitted the sharp contrast between his white teeth and dark complexion. His sharp, shadowed features were surrounded by dusty curls which blew back in the wind. His clothes were like those of a park bench bum. The puffy, wrinkled sports jacket and slacks were several sizes too big, and his once-black, pointed-toed, lace-up shoes blended with his clothes in the color of Chilean earth.

Dolphins swam beside the launch dashing under it and appearing on the other side. The launch sent a huge flock of seagulls flying low across the pale blue water behind us. Although the truck driver told us on the launch he was only going 8 kilometers, he signaled us to get on once he was on the highway and took us to Puerto Montt. Most of the men in the truck got off in a mud-street neighborhood at a house which serves as the Assembly of God church. We went straight to the office of CORVI where Andrés I. works and were lucky to find him there. He invited us to sleep on the floor at the place where he stays and planned to meet us later to take us there. Meanwhile we went to find out what we could about the transportation to Puntarenas. At least this time they told us there was a slight possibility of 3rd class passage on a boat of the Empresa Marítima Del Estado; but we would have to return on Friday to see what they had found out, since they rarely know until the boat arrives. The airlines are full for two more months. An American-born Brazilian guy of 19 came up to talk to us. One of his traveling companions was shot one night as they were trying to get into the house which they thought was the one where they were visiting in Santiago. He was interested in knowing about Vietnam (as most people around here are) and Israel. We sat talking with him in the Central Plaza where dozens of long-haired Chilean hitchhikers gathered with their mochilas and blankets to lean on. Some even sleep here at night or in school classrooms or on the beach. There were perhaps only two females in all. We saw a couple of people who looked foreign also but didn't talk to any. Andres and his friend Alejandro, who has the apartment, took us home, a three-bedroom place with no gas for hot water or cooking, no furniture, no hooked-up electricity, an appropriate stereotypical bachelors' flat, a good place for us.

We were so hungry that we returned to town to look for food and ended up at the Angelmo docks. We were taken by the atmosphere of this small rustic area. Now on foot we could see more closely the details of it. We ate on a two-story boat, one of the two floating restaurants there in the port. The upstairs view was of the small harbor at low tide. Boats of very different sizes, most with both masts for sailing and motors, sat in the mud. The marketplace shacks, built on a concrete dike, sat slightly over the edge. Their paint was sea-worn. Our soup (caldillo de mariscos) of varied seafood was very rich and very good. Onions, chili pepper sauce, and lemon spiced it. We went through a tunnel-like passageway of booths. Most of the stalls were closed, but at one we asked what they called a sea animal with a beak-like apparatus moving in and out of the hole at one end of its shell. "Picoroco" we were told, "raw or cooked, 50 escudos the dozen". Did we want to try one to see whether we would like it? I just made sure it was a cooked one before the vendor broke one side and pulled out the beak which had all the mussel attached. "Just eat the white part and put on lemon," one said. Another man said, "Eat it all and then suck the head." The taste was quite good, so Terry and I shared a dozen. The people there became very friendly. They asked us the usual questions. The children shared crab legs with us. We were given a few bites of charcoaled lamb (practically raw) and a couple of glasses of wine. One man paid our bill, and another invited us for an "asado" on Thursday. Later at the plaza, Isidro met us in his car and took us up the hill to the house which overlooks the town, the bay, and surrounding hills, and islands.

ANCUD, CHILE - JAN. 30, 1973

We went to a town named Castro yesterday and found it difficult to get a passenger boat south from there. One must wait and wait and wait and maybe there will be space available, so we hitched back here last night and got a ride in the back of a pickup of a guy running for congress.

It rained most of the early morning so we spent a while getting our tent dry; and, wouldn't you know, just when it was dry, a big cloud dropped another load on us. So, we are drying the tent again. We decided to travel to Puerto Montt to figure out the best way to get to Tierra del Fuego.

The island of Chiloe is one of the most beautiful parts of Chile, and it would be nice to spend a summer writing and drawing in one of its colorful ports. The atmosphere of these misty seaside villages with boats lining the beach seems good for mental stimulation. Chiloe is always green with rolling hills and sailing boats in the ports. Weather-beaten, shingle-sided houses and smoking chimneys are common scenes. It rains here a lot; and, because it is cold much of the time, the people are ruddy-cheeked, strong, and happy.

PUERTO MONTT - JAN. 31, 1973

It took two hitches to get from Ancud to the ferry crossing. We camped night before last on a wooded peninsula just outside Ancud. Our tent was protected from the wind by a natural tree line and the front faced a clear wide river. All the rivers I've seen on this rustic island have had clear water. Even the early morning rain did not bother us.

While crossing on the launch, we were raced by a sleek dolphin who looked like it was having an exciting time. We also passed through an entire flock of seagulls that were bobbing on the waves. It must be a wonderful sensation to slide through the ocean as a dolphin and glide on the breeze with seagull wings.

Danelle asked a guy with a truck at the boat launch area if he would take us to Puerto Montt, and he said he was only going 8 kms. As we were walking up to the main road after landing, he came by and motioned for us to get in the back of the truck. So there! We had our ride to Puerto Montt just like that without even having to try hard. Come to find out, there was a preacher in the front. Perhaps they felt bad about lying to Danelle, so they decided to take us. The preacher gave out a few religious pamphlets, and off they went.

We looked up Isidro A. who had given us his address while in Collipulli. He's a guy who gave us a hitch one day. We are sleeping on the floor in his house which is a typical bachelor apt. He and his roommate haven't paid the electricity bill, so the company cut off their service. They use candles and never eat here, so they have no gas connection and, unfortunately, no hot water. I really need a bath. My head is getting scaley and itchy, and my hair is dirty.

We might get a boat but will not know for sure until the end of the week. The airplane to Punta Arena costs $15.00. I do not know what we will do. We were treated to more Chilean hospitality last night when we went to eat seafood. We found a floating restaurant with inexpensive meals and had a bowl of mariscos (shellfish) which was superb. Looking out the windows we could see a typical old-world, harbor scene with sailing boats drydocked, lying on one side due to the tide being out. People were busy breaking open mariscos, driving horse-drawn wagons and building fires on their boats. Buildings hanging off the sea wall were supported by crooked poles, and seagulls claimed it all. It was an enchanting scene.

As we were walking through the fish market, we decided to try mariscos (shellfish) called Picoroscos. The lady let us try one first to see if we liked it. She said, "They are eighteen for 12 cents." Sure, why not? Danelle asked for a glass of wine, and we got three and some roast lamb to boot. All this cost us nothing. One of the old guys we were talking to paid for our food. When we tell these people how fantastically friendly and helpful Chileans are, they feel they must keep up the image. They are probably some of the friendliest and helpful people in the world. There is no end to their helping us. Funny thing is, this hospitality is reserved for foreigners and not for their own travelers, but it sure helps us out. People who ordinarily would not pick up Chilean hitchhikers will pick us up and treat us to the works.

JAN. 31, 1973—D.C.

Although we had bread and cheese in the house, it wasn't enough, and hunger drove us back to the stalls at Angelmo. We ate fried fish inside a restaurant hut (slanted-out walls for earthquake protection) with long benches at the tables and wood-burning stove. Digestion was somewhat disturbed by a violent fight in which a little boy was chasing and hitting his older sister with a board. Then for some reason or other the mother beat the little girl who soon got revenge by sneaking up on the boy and hitting him. It went on.

The old woman, who was serving, didn't know how to make change and oddly enough, neither did her customers. She short-changed one man, and the next time she short-changed herself. The pride of this restaurant was a magazine cover picture and the national championship certificate of feather-weight boxer Juan (?) Godoy.

We bought some small black cherries called "cerezas" as opposed to the large red ones called "guindas" (sour cherries). These we washed in the Plaza fountain where we sat eating them. Even a tea and water at a corner cafe didn't calm our hunger and thirst.

As we were opening the door of the house, the next-door neighbor woman asked us if we lived there, if everything was all right, etc. We quickly explained that there was no gas for cooking or hot water for bathing, so she invited us to go for a bath tomorrow and to come over later for a chat. We went soon expecting a cup of hot tea but instead were sat down with her husband, the head of the airport, and her nephews for a three-course meal of soup, rice with mariscos [seafood] (also tried these raw), salad, watermelon, and wine.

The Sra. Julie works in a dry cleaner her father left to her when he died. She was born and grew up here, so she knows everyone and has a very active social life. We saw something of the nature of it a little later when 2 couples arrived. Small drinks were served, and the subject of a lost umbrella developed into a fast-moving lengthy conversation which seemed funny to everyone but Terry and me. I was entertained listening to the Spanish.

When we heard thru the wall that Alejandro and Isidro had come home, we left. Isidro had been worried and had gone out looking for us. He soon came back and the four of us had a short conversation about life in the States as compared to Latin America. We were all very interested in this conversation; but it was late, and they had to work early tomorrow.

FEB. 1, 1973—**D.C.**

Washing clothes, answering the many questions of the neighbor children, and taking a hot shower next door were the morning's occupation. It felt so strange to be clean, I didn't want to touch anything for fear of the time span before my next chance for a hot bath.

We were crowded into the back door of a bus with the prevailing odor of fish, even on the people's skin. (Almost everywhere in this town there is fish smell.) We had a seat beside an old alcoholic who talked on and on to us although he could no longer remember most of the nouns he wanted to use in speech. Others on the bus laughed although nothing he said was funny to us. Before he got off he did say, "Chile is a very beautiful country. Here one can drink anything."

We went to the market to meet the people who had invited us to the lamb roast, but they had left town in the morning. At the same booth someone was cooking fried seafood pies (empanadas de mariscos), hot and very delicious. The booths were bustling with activity and stocked with crabs, sea urchins, picoroco, and mussels. We went back to eat at the hut where we ate yesterday.

At Hernan's (the airport supervisor) and at the shipping office we had seen some port-scene paintings that we liked very much. We were told that the artist's studio was in Angelmo, so we decided to visit there in hopes that we might see a few more of his pictures. Manuel Maldonado (Manoly they call him commonly) had a small name plate on the ceiling-high white wooden gate. We walked thru a long dark passageway with one wall artistically adorned with fish net, oars, other implements and parts of boats and ships. This hall led to a yard with plants, a fishpond, and steps to a new-looking, well-varnished house.

Nothing in this indicated a public studio to me, and I was beginning to feel very embarrassed about intruding on the privacy of the painter's home, when a woman opened the door. She asked us whether we minded waiting in the front room. A couple of paintings hung on the wall, but otherwise the room was well-furnished with expensive furniture. A middle-aged man with a pleasant face, short black hair and a moustache introduced himself as Manoly. Although we were dressed in our dirty traveling rags, he treated us as friends and important guests. His manners and social graces were highly developed. Climbing the stairs to his workshop was like entering the quarters of a ship's captain on board. We soon saw that he was a collector of warship plaques and other sea-faring remnants. His interest had been stimulated by years of living at the port.

Only one small corner of his studio was occupied with shelves of paints and brushes and his easel. He explained that he always painted outdoors when possible and only finished when necessary indoors. A gray painting of people gathering wood in the typical cleared forest of burned tree trunks (that we've seen so often these past few days) stood on the work stand. Another corner was occupied with his writing desk. The rest of the room was his exhibition salon where he invited us to sit. He put soft music on the stereo, and all the lights were low except the ones which illuminated the paintings on display. He showed us several types of scenes, all typical of this area. There was a still life of sea urchins, lemons, parsley, and butcher knife; Angelmo port scenes of boats, vendors, booths, and carts, seaside houses, lonely clam diggers, plowed hills near Puerto Varas, even a surrealistic painting called The Fisherman. Manoly explained that the small fisherman inside the giant one stood for the feeling of bigness that a man has when he is accomplishing and doing what he enjoys. He talked about his constantly changing technique, his struggle to capture the moist atmosphere of these scenes, his striving for perfection in each technique, the studying of details to form a general atmosphere, and of his successes as well. He claimed to be the best in Chile. There was no lack of ego in his statements, however graceful; but all he said was very interesting.

Then his interest turned to our careers and education. When anyone entered the room, he told them these things about us and explained the on-going conversation so they could continue with us. With the traveling talk we discovered that he knew Jan West and Manuela who had sent Jan to his house. Jan had spent quite a long time in Puerto Montt waiting for a boat and finally left for Bariloche to go from there to Punta Arenas. He had spent many hours with this family.

A surgeon and his son joined us, and we were all invited for tea. Doctor talks about Chile's medical care system, an effort at copying England's. There are six thousand doctors for 10,000,000 population, even less nurses. Most want to be in Santiago although pay increases with distance from the capital. High infant mortality rate mostly from malnutrition and attributed to frequency of unwanted children. Women usually don't use pill, etc. correctly so control is minimum. Hospital boat is costly to run because of seventeen crewmen and ineffective since the time span between visits makes care of urgent medical needs a matter of luck. Mostly works in distributing powdered milk, weighing babies, vaccination, this sort of routine thing. Dr. says it would be better to have three small launches with outboards that would be less expensive to maintain and quicker to deal with emergencies. We were shown a hut in the yard and invited to an asado on Saturday. Then the doc drove us to town.

We saw Isidro, drove around, chatted a while with him, sat in the plaza, then crammed in a bus again to go home. We were looking forward to rest and quiet, but upon arriving we discovered that Isidro and Alejandro had loaned the house to all the neighborhood teenagers so that they could have a party. The record player was already blaring, and the usual hassle over which records and what kind of music to play had already begun and continued all thru the night. The younger group liked the more modified popular rock while the older ones liked the very heavy, acid-rock and soul. At one point one little girl was fanning the record playing some Woodstock acid music, as though to cool it off. I couldn't last too long at this party since the stage of subtle romances of one dance, or a look, etc. has long passed me by. But even after I came to my room to write, then sleep, the younger girls still came in and out and made a general nuisance all around the house since they weren't in on the romance either. This party drug on until about 3:00 AM.

FEB. 2, 1973—D.C.

Again washing clothes, writing, etc. occupied most of the day. I had to hang out the door of a bus to get to the shipping office where there was little added information. "Come back Monday or Tuesday."

I visited another market, again predominantly of fish, but discovered it had small kitchens for eating fried fish, etc. I went to buy menstrual supplies which are in great shortage, like so many other things. I managed to get at least some cotton for 75 escudos. In the plaza people were gathered around a young, preaching, "Jesus freak." The generally black Cubans we've been seeing around town for several days now, all sat on a bench observing this plaza spectacle of vacationing hippie types and many others all idle at a time when the country is practically desperate. We would like to talk to the Cubans, but l haven't quite gotten up the nerve.

I waited a couple of hours for a bus which was so full it wouldn't stop when it finally passed. Many others waited also. Once an old man with no lower legs passed by on pieces of car tire. He was carrying heavy, full, burlap bags, and leading a little dog on a string. I finally decided to walk home which turned out not to be a great distance but all uphill. Others from the neighborhood were walking also. Terry came in late from his excursion all excited and describing in detail what he'd seen during the day down to the drunks. Meanwhile neighbor children peeked in the windows, knocked, hollered at us, made all sorts of noise in general. We are getting pretty fed up.

ON AN ISLAND SOMEWHERE SOUTH OF PUERTO MONTT - FEB. 2, 1973

I am constantly amazed at how beautiful life is and can be. It's there. All one must do is take it by the hand. Our good fortune seems to be growing instead of diminishing because of these wonderful Chilean people. Two days ago, we asked for information concerning a bus we had to take to get home. The old man who gave us help was very cordial and helpful. Yesterday I saw him on the street, and he invited us to take us on a boat tour of the islands. He said he was the boat captain. He would pay for the pass or give it to us free, and we would only have to pay for food. Danelle did not want to go; so here I am by myself, on a brisk ride on an old oil-burning boat slicing through turquoise color water framed by green islands. Old houses, new houses, all of wood, standing among the sea air, are all parts of this colorful day. The sun is bright, the breeze is fresh, and the ocean is a deep bluish green that looks as if it has never been touched by pollution. On the boat we were entertained by music squeezed from a shiny black and chrome accordion. Large dolphins called "Tunina" swim with great strength and agility, racing the prow of the ship as if challenging each other to see which one could come the closest to the boat. What fun it was to watch these wonders of the sea!

Upon anchoring in a bay, we were ushered into a rustic room with tables covered with oil cloth. Plates of food containing sausages, pork,

potato pancakes, bread and soup were placed before us and then here come ladies with buckets full of steaming shellfish. It was like a dream prying open those delicacies, putting a little peppery sauce in the natural curve of the shell, and downing the succulent mussel. When that first bucket was empty, they brought another. I had a beautiful 18-year-old girl waiting on my part of the table. She didn't charge me for my meal. I took a liking to her, and I think she to me. She had a fresh, glowing, lovely face and seemed very much alive. Their house was on the side of a hill overlooking a curving harbor and island.

I followed a trail through the meadow and crossed a small stream of clear water flowing in a trough to an ancient water wheel. The mill house was built of wood, now sagging, time weathered, and worn nestled in a flowery meadow above the rocky beach. The girl who waited on me, Angelica, picked some green apples and gave them to me. We talked a while. I told her this was the kind of place I'd like to spend a Summer exploring and enjoying.

The trip back to Puerto Montt was warm and sunny with more dolphins playing in front of the bow. The impressive views of the mountain range and snowcapped volcanos glimmered and changed to an orange hue as the sun dipped lower and lower.

The trip was about nine hours and every bit worth the time. We arrived back to the market where the strings of dried mariscos (shellfish) are always hanging in the little fish stalls. Fresh vegetables and dried fish color the scene. Horse-drawn wagons carry goods to the small row boats where the cargo is unloaded while the horse is knee deep and wagon up to its axel in the water. The sailors all wear warm sweaters and a brimmed hat, with pants tucked into rubber boots. They fit the classic picture of fishermen from Chilean ports.

Also hanging in these stalls are woolen blankets, rugs, and sweaters, all woven or knitted by hand in mostly natural-colored wool. This is a very colorful port.

FEB. 3, 1973—**D.C.**

Even the Central Plaza was almost deserted this Saturday afternoon when we went to the post office. Only one man sold postage at a dark corner window. We were surprised that a stamp for a letter to the U.S. was less than in Santiago, when, logically, you would think they would be the same or more.

There was the usual amount of afternoon activity at the Angelmo market. A strong breeze whipped up dirt and sand. Gulls precisely salvaged floating bits of garbage. Their bodies formed a strange arch and only their feet and beaks touched the water, never a wet feather. Small row boats full of sheep were unloaded onto 2-wheeled, horse-drawn carts which backed into the water. The shoes on these skinny, resigned horses had a metal piece on the front edges of the hooves to protect them from the stones on the incline leading out of the water. Across the street small wooden souvenirs were being sold to tourists.

Although it was 15 minutes after the hour that Manoly had told us to come for the asado, we were obviously arrived too early. His mother-in-law, a nephew, and his oldest sister (they are nine siblings), an attractive single woman with gray-streaked black hair, bright brown eyes, and slightly wrinkled face, were sitting in the sun in the back yard. There was no apparent preparation being done for the asado (steak). We were there quite a while before even the first beer was served.

Somewhat more bohemian-looking than Manoly, the painter Flavio arrived dressed in clean but worn, patched Wranglers and high-topped black shoes which appeared to be special for some abnormality in his foot. His long hair, beard, wrinkles at the bottom corners of his bloodshot blue eyes, presented the image of the hard-suffering, sensitive, poverty-stricken painter who after 10 years of intense work has had little success. He told us that he had no education in painting but was self-taught. He was very quiet and would say nothing about his painting except the most basic answers to our questions. He didn't seem to want to talk, so we didn't question him very much.

The doctor came with his two children: Aurora in the 4th grade and a younger little boy. They brought a guitar on which we enjoyed playing the remaining remnants of mutilated folksongs from our guitar-owning days. The doctor played an apparently well-known, Chilean song called Río Río. "Me mande a hacer una manta, de negro, verde y rojo." The colors were remembrances of aspects of the sweetheart "Río, Río, traiga la amor mío, estoy cansado de esperar."

Manoly told us more about himself. Since childhood he had wanted to be a painter and drew and painted often. But since painters were bohemian and scarcely earned enough if any money in those days, his father was against it. So Manoly practiced, took correspondence courses, and then paid his own way to school. The rest of his brothers are professionals although one of them has also recently begun to paint. Later while drinking, he told us a story of a trip he had made in a ship during which he and several other painters got very drunk with the naval officers. The captain asked the painters to all paint portions of a wall with whatever they most felt like painting. The result was such an indecent mess that the captain then asked Manoly to do what he could about fixing it up. First Manoly asked for music to be played, and a small band came. Then he had to have his jockey cap on and began to paint. From that point, however, he remembers nothing until the next morning he woke up; and seeing all the paint on his and Flavio's fingers, he was reminded of the evening before. Washed and trembling he went to see what he had done and found a painting of an enormous, charred, tree trunk with several wood hunters chopping away at it with live expression of movement. He says it is the best thing he has ever painted. When the ship was old and torn apart, this wall was taken and put in a museum. We laughed very much at this story; Manoly was very humorous in his telling it.

The lamb meat was roasted on a long flat metal pole with a circle for holding and turning at one end and a point at the other, supported at each end by metal forks sticking in the ground.

The pole was constantly being turned by the "asador," a humble man named Luis who works for Manoly. A wide row of hot coals lay on the ground parallel to the cooking rod. As the meat was close to being done after about 45 minutes, the coals were moved closer and closer until finally under the meat; and then the forks were hammered down closer to the ground. At this point, the first white wine and cheese were served.

While the meat was roasting, a basting sauce of ground garlic, chili pepper, oil, butter, pepper, onions, and white wine was applied to it with a bunch of oregano branches. Boiled potatoes and tomatoes a la chilena (Chilean style) were served with the lamb. Our appetite was so wetted, by not only the beer and wine but also by several days of eating only bread and cheese, that we devoured it all with excess appreciation and weren't deterred by the surgeon's comments on how so much of this type of fat caused many Chileans to eventually have to have gall bladder operations, the most common type of operation in Chile. There was singing and playing guitar, joking, and talking, more white wine, then red wine, and as the final push into drunkenness, champagne.

The doctor offered us a ride home, and Manoly rushed us up for a short exhibition. We were all overly enthusiastic, and our state made us amazed at all we saw. The painting we had seen on the easel was even more impressive than before. On the exhibition stand was one of a river and trees in fall colors. It seemed alive. Then we saw the inside of a burning woods where land was being cleared. Manoly had given this one to his daughter; she has the privilege of keeping the paintings she wants. As though gaining more confidence in our taste for the unusual, he set up a most lonely and eerie painting of a shredded scarecrow on a cross, with a name something like "Ingratitude" (painted in 1958). The crop had been harvested, the black winter sky stormed in the background, and the scarecrow, whose usefulness had passed, was left to waste in the rain. While Manoly's daughter, Terry, and I both commented that Van Gogh was our favorite painter, Manoly named one of which we had never heard. (Now I remember Manoly telling us how he felt sorry about having sold a painting very soon after he had painted it because he wanted to keep it and learn from its mistakes.) Before leaving, the daughter showed us the wooden sculpture of the head of a fisherman smoking a pipe; she had carved this very well and made a lamp base of it.

With very affectionate farewells we were told to come by anytime. The doctor invited us to his place sometime. He dropped off Manoly's sister at a huge, dark, 2-story wooden house with a "relojería" [clock store] sign over the door and waited until she was inside before leaving, saying that there were many drunks on the street in this area.

FEB. 4, 1973—**D.C.**

Maggie walked down to the plaza with us. She is a child developmentalist, going to teach kindergarten soon with specializations in testing and certain areas of psychology. After some months of working, she will study for her doctorate at the Sorbonne in Paris. Only 22 now, she spent eighteen years of her life learning classical ballet. She had a scholarship to go to Russia when a guy, who was in love with her ballerina boyfriend and jealous of her, hit their car with his, causing it to roll. She was crushed under it and almost killed. Her face was lacerated, all ribs broken, and legs immobilized for a long time. She had to learn to walk again and from that time on has dedicated her time to studying and especially has avoided romance, fearing the violent passions sometimes a part of it.

The plaza was full of people of diverse types seated on benches, walking round and round, running in mobs down the street to see a fight, etc. We saw John and Mary walk by with their packs, and they stopped to talk a while. Terry and John went off to look for a room while Mary, Maggie, and I sat in the park eating "avas" [large lima-like beans] and talking about our trips. Mary and John have been traveling around the lake district ever since we saw them last, camping, and buying food from farms. They gave us their address in California.

This week is Puerto Montt week, and various activities are supposedly going to take place. We saw a big boat come in today and are hoping it is the one we're waiting for.

The word for belly dancer is "vientrista." Among the interesting Chilean verbal idiosyncrasies are the words "lolo" and "lola" for teen-age males and females (most often used for the stylish ones) and other words based around it. "Pololear" means to court or romance. "Polola" is a female sweetheart. "Loladromo" is a main street where people gather, walking up and down. A "viejo loladromo" is one where older people shop and walk. Bell-bottom pants are the main fashion for these young people. Most of the "lolas" have the high heeled, thick-platformed, Scandinavian-type shoes and closefitting, knit, sometimes backless, braless style blouses and mostly long natural-looking hair. The difference between these stylish people and the those in Argentina is that here the clothes are much cheaper looking, certainly more worn out and often patched. It's strange how many people ask me if I "pololea".

PUERTO MONTT - FEB. 5, 1973

We just found out this morning that we will have to wait until Thursday to learn if we will get on the boat south. That puts us in a pickle because tomorrow we arranged for a ride in a car to Bariloche. What we will probably do is take the ride to the border and hitch back, check the boat situation, and figure out what to do then.

Two days ago, we went to an "asado" at Manoly's, the painter. It was a tasty BBQ meal of lamb, boiled potatoes, Chilean salad of tomatoes, onions, oil and vinegar. The freshly killed lamb was cut into large sections and skewered on a ten-foot-long steel bar. The helper, Don Lucho, started the coals and carefully turned the skewer by hand for an hour and a half, watching it very carefully so as not to let it cook too fast at first and burn on the outside before the inside is done. The smoke rolling up in the little shack with benches all around the sides added an atmosphere that Manoly took pleasure in exclaiming. He felt good, I felt good, and everybody felt good. Oh, how rich that food was! The meat sauce consisted of white wine, garlic, onions, chili pepper, butter, and oil, and was brushed on the meat with several applications using oregano twigs formed into a brush.

Stories were told by people sitting by the warmth of the glowing charcoals and smoke with the long skewer and freshly cooking meat. It was a mellow evening spiced with Chilean wine and watered-down beer. Manoly told about when he and a group of other painters were having a party on a boat in which they and the captain all got sauced out of their minds. The captain asked them all to paint pictures on the boat. As it turned out, the painting was so gross that the captain asked Manoly to paint over them. Manoly remembers painting most of the night and when he awoke from a short sleep, he found all his tubes of paint expended and to his surprise, the best painting he has ever done. He said they displayed that painting in a museum where it is still hanging today.

After all were getting ready to leave, Manoly took us back up to his studio where he brought out paintings that he had not shown us previously, all typical of Chile. One he did six years ago was a smoky scene of forests near here. The forest was being burned. The entire scene was a beautiful night cap to a warm afternoon and evening.

FEB.5, 1973—**D.C.**

It was a cold, cloudy morning, and torture to drag ourselves out early to the shipping office. The boat we saw yesterday was the one going to Punta Arenas, but the tickets won't be sold until Thursday morning; we have no way of knowing until then whether we can get a place or not, and there are few. The office was full of people asking about it! We saw John the Brazilian in the plaza again, this time with his friend who was shot. They also want to get on the boat.

At the market near town, we sat at tables crowded with people and ate fried fish again. There was soup also, mostly of meat and various starch foods and oil. Near here along the edge of the street, farm women sold their small quantities of apples, onions, carrots, potatoes, seafoods, etc., cheaper than at the stands. Small green apples are starting to appear everywhere now. I am getting very restless and hoping to visit the lakes within the next few days.

Maggie came over with Terry, and our conversation about psychic powers included a variety of them. It began when Maggie told us about the peritonitis operation she had without anesthesia not long after her accident. Besides that, her lacerated face was repaired also without anesthesia. She will have another operation very soon for a rib which is gradually pushing into her lung. Without these two operations she would have died. Anesthesia would kill her also because of antibodies she has from having had blood of the wrong type put in her after the accident. (I'll certainly never complain again about the local Novocain shots and subsequent operation I had for my hernia and appendix.)

She believes that she was able to go thru with this first operation she had without anesthesia because, when she was 14, she began to have sessions to learn to channel her psychic powers with a certain very psychic, learned "doctor" who has been in prison now for several years (Carlos Mariani) because of his exercising of his powers in the once hyper-conservative Chilean society. He taught Maggie self-hypnosis. It happened that from early childhood she had startled parents, acquaintances, teachers, everyone with her prediction of future events thru dreams and other e.s.p. manifestations. Her mother was psychic also; and when she saw a psychiatrist because she thought she was insane, she was told to watch out for these powers in her children.

Maggie read mine and Terry's palm. The reading was incredibly detailed and fascinating as she pushed together, pinched stretched and bent distinct parts of the palm and wrist to see even the smallest lines. The right palm is your born potential while left shows actual development of possibilities. My destiny line on left hand shows that I can have some control over the destiny that is shown in my right-hand lines. It is developing, but still has room to go much further. Hand, finger shapes and forms, even nails, show something.

Maggie over and over emphasized my being closed to other people, hiding my feelings and other characteristics, the general lack of openness and all its suffering that, although I was able to divert it for some time with the attitude of learning, related (or unrelated) distracting questions and comments. Maggie is sensitive; none of this escaped her. Instead of leaving the uncomfortable situation I was in, she hammered on it, advising me to learn to give, telling me (as many other people have) that my eyes reveal very clearly my thoughts and feelings. She said that yesterday and today both she had felt vibrations of worry coming from me.

Well, I felt that all the things she told me could be said on any palm and sound perfectly feasible; but, when she read Terry's palm, it was hugely different-looking and very differently interpreted and described him as perfectly as mine did me. She spoke of other kinds of psychic abilities. She divined Terry's hunger by his handprint pressed on a printed page.

The silver ring she gave me yesterday is a good luck charm which modifies bad vibrations. She removed her own vibrations from the ring by wearing a gold one with it before giving it to me. We spoke briefly of astrology; though Maggie says she knows little, I suspect it is much more than the average. She is a Virgo also, Sept. 1st. She said among other things that Leo heavily influences Virgo during times of full moon, that always Virgo is heavily influenced by Aquarius; and that Aquarius, while not always accepting criticism from others, will accept it from a Virgo who is highly critical.

Maggie says that she would never exercise her psychic powers for money, which would be like selling her soul. She sees opportunities to help people often but cannot take this responsibility so only does so when she wants. For a living she can write if necessary. Since childhood, her poetry and children's stories have been published with the pseudonym of a male, and the money is given to poor children's homes. Her father is a mathematical genius, her mother a psychiatrist, and Maggie has scholarships to study; so, there is really no problem with making a living.

Later the little girls across the street brought us hot coffee in a pitcher. Alejandro came in terribly upset and fed up with his work and the state of the country. It is very difficult, if not impossible, to get materials to do the construction, so their work is practically wasted. They are very frustrated with the lack of accomplishment. (We played the guitar outdoors today.)

FEB. 6, 1973—**D.C.**

We had intended to go Lake Llanquihue today but woke up to thunder and pouring rain and chill in the house which caused me to savor even more the comparative warmth of my sleeping bag. The neighbor girls came again with coffee and this time with bread and jam and sat in the floor with us, eating apples and speaking a sort of Spanish pig Latin which consists of adding pe, pi, pa, po or pu after each syllable depending on which letter the word ends in. Some of the girls were over-doing this game, but we didn't complain since they kept the room warm. When lunch time came their mother invited us over, and we feasted again. We were all very frightened when the youngest girl pounded on the door and was screaming in a most horrified manner; she was afraid a big dog was going to eat her pup.

After an afternoon rest we accompanied Maggie to the bus station to take the 7:00 bus to Santiago; but, as it sometimes or often goes in Latin America, the bus would be delayed until 11:00. It finally did leave at almost 1 a.m. I asked Maggie about the magic in beads. She said they were amulets but different from the silver in that the colors brought the type of fortune that they signified, and that combinations and use of designs intensified, modified, or changed color powers. Blue is for peace, white is even calmer tranquility, almost empty, red is passion, black is mysterious, orange is hypocrisy, yellow is "desprecio" (scorn). In the bracelet that I made and wear, a mixture of blue and yellow show the modification of scorn by peace and tranquility, a reflection of something in my character, she says. Crosses seemed to be an important magic design from what details I can remember. The cross in yellow nullifies the scorn. A black cross is especially strong (in what way I don't remember exactly, but evil I think).

We went walking thru the plaza on our way to see John and Mary. There was a firemen's parade with fire trucks of various sorts, one incredibly old but well-kept. Then there were the brigades of firemen in black boots, white pants, heavy black jackets with towels for tucked-in neck scarves, and black helmets crowned with a tall wedge of chrome. On the second-floor balcony above the post office stood the chiefs in fine uniforms and metals. We didn't stay around to hear the speeches. We stopped at the crowded Cafe Central for a snack. The waitress almost scolded me for having torn one ridiculously small paper napkin in half to use for writing Maggie's and Doctor Mario's address on. Here there is milk, sweets, soft drinks, ice cream; the other cafe only has weak tea.

At John and Mary's room in a big house which offers "alojamiento" [lodging], we sat on the bed travel-talking of markets and things to buy, things to see, roads and routes traveled, money exchange, and possibilities for Mary to work belly dancing. She has already danced in several places and earned quite a bit of money, especially in Quito. She showed us photos in which she was dancing. Her hair was combed out long, abundant, and curly. Most incredible was her face covered with gross stage makeup and false eyelashes, almost clownish. No one would recognize her once she cleaned her face down to its dark, suntanned naturalness, pulled her hair back leaving only a few frizzy curls on her forehead, and wore her loose, plaid, men's shirt. It's sometimes very convenient not to be recognized she said.

While we did all this talking in English and looking at maps, Maggie talked to her cousin Liz and wrote a great deal in the notebooks she carries. She writes whatever she thinks. One sheet she tore out and gave to me. [It is a poem and farewell note in Spanish, with my English translation.]

Desde muy lejo vienes con tus suenos [From very far you come with your dreams]

Andando siempre para hacerlos realidad [Walking always to make them a reality]

Nadie sabra jamas que fuerza te alienta [No one will ever know what force feeds you]

Ilusiones que aumentan cada día al despertar [Illusions that grow every day upon awakening]

Es tu senda muy larga [It is your very long path]

Lento tu caminar; en tu mochila [Slow your walking; in your backpack]

Ansias y sueños que son de viajera [Hopes and dreams that are of the traveler]

Que hoy viene y manana se va. [That today comes and tomorrow goes.]

Siempre me sucede, quiero decir muchas cosas, y solo logro balbucear, pero son palabras que encierran un cariño sincero. Poco tengo que ofrecerte solo mi Amistad. Con cariño en un rinconcito de Puerto Montt 6-II-73

[It always happens to me; I want to say many things and only succeed in babbling but words that enclose a sincere affection. I have little to offer you except my friendship. With affection in a little corner of Puerto Montt. Feb. 6, 1973]

She talked a little of other things she has written, an article or book called *From Adolescent to Adult*, some children's stories, one of which she just wrote using my name and taking the child-like quality of my face to form the ideas.

We joked briefly with John and Mary about how we were going to form the line to buy tickets for the boat on Thursday. We want to be there very early, perhaps the evening before. John is a wheeler-dealer who would do anything no matter how foolish or out of place. I'm very anxious myself about the whole hassle that will probably be involved.

PUERTO MONTT - FEB. 7, 1973

We met a young lady named Margarita (Maggie) who has turned out to be perplexing. She is 22 and seems to have lived beyond her years. She is gifted with extrasensory perception and has a profound knowledge of the occult, palm reading, and signs. She is to have an operation to correct a part of her rib cage that is somehow damaging her lung. The doctor has given her four months to live if she does not have the operation. If she has it, she will not be able to have any anesthesia whatsoever. That is difficult to imagine. She told about being in a bad car wreck a little over a year ago in which the car rolled on top of her. The car rolled three times; and after the second role, everyone was thrown out. Maggie jumped back into the car again to turn the engine off, was thrown out again, and watched in frozen fear as the car came down on top of her, smashing all her ribs and her pelvis and tearing her face. She had been planning to go to Russia to dance on a ballet scholarship within two months. She has not danced since the accident.

A jealous gay person caused the wreck. He was in love with the guy Maggie was with, so he forced them off the road. He is still in prison, and the authorities have not looked at his case yet. When they lifted the car off her, she blacked out from pain. Before that she was wide awake and did not feel any pain.

In the hospital they pulled her flattened ribs into place and set her broken pelvis and put a body cast on her. They put a plastic bandage on her face, and she slept for 15 days as her body healed. Today, she does not have a mark on her face. Unfortunately, she needed a transfusion. She has a rare blood type, very rare (universal donor negative); they had to give her another type of blood. This caused her system to build antibodies to heal. She says she has something in her system that will not allow her to have any type of anesthesia. Soon afterwards she developed peritonitis, an inflammation of the stomach lining, and had to be operated on without anesthesia. She watched them cut her open, haul out her insides (stomach and intestines), and place them on the table beside her. She blacked out then. She said she wanted to watch. Her father and mother were watching also, but her mother fainted when the doctor made the incision. [Maggie's entire story sounds fishy.]

The doctor operating on her was a friend of hers who was also in the car during the wreck. Now that she needs this other operation, he is looking for another doctor to help him, one who can successfully hypnotize her. He is still in love with Maggie; but, since the wreck, her love for him has died. They had been thinking about or planning a marriage.

Since then, she had come to Puerto Montt to rest up for the operation, but she was not having an enjoyable time. She said she would like to die. Since meeting Danelle and me, she has been a different person. She says we have changed her whole outlook. I really felt strange after she told me that.

The guy who has helped her with her psychic powers is a man of the occult, and he himself has these powers. Maggie's mother has ESP also and thought, at first, that she was going crazy; but a psychiatrist told her otherwise and that she had to try to help her daughter because these powers are often inherited. Her mother introduced her to this Dr. Mariani who opened her mind.

While taking an exam, Maggie could read the questions and answers on exam papers lying on the teachers' desk, etc. Dr. Mariani could help her put her mind at ease so as not to feel anything during an operation, but now he is in prison charged with the death of his girlfriend. He had hypnotized her one evening and then fell asleep. The gas was on and filled the room. An explosion killed the girl, but the doctor lived. I am sure there were people who would have liked to see him behind bars, and this was their chance. Maggie said he would go to parties and use his powers to let people walk on water and in the air amongst other mind feats. She knew she was going to have a wreck during her 21st year and had seen it all in a dream, but she did not think it would happen seven days before her birthday.

One more thing, she said her ex-boyfriend, Mario, the guy who operated on her and is going to operate again on her, is a typical Latin lover. He is still hanging on after her fire went out. He said he would take Danelle and me anywhere if that is what made her happy. He was perplexed at how we could make her happy. Anyway, if we do not get on the boat to the Straits of Magellan, he is going to take us to Bariloche and even south if that is where the doctor is that she is looking for. This other doctor is supposed to be a very young Brazilian. I am completely bemused by the details of this story. It is like a far-fetched soap opera.

Danelle, John, Mary, and I are going to the shipping office about 6:00 PM to begin our all-night vigil on the sidewalk in from of the shipping office. We want to be the first in line to buy our tickets to the Straits of Magellan because we have been told they do not have many available tickets. We MUST get on that boat.

FEB. 7, 1973—D.C.

Tried to sleep enough this morning to get ready for the vigil tonight. The weather doesn't look very promising since it is quite overcast. Must remember to contact Dr. Mario L. at Hotel Vicente Pérez Rosales about the ride to Bariloche. We weren't in town very long before it started to rain but slowly made our way to the market, then to the school/hostel, and then to the shipping office where we prepared for a long wait in front of the door.

Mary came with a bag of food and little stove for tea. Once again I found myself confronted with my ego in this group situation. I realized that my self-observation and efforts at awareness had been neglected during these past few days of magic, art, and intelligence. A Dutch guy, Robert S., joined us before long. The line was growing and could no longer be very inconspicuous, so the night guard came out. We politely explained that we were in line to buy tickets for the boat.

John who likes to take advantage of whatever situation arises, hinted as to whether we might sleep just inside the door. The guard, who was worried about the women sleeping out in the cold and rain, decided to (when the bosses were home asleep) sneak us into a back office where we could sleep, make tea, and use the bathroom. Once inside the building we told stories, e.g., Robert and girlfriend were robbed by armed men at the Chan Chan ruins in Trujillo, Perú, and his nose broken. We shared cheese, bread, and wine with the guard. At first I did not want to go inside and lose our place in line when we left the building in the next morning, but the guard said there were never any lines in the morning. When I saw rain pouring very hard most of the night, I was more grateful.

At 6 AM, twelve hours after he had arrived, the guard let us out; and just like he had told us the night before, there was no one waiting in line yet. Brazilian John and friend Hugo had just arrived. An hour or so later the first Chileans began to arrive. Being first in line, we got tickets as quite a few people behind us did also. At any rate we felt very lucky to have them after so much worry and dread of having to take an alternate route and miss seeing the canals.

We went by to see Manoly and Norca in case we didn't get another chance. Manoly was preoccupied and restless; he had probably just started to work. After our tea he showed us the four paintings he had done yesterday. Obviously three were hurriedly done (all were from memory) and were very common (for him) port scenes of which he does so many. The other, much larger, and more pastel, was a lonely, tranquil scene of a bay shore and large figure of a female shellfish digger and little boy child. She is a lonely, isolated figure who must support herself, children, and drunken husband by searching the beach for their daily food.

I mailed a letter to Steve E. today, long overdue. We ran into John and Mary again; and while we were with them, a young Chilean man named Juan began to talk to us and tell us he was married to a woman from Dallas. He then invited us home for lunch; so very soon we met Helen, a thin, blonde woman with very light eyes and a very slender, delicate look about her face. She had lived in Algeria, Switzerland, England, and France; her speech, form of being, and manner certainly wasn't of a typical Dallas woman. Juan teaches sociology at the University in Puerto Montt; Helen teaches English and is developing her skill in photography. The bookshelves with books like Sylvia Plath poetry drew us all to them. Juan put on some music, Bob Dylan, James Taylor, others. We shared a very meager meal. "Money is very scarce this month," Helen said.

Outside rain kept pouring, and the atmosphere inside gave me a familiar dread, a fear of trapping oneself in obligation and the boredom of day-to-day settled life. We chatted about Helen's life in Paris, about Mary's belly dancing experiences, like when a dancer shakes up close to a man, correct custom is for him to tuck money in her belt or bra. We were all invited to stay; John and Mary accepted the invitation.

We walked to Población Lago Chapo passing down embankments, thru the back alleys of an orderly slum with chickens in the yards, thru an old neighborhood of 2-story wooden houses, some containing night clubs with odd inappropriate names like Club Tropical, others with fruit crowded against the windowpanes indicating a small neighborhood grocery, then finally up a steep hill with damp, mossy stone, wooden steps, and trails bordered with weeds and bushes.

There we met Raul, an American from New York/San Francisco who grew up in London. He had been in Chile this trip for only 4 days, had come by plane on a ticket that also includes Tel Aviv, Paris, London, and New York; and he looked it. We assumed his appearance to be the latest in American male fashion. His hair was very short like Julius Caesar in the way it was combed toward the face. A huge ring with an abstract design formed by sheets of gold, which looked like scrap metal, surrounding a large diamond attracted the eye to his clean white hands and well-manicured nails. Another gold ring, big diver's watch, gold bracelet and gold chain at neck adorned his spotless, tight, denim suit and tight, knit shirt beneath. His pants had no belt loops, and his leather belt hung off his hips. His purse was like a large pouch with long shoulder chain put through the belt loop. His shoes were masculine but with platforms and very high heels. He only briefly mentioned that he works in graphics. When he left us, he walked fast like he was on his way to work in New York. It took Terry and I all day to get over the surprise of meeting this person in Southern Chile.

We had to wait in line to buy bread today. The owner of the bakery says he can't get enough people to work for him to meet the demand. We couldn't get toilet paper at the place Terry bought it before.

Terry gave me a lesson on perspective drawing. Vanishing points are on the horizon. All lines which are not in vision always are parallel, vanishing to the same point. Then he talked about basic interest and composition. Horizons are best above and below center. Central object is often best off center. The shape of the negative space is very important to the interest. Diagonals are sometimes uninteresting and lead the vision off the picture unless it is blocked by something at the edge. Some good compositions are a sort of L, a curve C, an X with action going in. Movement on the canvas should be toward the center of interest, at least not leading off the page. This applies to roads, streets, etc. Something can be placed to block the movement. Very dark against light makes interesting contrasts.

PUERTO MONTT - FEB. 8. 1973

Just before six last night, Danelle and I went to the fish market on the way to the shipping office to have a meal of fried fish, soup, potatoes, lettuce, and coffee for 15 cents, before we started our all-night vigil. It was raining as we walked to the market and the shipping office, but we did not mind. I knew that I would have a dry place to sleep in after our vigil. Besides, just the thought of being first in line and getting a boat ticket south gave me all the strength I needed. We bought a couple of loaves of bread for 3 cents and ¾ kilo of cheese for 40 cents and were set. John and Mary came about a ½ hour later after the rain had slacked off a little. They had their little camp stove, food, and tea.

About an hour and a half later a Dutch traveler named Robert S. joined our group. Our conversation switched from surfing on the hot-dog beaches of California to internal uterine devices. After a while, the caretaker or night watchman came outside and offered us the luxury of sleeping on the floor in one of the offices. We were leery at first because we felt that when we got up in the morning, there would be line of people outside the door and a big hassle with us trying to take our earned first-in-line position. The caretaker said, "Don't worry, nobody comes before 7:00 AM." He was right, to our amazement, when we got up at 6:00 AM, no one was waiting outside. But when we finally got our stuff together and were walking out the door, our two young Brazilian friends were just arriving. Boy, they were sure surprised to see us coming out of that building!

One of the Brazilians named Hugo, an 18-year-old, was shot in the upper leg when in Santiago. He was trying to get into a room that was lent to him and his friend; but, unfortunately, it was the wrong place. As he was trying to climb up to the window, the old man inside fired on him without warning. Their impression of Chile was low.

We were thoroughly amazed at the old caretaker letting us stay in the building overnight, us being a bunch of "hippy freaks." A government office at that! This is pure Chilean hospitality in its purest form. We could never get that treatment in the USA. He took on a great responsibility to help us, which most people just would not bother. It rained most of the night, so I am pleased to have had the invitation to sleep indoors instead of being huddled on the sidewalk under a plastic sheet all night.

Before we went to sleep, Robert told us a harrowing tale about him and his girlfriend being robbed while strolling through the great ruins of Chan Chan in Trujillo, Peru. Three men jumped them as they passed through a huge gate. A knife was held at his wrist and a broken wine bottle was thrust at his face while they searched him, robbing everything of value he and his girlfriend had. He started to struggle with them but was slugged in the stomach and kicked in the face which broke his nose. The robbers ran and left him and his girl, two very nervous people.

After watching a warm sunup, I had a good feeling when the doors to the shipping office opened about 8:30 AM. I walked up to the ticket seller second in line behind Danelle. John and Mary were next, followed by Robert, the two Brazilians Jao and Hugo, another American, and a Norwegian. All hard-core travelers were first in line. The Chileans started coming about 8:00 AM when the door was opened. Strange! They were not as anxious about getting on the boat as we were.

We were happy travelers with tickets in hand after that was over. Our third-class boat ticket cost $1.75 US for a one-week cruise of 1,000 km. The value of changing money on the "mercado negro" (black market) helped us. It is amazing. We are going south on the boat; and, if it is not cloudy and rainy the entire trip, we will see the most wild and virgin scenery Chile has to offer. I am excited about not having to go down the Argentina side of the Andes by land to Tierra del Fuego. Best of all, Danelle and I are going to pass through the Straits of Magellan to Punta Arenas. I have always dreamt of that.

After we got our tickets, we went to visit Manoly again who said he had been painting diligently over the last four days. He took us up to his studio and showed us his latest, even the one that was not finished, which he usually never shows to anyone until it is finished. What warmhearted persons he, his wife Norca and his daughter Norcita are!

So full of praise and sincere warmth! They even invited us to spend our last afternoon in Puerto Montt at their house for another cookout, only this time with mariscos and fish.

It is raining now, as it seems always to do. We are sacked out on our sleeping bags, eating our customary cheese sandwich, and writing our reflections. My journal is coming along nicely. I am constantly adding to the notes whenever I think of something worth remembering or something worth reminding others of.

PUERTO MONTT - FEB. 9, 1973

The bread store has window boxes where once were displayed varied breads and cakes. Now the shelves and grey window boxes are bare except for flour dust that has collected. One of the walls is covered with mold, and the three neon light fixtures are nothing but bare metal boxes with shaky wires hanging loose. Only one long fluorescent bulb throws a soft light over part of the long counter next to the cash register. This is where the bread is lifted from the basket on the floor and placed on the counter in front of the line of patiently waiting customers. They wrap their fresh warm bread in their own paper which they had tucked under their arms or in their pockets. In other words, the baker is still doing business but barely. He says he cannot get enough help. I wonder what he pays them for their long hours by the hot ovens, starting work at 1:00 AM and working until 7:00 or 10:00 PM.

It is unbelievable what people will do to buy cigarettes. Standing in line for an hour is nothing to them, and they can only buy one pack at a time. Unfortunately, that is not all these people have to stand in line for. It is getting harder and harder to find items that once people took for granted, such as toothpaste, sanitary napkins, toilet paper, cooking oil, meat, butter, sugar, car parts and tires. It is as if the country were at war, sending these things to support the Army.

We went to Puerto Varas today on a modern bus for less than the price of a pear. It was a small rustic town built on the side of Lago Llanquihue. A tremendous view of Volcano Osorno can be seen from there, but it was clouded over except for the sparkling white peak. I had seen the volcano during my boat trip to the islands. It is perfectly shaped, tall and an impressive sight.

We talked to an American guy whom we met at the market. His outlandish style of dress shocked us. He wore the latest styles from America and a heavy odor of sandalwood incense or perfume. Overall, he looked overly stylish in his jean jacket with gaudy diamond and gold jewelry on his hands. If he traveled in Colombia and even here, he might lose his fingers to thieves. To top it all off, he had high-heeled, wooden-soled shoes like the girls wear here. Only the shoe tops appeared to be for men. What a strange sight! Even his short Julius-Caesar-style hair cut was over-the-top fashionable. He's flown from New York City to Santiago, and plans to travel next to Tel-Aviv, Paris, Rome, and San Francisco, CA. He said he wasn't having a very good time, and I can see why.

CASTRO, CHILE - FEB. 11. 1973

We boarded the ship! What a comforting feeling to explore this huge ship as if I were a little kid experiencing all the nooks and crannies of unknown frontiers: the narrow halls, my room with three sets of bunkbeds and two porthole windows, the green dining hall, and the filthy bathrooms at the bow of the ship. I am in the old second-class section. Under us is the fourth-class section which has 8 to a room instead of six as in my room. They have no porthole windows or ventilation. The place has an odor, and the air down there feels heavy.

People are sleeping all over the ship, on the floors, in the halls and in the lounges because they only worried about getting on the infrequent ship; that was all that mattered. There are no roads in southern Chile.

Many travelers somehow boarded without assigned bunks after the island port town of Castro. The Port Authority officers were scouting the entire boat for stowaways but never found any. All international travelers were very neatly entertained in the first mate's cabin until everything was cool. Some of the girls are sleeping in the officers' quarters; the guys are sleeping on the floors in our rooms. It is all working out beautifully. It's a comfortable feeling being with all these international "viajeros" (travelers) who originate from Norway, France, Holland, Brazil, USA, and Chile.

FEB. 10, 1973—**D.C.**

We are at last aboard the ship Navarino. To have passage on this boat is certainly not as difficult as we were led to believe. Even now at the last minute people without tickets are arriving and are being accommodated in the lowest portion of the ship more than 6 to a cabin (where we are in fact very comfortable) and must use their own bedding. A few even were able to get 1st class or 3rd (like ours). A Canadian woman, friend of Terry's since Peru (we ran into her yesterday in Puerto Montt) got on this way. A few others just jumped on without being seen.

This new port with its big warehouse which seem so obstructing and dead from outside is quite interesting inside. Tall gray cranes standing on their 4 legs remind one of spaceships. The operator's glass cabin revolves with the movement of the crane arm. From the big Greek ship near the Navarino, bundles of bags are tied and attached to the dangling hooks of the crane which transfers them, setting them down on a loading cart which is a platform at the door of odd, faded gray and brown box cars. An old black steam engine, chucking clouds of smoke and blowing its traditionally mournful whistle, will later fetch these cars and pull them across town between Costañera Street and the bay, then pass near the plaza on to the station and toward the north.

Watermelons are being loaded onto our ship. Broken ones are given to whoever asks for them. John managed to wrangle a good whole one that was badly cracked. People with bundles, suitcases, or back packs crowd in the line to go aboard and to check tickets. Besides the travelers we met in line at the office, there are also 2 French female hitchhikers, Odile, and Elaine, who have hitched down from Canada in 4 months, plus 4 French people with a car. An aura of quiet excitement surrounds the ship. There was a fine mist falling all day today, and now Puerto Montt is covered by fog. This gray, ephemeral background intensifies the black of the pebbly volcanic beach and the deep green of the trees and bushes on the islands across the harbor, where boats are drydocked to be painted or undercoated. In a lighter green clearing a few figures stand near a small fire. A smaller boat, the Rio Baker, leaves after dark sounding its foghorn; the Navarino answers it.

Earlier this afternoon we walked one last time through the Angelmo market before going to Manoly's house where we had been invited to a fish bake. There are many abalones on the stands today. We watched an aproned man putting sea urchin flesh in old wine bottles and corking them. Other people walk by eating the inner base of artichoke leaves. Bowls of sea urchin flesh sit ready to eat on display with abalone shells for spoons and lemon halves to spice. Crowded inside a small dark stand behind the display table of the bizarre picorocos was a group of middle-class, Chilean tourists enjoying the seafood and passing glasses of wine. We stocked up on apples and cheese because we have heard that the food on board isn't always too good. We found Manoly' s place strangely quiet and dark. Only his suegra (mother-in-law) was there. We thought that maybe they had forgotten, or we'd come too early but soon found out that a relative had died. Since people had to be notified, papers arranged, and the body transported, Manoly wouldn't be able to have the fish bake. We were invited to have tea with the suegra instead. Before too long Manoly came back to tell us good-bye before returning to his duties. He offered his house for when we returned. He said he might be exhibiting in Caracas in September. With the loud ticking of the cuckoo clock all our thoughts and conversation swung back and forth from life to death, death to life.

FEB. 11, 1973—**D.C.**

We haven't been able to locate the *Time* magazine which disappeared from my bed yesterday. It's odd that a magazine in English with no pictures of nude women would be taken. We imagine that it's to be used as toilet paper. One of our distinct memories of Chile is that practically every poster, magazine, newspaper, and even comic books have pictures of naked females. One comic book called *Viejo Verde* (Dirty Old Man) usually has a nude on the cover.

What I thought was our dining room is the officials.' Ours is like a marketplace-affair with the long tables and wooden benches at which we are sat down like prisoners in line to a breakfast of one bun and half a cup of coffee, a lunch of 2 half-courses and later a tea with bun. We are already talking about buying some bread when we put in at Castro. There is a third-class lounge at least which has a small bar and nice windows to look out. I still haven't investigated much of the boat; instead, I've spent much of the day writing and sleeping. As I write about these daily events and my surroundings, I am becoming aware that the undercurrent of life with its thoughts, searches, struggles, impressions, and interpersonal relationships is lacking in my expression. For me writing of these details and attitudes from another plane is very difficult. I even hesitate to do it because it is a sort of uncovering of myself which I believe will leave me open for later self-ridicule. Because my writing doesn't invite others to read it very thoroughly, I shouldn't have to worry about writing personal matters at least.

We left the Navarino when it put in at Castro. The dock was covered with stacks of seaweed bundles, potato sacks, and many people and their baggage. John (another one), an American traveling companion of Holland Robert, was there also and had bought a ticket from someone on dock who had decided not to go. Predictably, the military flight he was waiting for didn't come. Later a check was being made because some Chileans reported that there were 2 gringo rucksacks in their cabin that didn't belong. John was asked to show his ID so was caught with his ticket but wasn't thrown off. Others, who had come under the condition that they try to arrange matters in Castro, were hiding in the ship cabin. Passenger cabins and other rooms were locked, but many still managed to stow away. When the ship finally left Castro, it was crammed with people sleeping in every corner that did not block the passageways, families in the floor wrapped in their Chiloe blankets, people sleeping double in the small bunks, bodies on the tables. We now must wait twice as long for a meal.

SAILING SOUTH - FEB. 12, 1973

Just before we set sail from Puerto Montt, I sneaked into the first-class section and had a very hot, relaxing shower. I really needed that.

This morning, we had a section of open sea to cross. I never thought I'd get seasick, but I too ran to the railing. I didn't throw up, but I felt my stomach getting upset. I could not eat breakfast because of my nausea. A few of the Chileans in my room, who are sailors, gave me half of a lemon to suck on. That did it. Tonight, we are supposed to head for high sea, and it is said to be much rougher than this morning. Maybe I will take some of Danelle's pills.

The strangest thing, also on board is a wonderful young Canadian lady I had met on the bus ride from Huancayo to Cuzco. Her name is Helene K.; she is working on a master's degree in Santiago. She's very warm and affectionate, and I feel good being with her. We rolled around as much as we could in my non-private bunk.

I am sure I will say this again on the trip: these canals are immensely beautiful. It's a cloudless day, and the islands are covered with virgin forest growing on sharply rising hillsides and set in a transcending flow of blue coloring starting from the crispy brine and flowing upward to the endless mountain ranges stretching to the clouds and sky.

Our meals are definitely not first class, frankly, they are not 3rd-class fare either. Breakfast, served about 7:30 AM is bread and coffee, no sugar. At 12:00 dinner the first course is vegetable soup. You keep your spoon which is also used for the second course of beans. Tea or maté is served at 3:00 PM. Five PM is supper consisting of a thin starchy soup and spicy noodles and meat. Not bad, could be worse! The head cook of the 3rd class mess is a man with a rotund stomach. He and the stewards like keeping everything orderly as if it's a military mess. "Fill these seats first; keep in file." Extra bread and cheese, salt, aji, etc. must be furnished by the passenger.

I'm beginning to feel very adventurous riding on this boat and being this far south.

FEB. 12, 1973—D.C.

Since there was so much talk today about how seasick we might get while crossing the angry Gulf of Sorrows (Golfo de Penas) tonight, many of us avoided sleeping today so that we could get to bed early and sleep thru the worst part. Even so, this morning one of the little girls in our cabin woke us up with her vomiting. Few people ate breakfast. It was a good day to spend away from the cabin where 4 children and a man passed in and out all day doing everything from peeing in chamber pot, then accidently turning it over, to bringing in first-class meals for themselves while we drooled and tried not to think about it. Not that there is anything so bad about the food we get, it's just so little. A little sun outside encouraged us to brave the frigid wind a while as we lay on the top of the hold and watched the ship pass by the near coastline of low mountains, some with snow, which rise straight up out of the dark metallic-gray water. I had my turn at the *Time* magazine, same as the one we lost. There was an absurd-sounding article about Chile's desperate economic situation which could have been written by any half-educated, middle-class Chilean of the opposition. There is the usual frightening quantity of international violence, pre- and post-cease fire in Vietnam, Laos and Cambodia, fanatic North Ireland murders, conflict at the border of Zambia and Rhodesia, counterinsurgency against Moslems and Maoist revolutionaries in the Philippines, and, most frightening and sad for me, a now world-wide scope of terrorism between Palestinian guerillas and Israelis. Since guerillas can no longer work very effectively thru Arab country borders, they have decided to take the fight elsewhere; and Israelis respond in like manner.

Conversation has been rather difficult for me lately, self-conscious, stammering, lacking enough clarity for communication. It's only natural that this stage should reoccur in me at this point since I have been so critical and conscious of Terry's manner of expression during this trip. We are getting to know each other very well. It has been a fantastic, continuing lesson in individual tolerance for me. I have learned to admire Terry's outward appearance of not being bothered by my largely intolerant criticisms. He remains himself and doesn't try to change his character or manner to suit me. Thus, I learn that, although I can arrive at spontaneous-though-curt suggestions, not everyone will undertake following this feedback (fortunately). Terry goes on talking too much, sometimes interrupting, and somewhat aggressively questioning; barking aloud friendly greetings; hee-haws; and comments passing judgement on all sorts of things with a now-predictable phrasing. A distinct number of comments begin with "Strange how" or "Funny how." Superlatives are constant like "The most, the best (or some sort of maximum) I've ever seen." Any small detail will evoke a "First time I've ever seen that". The word fantastic is hard not to pick up after hearing Terry say it as often as he does in a day. An affectionate laugh and a "Look at that dog" comes with every dog that we pass within seeing distance. Every time Terry needs a bowel movement he announces it as a big event of the day, "Guess I'll go take a big hairy one" or "greasy one" or "I really have to go take a shit!" When he came back talking about his turds, I thought things had gone a little too far. Mary tells me that she and John talk a great deal about their shit. It seems that while traveling in South America, Americans find the nature of their shit assumes even conversational importance. Anyway, I am gradually coming to accept these and other idiosyncrasies of Terry's, but what really bothers me is that I tend to pick them up myself. Terry has certainly been very tolerant of me (or at least appears to be) and rarely slashes back at me to my face. At times like this when we are separated most of the day, I am glad to see him now and then. One technique I've learned for reducing irritation and resentment is that after every bad thought I have concerning any given behavior of his, I counteract it by finding something good in that same act. Still, I must be constantly alert so that my hateful feelings aren't allowed to accumulate and separate me even more from others than I am now.

STILL SAILING - FEB. 13, 1973

I heard this morning that, when we crossed the Golfo de Peñas, the waves were washing over the bow, and the ship was rising to great heights and crashing down, rolling side to side. All through that I was sleeping like a hibernating bear. When the sea began to get rough about 9:00 PM, I took a couple of Danelle's sea-sickness pills and was a goner. It's a good thing I did because my stomach was getting queasy. The pills must have knocked me out. I got more than 12 hours of sleep.

As the sun began to press the horizon, the world glowed a warm orange. This caused a spectacular panorama of colors to unravel across the wide expanse of jutting mountain ranges. The warm, yellow, morning light began changing across the mountains, receding to greens and then to varied hues of blues ending with the icy, snow-capped peaks. I will never forget that warm-appearing, bone-chilling cold scene, while I was standing on the bow, boldly heading into the

Antarctic winds. The sun had set as we ended our sail through the Darwin Canal. Waterfalls were cascading in thin ribbons from high steep cliffs. The misty mountains were spiritual in their mystic serenity.

Coming to Puerto Eden was a strange feeling after sailing by miles and miles of virgin land. There waiting to our right, nestled on the water's edge, were a handful of small colorful houses painted blue and yellow and red. When our huge ship was easing into the harbor, men in small skiffs were pulling at their oars and arriving at our lowered steps. Then a thriving business began. Mariscos and fish were the order of business. The sailors on our ship, being known to these fishermen and having connections with them, quickly bought up all the king crabs and fish. The passengers were bartering from the ship rails above. When a sale was made, the vendor in his little boat bobbing below would throw a rope around a bag of "cholgas" (mussels, shellfish, clams, prawns, etc.). The buyer would haul it up, throw it on his shoulder, and haul it off to his room. I was invited to open raw oysters and let them slide down my throat with the rest of them. It was a pretty good taste but left my throat begging for water all afternoon. The Chileans say, "One is not to drink water after eating mariscos raw." I think it's because this is a good excuse for men to drink more wine.

As for wine, it was incredible to see the total amount of huge wine jugs that were hauled out of the ship's hold and loaded onto a boat to be shipped to Puerto Eden. These people live in one of the most desolate climates and locations in the world, isolated from the world except for the occasional ship that comes by and does a little trading. Perhaps a few cargo ships come by as well, but I doubt it.

The sky appears to always be overcast, and snow blankets the land whenever the rains stop. I tried to mentally place myself there for a year, or a lifetime, but found it difficult to think of all the problems one would have to overcome.

We sailed through the "Angosta Inglesa" which is a narrow, dangerous canal that required precision steering with a couple officers on the bow keeping their eyes peeled. It's always cold here, and it's summertime.

Last night a bunch of guys made a raid on a large crate of watermelons on deck. It's amazing how many melons were skirted away to unknown corners of the ship. I counted seventeen melons in just one room. I happened onto one of these scenes; and there I was, eating cold, sweet, juicy watermelon with about 20 gringos and Chileans. We were scarfing that juicy pulp like we had not eaten anything for two weeks.

FEB. 13, 1973—D.C.

I shook badly after finally sleeping off the effects of the motion sickness pills I'd taken for the Golfo de Penas, but at least I slept well and didn't become seasick.

I spent a lot of time today waiting for meals in a line (so-called) outside the dining room doors. At one point we were made to wait extra-long because we knocked somewhat violently. We were soundly scolded by the huge cook who told us he would let us in when he was ready for us.

Mary and I spent some time on the captain's bridge looking ahead at the maze of canals which stem out to end at the feet of black and gray rock islands but around the bend they stretch on and on around these misty sea mountains. Some of the waterways are in fact fjords; and our imagination floated back to the silent, fearful explorations that must have been made to discover the passage thru these channels from Puerto Montt to Puntarenas. It's summer here now, but a frosty, salt wind caused our faces and ears to ache.

Later we were out to watch the passage of English Point, a section so narrow and so shallow on the sides that only one ship can pass thru there at a time. Foghorn signals sound our approach. On the small, low islands which form one side of the strait there are markers and lights for careful navigation. The ship had to make some sharp turns to maneuver into the passage.

Not much later in the evening we went thru a pass with steep mountain sides and cliffs surrounding us. Both melting snow and rain dropped from the smoky clouds which blanket these tall islands, feed white-threading waterfalls which stream down these massive, moss-adorned, stone sculptures. The vegetation we see on the hills today is different from yesterday's abundant pine growth. There is less, and the broad-leaf trees are sometimes snarled, shrub-like, and pale as they struggle for life out of stone and hidden sun. I went to stand at the back of the ship to see the teared mountains each an assorted color: nearby dark green, then darker, then deep blue, and deeper, back to the most distant ones which were covered with light gray mist as they seemed to close the passageway behind us. (Our earlier illusion from the front of the ship was that these mountains slowly parted as we approached to let us pass thru.)

Three gulls with velvety, black wings trimmed in white scanned the churned water behind us. They flew in varying patterns sometimes straight at me so that the roundness of their white bodies and the yellowness of their beaks impressed themselves in my memory. Yellow, black, and white with gray silver, green and blue, the areas we have seen yesterday and today look uninhabited.

When we approached the tiny village of Puerto Edén with its few small houses scattered at the base of a low scrubby island, the passengers acted excited at this sign of human existence. We ran to the ship railings, hoping that the ship would dock, so that we would be able to walk around the town and speculate as to what life might be like in a place so far surrounded by desolate mountains, icy-cold, gray sea, and mist. Instead, the ship anchored in the channel, and inhabitants of the village enthusiastically approached in small fishing boats or row boats. Some came with luggage and boarded while others came to take ashore those, like our cabin companions, who were coming home and were greeted by all with friendly handshakes. Still others had come to carry away potatoes and enormous quantities of wine which are probably their only additions to a diet of seafood like fish, shellfish, and seaweed. Their excess of seafood, smoked and strung or in shells, was being sold to passengers who leaned over the ship rails bargaining with them for very cheap prices.

The isolation and desolation of this site repeatedly stunned me as the thought of it returned like waves. I found out that there was at least a doctor there, a church was being built, and wine made. Tonight, I saw no sign of the sunset as darkness came, unlike yesterday when bright yellow rays cut into the gray of sea and sky and the island's shade of blue.

Terry was already in the first-class cabin of some friends who live in France, a stage-backdrop designer Swiss man, formerly Chilean woman living in France 13 years and her 14-year-old, flowerchild son who likes to do psychedelic drawings. He had spoken to me several times earlier as we watched the scenery. "What things a person can imagine while seeing all this! Surely no man has ever stood there. There must be wild animals there, free, and unafraid of man." Was it so many years ago I contemplated those same things? Is age a forceful focusing on the reality of what the senses perceive and little beyond? Anyway, it was pleasant to talk with these people and share wine from their glass. "I met my father in Santiago," says Sven. "It was fantastic." No apparent uncomfortable feelings in the room were caused. We saw some very shadowy ink drawings of the area. Talk was casual, much about the lonely and frustrated, "monstrous" old women who live in Paris, intimidating each other and anyone else who has contact with them (very similar to Helen's stories).

A group of travelers sat in the second-class lounge passing wine, chocolate, reading materials, talking about how Sinatra insulted Cheshire, court ruling that abortion on demand should be available in all states, trips to hot baths in Southern Chile, etc. They were uninterested in the party going on below in the dining room. There I stood in the door hidden behind a man who was also watching, hoping that no one would approach me since I didn't feel like being sociable. The atmosphere was quiet and almost sentimental as an electric guitar accompanied by a tambourine picked out sad, romantic popular tunes whose rhythm matched that of the hardly discernible rocking of the ship. The young, city, mod types crowded around the band and microphone. Quieter, more mature men, and women of widely varying ages sat warmly dressed in coats and sweaters, sharing bottles of wine at the long tables. Several clear, bright, light bulbs illuminated the port holes and the sea green color of the ceiling, walls, and tables. Warmth from the close gathering of many bodies drifted out past me into the long, narrow, cold, white hallway. I was very tempted to go in, but I knew that once I accepted the open friendliness of the wine drinkers, I wouldn't be able to leave until early morning. Once the carabinero's family got off at Puerto Edén, our cabin immediately filled with other passengers: English volunteer Shirley who teaches dairying at an agriculture school for campesinos near Santiago; French Odile; and a very close family of Chileans: a little girl of perhaps 2 who is fed and treated almost as an infant, woman who is usually in bed and boy of 10 or 11, who like the rest, hardly ever leaves the cabin. The man of this family comes in very frequently bringing food and hot water for coffee. Like the family before them, the man seems to like to stay near the family as much as possible; everyone seems to group around the mother. Fortunately, there is no enforced restriction on the coming and going of males in the female quarters or vice versa, although sleeping facilities are divided (more or less). John K. came in after we were in bed to pass out to everyone slices of melon which were being stolen from the ship's cargo while the men in charge are distracted with the party. So, someone somewhere, perhaps a person desperately in need of the money, will probably lose on this shipment; and the people in Punta Arenas, who so seldom have fruit of any kind, may not even enjoy a melon at a dear price.

Once when I went to the bathroom for Señoras (women), the man who sweeps the floor was in there leisurely talking to some women.

FEB. 14, 1973—**D.C.**

Perhaps it is a mistake that Terry and I sometimes read each other's diary. Today I read a description he wrote of Puerto Eden; it seems like something I wrote, and when I read my own, it sounds like his! The day was so sunny that even the water reflected blue. Small, white, lighthouses appear now and then. The rough, rocky mountain islands we see are barren and of a lighter gray than the almost black rock we saw yesterday. The sight of snow is much more frequent now. Low, jagged hills, not so far away, are covered with snow fields looking like the cut-off tops of the highest Andean Mountain ranges.

I ask Maruja a few questions about the political parties in Chile since about all I have heard is insults attached to initials. The Communist party is the most radical party, while people of more extreme revolutionary ideas (like violent take-over) are the Banderas Rojas (Red Flags) and the Movimiento Internacional Revolucionario (MIR, International Revolutionary Movement) which are not political parties but movements of guerrillas. (John K. told us an interesting anecdote about how the MIR robbed a bank by pretending to be making a movie of a bank robbery. They had stolen the film-making equipment, and the set was the locking of all employees in the safe while the "film makers" took the money and ran. A few months later they returned as policemen with their prisoners to re-enact the crime as a part of the investigation and robbed the bank again in the same manner.) MaPu is a sort of elite group of philosophers and intellectuals, a kind of democratic socialist movement. The Christian Democrats are the middle of the road party, while the Partido Nacional (National Party) is the conservative party.

We passed thru an area of the canals which is commonly called the Ship Graveyard. Here in a setting so surrounded by rocky gray hills that it appears to be a lake, several ships have lost course and crashed into small flat rocky islands. One lies on its side, the back half above water, its visible underside the orange shades of rust. A Grace Line, it was probably considerably more seaworthy than the Navarino. Our ship had to pass a rough section of gulf before entering the Straits of Magellan, so we rocked back and forth for over an hour on huge gray waves. Some of the port holes had been left open so that a little water stood on the halls outside our cabin. Unfortunately, we entered the straits at night and only the full moon gave vague idea of what might be seen on the coast.

FEB. 15, 1973—D.C.

I got up several times during the night and looked out the porthole to see whether I could tell anything about the coast but only saw somewhat low hills which didn't seem very close. I was awakened in the morning by the people in the cabin as they prepared their belongings.

We were approaching Punta Arenas which could be seen as many pale-colored buildings with the common red, corrugated metal (chapa) roofs and quiet streets gently inclined to the low, treeless, rolling hills behind. A dim rainbow added to the pastels of the scene.

The trip seemed very short to me. I was almost disappointed to see it at an end, but I knew from a visit I had made to the facilities below where country people stayed, it had been a long, miserable trip. For the same price that we were paying, many people crowded in the very dirty, unventilated compartments with crude wooden beds that had no bedding. The sound of crying babies was constant. At the bottom of the stairs which entered this section, people had established themselves in the hall, sitting and sleeping on their belongings throughout the five days. The bathrooms which were under the prow seemed to have never been cleaned. Certainly, I'm used to this sight and smell; but in a rolling sea I'm sure I wouldn't have the stomach to enter there.

We had to say many good-byes and exchange addresses. The captain and first mate and wives were telling the passengers good-bye like hosts and hostesses at a formal party. (Note the beautiful necklace of the captain's wife, strands of beads wrapped around a thick, soft cotton cord, 2 rows of white, 2 rows of mixed colors, again 2 rows of white, etc.)

Cows were being unloaded from trucks to ship by a crane lifting them by straps under the chest and belly. A wino crew member, whom Terry had befriended on the ship, gave us directions to the central plaza and walked off carrying a string with two long, stiff sierra fish.

The buildings downtown had a somewhat European flavor and with reason. Most of the settlers here were Yugoslavian. We saw several monuments and sculptures, one of Magellan in the Central Plaza with a mermaid and 2 strong Indian figures around the base of the central statue. Elsewhere we saw statues of the Condor, a shepherd with sheep and donkey and others. A stark church facing the plaza had distinctly stained-glass windows, two of Indians wrapped in the guanaco skin robes which were their only clothes. From our own situation we could hardly imagine how the Natives had endured the climate. I had on long underwear, sweater, denim shirt, long pants, boots, and my poncho and still didn't feel especially warm.

Outside of town we sat to wait for a lift. A freezing wind blew across the grassy pastures where milk cows grazed near a stream. Next we were left near the straits with the awkward dilemma of having to hitch 2 roads at once, one the old road that is smoother, and parallel the new wider one. We tried to stand halfway between them at a point where we might see vehicles coming on both roads, far enough away that we might run and reach either road in time to thumb. The wind that sounded thru the dry prairie grass and high line wires elated me with the sense of freedom that these only slightly rolling open stretches have given me from my distant past. The wind also tangled and flapped my Andean poncho around so much that I felt like a bat.

In the pickup that gave us a lift, an instrumental of "Don't Fence Me In" was playing. The road passed thru the headquarters of a huge, now state-owned ranch. Titles over each door indicated the use of each building, sheep baths, dining room, different storage barns. There was even a control station checking the passing automobiles. Other farms we saw were situated near the low hills in an effort to minimize the effects of the fierce winds. Horses and sheep grazed. Occasionally we saw a small oil field.

Our next wait was a 3-hour one, but when I put back on the lucky ring Maggie gave me (we later noted), another pickup stopped and took us to the ferry which was just leaving. We hurried on, on foot, just in time. The ferry only runs when the tide is high; but, since this is the narrowest crossing of the straits and an inexpensive ferry (Punta Delgada), many cars and trucks come here. They sometimes wait several days to get on the ferry.

We spoke with an Italian guy Ferreto, and French woman Chantal, who have been traveling in South America with a Land Rover. As we hitched off the ferry, they stopped for us and took us to Río Grande where we ate and camped with them. During this interesting ride we heard much French spoken, and I began to recognize many words. We continued seeing the wind-swept prairies which became increasingly sparsely populated it seemed.

At sunset we were passing a very green, marshy valley. We saw a herd of wild guanacos, an animal related to the llama. Fires burning the oil wastes broke the darkness and reminded me of the earlier fires, those of the Natives' warning system which Magellan saw, those which gave the island its name.

We felt a small degree of anxiety at crossing the border because of the money exchange problem, but surprisingly the guard only tossed our bank slip under the counter, smiled, and said, "Is that all?" and let us go thru with no problem even though we didn't show him our letter from the bank. We were happy, appreciated the cold windy silence and moonlight outside. Although we were sad at leaving the friendly Chileans, we were also very glad to be back in Argentina. The atmosphere of the country soon came back to us as we passed thru the wood-paneled border station, heated and clean. The clean toilets with paper and soap, the table service, the new concrete buildings in Río Grande, all reminded us of where we were.

USHUAIA, TIERRA DEL FUEGO - FEB. 16, 1973

It's unbelievable, but here we are in the southernmost city in the world. Summer is here, but Winter is in the air. I'm freezing.

I must backtrack a little bit to capture the scenes from a couple of days ago. After the big watermelon raid, eating juicy red slices and drinking wine, I remember having to get up and piss about 3:00 AM with a bursting bladder. I don't think I've ever peed so much in my life.

The next day started off with a wine-marinated melon that we doctored the night before. The melon was like a cantaloupe; but the fruit was green and so sweet that with the added wine, it was bursting with flavor.

It was a perfect sunny day to watch seals playing in the water while we sailed past jagged, snowcapped mountains. Colossal, knobby, granite cliffs appeared to be the aftermath of huge volcanic eruptions flowing with the buckling savage earth. Time has been hard on these mountains where the weather shows no mercy. There were very few trees as we neared the entrance of the Straits of Magellan, named after the Portuguese sailor, Ferdinand Magellan, an explorer who is famous for leading the first circumnavigation of planet Earth.

We entered the Straits shortly after the sun began to settle on the horizon, and we had just finished the "supper" soup which a Chilean in my room called jugo de las sabanas sucias (juice of dirty sheets). It was the juice from the cooked lentils we had this noon. The cook called it soup. We also had a few specks of meat which was still clinging to the piece of backbone each one of us had spooned in our bowl of watery juice. Oh yah, a piece of bread was given to each person. I began to really catch the flavor of the place about then. The sick-looking light green painted steel walls, tables, benches, walls, and doors, all reminded me of what a Chilean prison dining hall must be like. Even the way people are filed in and given only a spoon to eat with seemed like being in a prison.

As we entered the mouth of the Straits, the waves grew larger. We were rolling and dipping but I never got seasick. It was a smooth-flowing experience to ride those waves and feel the power of the ocean. I had read about Magellan, the first European to pass through these straights in 1520 when I was in the sixth grade and longed to see this part of the world.

I was disappointed to sail into the Straits of Magellan at night. However, it would have been anticlimactic to see these Straits for the first time, during the day. On a map, the Straits appear to be a narrow passage. In fact, this passage is comparable to a long wide lake. We would have only seen the banks in the distance.

We arrived in Punta Arenas, Chile, during the midmorning sun and were greeted by a full rainbow arching gracefully over this handsome town. As we deboarded the Navarino, workers were loading live cattle onto another boat with a crane and sling. Carpenters were busy nailing wood frames around them. Some of the cattle were squirming violently in the sling, and others were taking it calmly as if it were an ordinary event for them.

Punta Arenas is a handsome, eclectic, clean town with old Victorian buildings and many enormous outdoor sculptures, all exquisitely crafted. The Plaza de Armas, (Central Plaza), has a mammoth bronze sculpture of Ferdinand Magellan, noted for discovering the Straits of Magellan. The base of the statue has a mermaid, and two huge sculpted Native Americans around the base. One of the old stone Victorian buildings on the central square had a green house, a marvelously delicate green house, on the side of the plaza.

As we walked along a paved road leading out of town to Tierra del Fuego, we passed several more handsome sculptures; one was a sheepherder with his dog and burro walking along after his herd. Another was of modern, Le Corbusier-style, sculpture of people with outstretched arms, the style one might find in Brasilia.

So, there we were again, hitching our asses off, but this time near the end of the world with our goal nearby. Our second ride left us off in the middle of nowhere. There was an old road on one side of a grassy area and a new gravel road on the other. Our trouble was, we had to hitch both because they were both traveled, so we waited huddled beside one road to be out of the frigid wind and if we saw someone coming down the other, we took off running over to it and stuck out our thumbs. We caught a long ride in a pickup to another out-of-the-way place and waited about three hours for a ride.

That's when Danelle put on her lucky silver ring that Maggie gave her. Our luck hasn't stopped since then. We caught another ride in a pickup truck, just like that, which took us to the ferry to the island of Tierra del Fuego. As we zoomed along in the pickup, we passed houses nestled in valleys or on the leeward side of a small mound of earth or a hill, anything to protect them from the cutting wind. The singing wires and windy plains are a perfect touch to this treeless area along the Straits.

WHERE FANTASY AND TRUTH MEET THE ROAD

Highway, highway run along
Carry us through the next small town,
Past fields of grain row upon row
What's at your end I want to know.

Highways are made for you and me
Hitching along by light of day,
Eating cheese sandwiches at high noon
And oftentimes under a shining moon.

Sometimes when the sun beats down
And the dust and heat choke me dry,
I feel the shivering, shivering cold
But then I was longing for burning coal.

Danelle's going through the soles of her boots
And the knees of her pants show miles of wear,
My hair and beard flow long and dry
We're hitching a ride to the town of Ushuaia

At times we're in the comforts of home
But often we're sleeping beside the road,
A road to where the unknown lies
Where fantasy and truth meet eye to eye.

On my shoulders my sleeping bag hangs
And a few other things I need,
The robbers were swift, and I was slow
They took things I used to know.

That was in Mexico a year and a half ago
And I still carry more than I need,
A passport, map, and a pack
Is the magic carpet on which I act.

To go and go in a constant flow
Is my idea of a life aglow,
Resting here and resting there
Is just as important as breathing air.

It's not a rainbow I'm looking for
Nor am I searching for a pot of gold,
For where I go there is no end
To the flowing life which I contend.

Sitting in the back of a pickup truck
With us and the clouds rolling by,
Ponchos and sleeping bags keeping us warm
As we watch the black ribbon endlessly form.

It was a happy feeling to be on the road again while hitching along the Straits. Hitching is the only way to travel here because there is no public transportation. The countryside resembled that of the Montana plains. It had that nowhere feeling as we passed by wild birds and ostriches, sheep, and horses, all grazing without fences.

When the ferry landed, we started walking on the island of Tierra del Fuego; and then, within a couple minutes, we were given a ride by an Italian guy and his French wife in their Land Rover all the way to Ushuaia, another stroke of luck.

Tierra del Fuego is a land of change. Windy and barren terrain gives way to the lakes and snowy mountains. We passed so many flocks of birds that, at times, I thought I was in a wildlife preserve. In the summer months, we were told there are 152 distinct species of birds on this island. Scrubby, twisted trees and rolling plains give way to the craggy, snowcapped mountains as we jostled our way farther and farther south. The roads are all gravel. Most of the cars and trucks had wire-mesh screens in front of their windshields to protect the glass from flying rocks. The drivers say the best way to meet an oncoming car is to pass as close as possible to it. This keeps one out of the line of rocks being thrown up by the tires.

We crossed the border to the Argentina part of this island late at night without any official border hassle and camped on the seashore of Rio Grande, a town where we heard people support themselves by cross border smuggling.

Through the inky blackness, I could see small fires, said to be gas flares, in the distance. They remind me of the nomadic Yámana people who navigated the waters of the area surrounding the Beagle Channel. They navigated in canoes, keeping small fires burning in their hulls for warmth and light. Uniquely, when the explorer, Ferdinand Magellan sailed this area, the Yámana fires were so prevalent that he named this island Tierra del Fuego, (Land of Fire).

Topping the mountain ridge and seeing the Beagle Channel and Ushuaia in front of me was an emotional feeling. I finally made it to the southern tip of South America after a long year and three months of hitchhiking, walking, traveling by car, pickups, long-haul trucks, bus, trains, boats, and plane.

The windswept town of Ushuaia is sited along the Beagle Channel and is settled on the sloping base of the craggy, snow-covered Marshal Mountains. The town is aptly nicknamed the "End of the World." It is a small town, about five blocks wide and fifteen blocks long. The side streets slope steeply down to the channel. It's cold here, and with the wind it's almost unbearable. We found a place to sleep on the floor of the Club Andino (Club of the Andes or Mountain Climbers). The building is under construction, but the walls and windows are installed and protect us from the wind. We have no stove, so this concrete floor we sleep on is very cold. I can tell that we will have to hunt for some boards or cardboard to place between us and this icy floor.

FEB. 16, 1973—**D.C.**

Although we slept on the coast last night, our tent protected us from the chilly wind; and we were able to sleep well. Chantal gave us hot coffee, and Ferreto offered us a ride to Ushuaia which we greatly appreciated. Along the way we saw several species of large birds and more herds of wild guanacos. The wind-swept prairie scenery gradually changed to low hills covered with short, very gnarled trees with some bare protruding branches among the scant leaves. Pale green strands of moss hung from the wood. Soon we were able to see jagged peaks patched with snow. We passed various mountain lodges and stopped for tea at one which sits on the large Lake Fagnano surrounded by peaks and trees. Young road builders waved at us as though they were very glad to see another person. We passed near the pointed Mt. Olivia, the highest peak on the island. Ushuaia impressed us with its beautiful location at the foot of the jagged mountains and its main street along the edge of the channel harbor. We were able to get permission from a Sr. M. to sleep on the floor of the unfinished Club Andino. The first people I saw there were a couple

I had met in Cuzco. It took us a while to recall that we had met there at the Comedor Nacional [National Lunchroom]. Their rings, Mike's a Persian antique with inlayed astrological symbols and Jane's copy of it, helped to place the scene of our meeting and conversations there. I went out to the post office hoping to find a note from Nito; instead, I ran into Peter G. who recognized me and called my name. I was thoroughly surprised to see him and Pattie. They had looked for me in Buenos Aires. We had tea together and exchanged what gossip we had from our mutual Peace Corps friends.

When I returned to the Club Andino, a circle of travelers sitting on empty coke cases were engaged in a conversation with an American named Henry who had turned down a $4,000 a year scholarship to get his doctoral degree at Harvard in theology. He also left a girlfriend whom he claims to have loved very much. Soon we were off to the movies to see *Gimme Shelter* which was depressingly irrelevant to the peace I felt in chilly Ushuaia. Felt good to be far away from the USA.

FEB. 17, 1973—**D.C.**

I was trying to write when in walked Joe W., another ex-Panamá Peace Corps volunteer. I heard here and there that he has been traveling in South America. I missed seeing him only by a few minutes the last time I was in Panamá. He met Jan W. in La Paz (Jan had traveled by land through Argentina to Punta Arenas and had gotten a boat to Puerto Montt.) Joe and Rita lived for several months in the Galápagos Islands where they also ran into Tom H., who wasn't drafted as I had been told before, but got a job working on a boat in the Pacific.

FEB. 17-20, 1973—**D.C.**

The distractions, and the discomfort at the Club Andino were such that I let the days pass without writing about them. Now, the

23rd, they are run together and blurred in my mind even more than they were then.

In the 2nd floor room of the unfinished Club building, along with other travelers from the States, Argentina, and Ireland, we spread paper, cardboard, boards, whatever was available on the floor to insulate us from the very cold concrete where we laid our sleeping bags. Near each person's (or couple's) sleeping bag were scattered various belongings: food, dishes of tin, small gas, or alcohol stoves, drying or dirty clothes, reading and writing materials, near-empty back packs, even a guitar. Only furniture was a lone table in the center of the room under the one florescent light bulb. We sat around it on Coke cases and large cans as we ate, talked, drew, and tried to write. Now and then, someone would play a few tunes on the guitar. I even learned to play the simple "Let It Be."

Until the sun shone warmly through the big windows (around 10:30), no one got up. When we finally did, the conversation began and lasted until late at night. Each new arrival added variety to the many topics discussed. Among the more frequently appearing subjects was the anxiously awaited arrival of Jacques Cousteau's ship the Calypso which had been hit by an Argentine naval ice-breaker; the tourist ship in port which was taking mostly retired Americans for a 2-week excursion from New York to Antarctica for $3,500 (the price grew with each telling to $5,000 then $7,000). The hitchhikers talked derogatorily of the tourists, and the tourists did the same (perhaps more cleverly) of the hitchhikers.

Thanks mostly to Jane and Mike there was very interesting information about Tierra del Fuego itself concerning its plants (many edible) and animals (like 152 species of birds in summer), its history, the Natives (of whom only very few pure breeds are left) and good books to read about it, like the highly recommended *The Uttermost Part of the Earth* by Lucas Bridges. One of Mike's accounts was of his knowledge of the Tarot which he has studied for several years. One type of deck he mentioned was of Aleister Crowley who composed each card of symbols from a page of the

64th Egyptian Book of the Dead, a lost book, which taught the use of psychic powers. Egypt magicians were very powerful because of their exclusive contact with this book (see story of Moses in Bible and his round of tricks with them).

Among the few activities I was able to drag myself into was the buying of air letters and post cards to be sent mostly as thank you notes to people in Chile. There were many beautiful cards sold with envelopes of both Tierra del Fuego and Antarctica. Always the people in these stores and the small bakery (with its large flat pans of sweet and grease breads sitting on the counter) were very friendly and trusted us to owe them the few cents neither of us could produce in change. Once when I mentioned my lack of money, the young male vendor at the bakery jokingly suggested that I stay in Ushuaia and dance in the streets disguised as a penguin for tourist coins. One day we ate a very big, long-legged crab which Terry bought for 5 pesos from the fisherman's boat. Jane cooked it live on her small stove [which horrified me as it tried to escape the pot].

Twice I used an Ushuaia name we were given, under the pretext that I was looking for this man, as an excuse to enter the expensive Hotel Albatross and use their bathroom (since we had none at the club). Besides using the toilet there, I could brush my teeth and wash my face and hands with soap and hot water! Several times I tried to get into the public library, which was heated, quiet, had chairs and a toilet. When I finally found it open one day, I was distracted from my writing by a fancy new reference book whose maps showed some cities in the wrong location, whose picture titles were sometimes incorrect, and all with very slanted information using words like primitive and barbarian.

One day several of us took the hike to a nearby glacier on one of the mountains behind the town. Mike and Jan pointed out small ferns and berries near the path in the foothills and turned my attention to the details of the vegetation around me. The path was well-cut by the many tourists who go there. It continued up to the deciduous woods always near a small rocky river.

Crude bridges of logs and branches were built over some of the marshier trails. By staying to the left of the river, I took a short cut which led thru a thick, near tree-line woods where the low trees had sharply curved orangish maroon trunks with little, short white streaks raised on the smooth bark surface. The leaves were small, almost round, all growing on the upper side of the twigs and branches facing the sky. The clusters were like thin flat sheets lying parallel to the branch. The valley where we reached the first snow was green and marshy, and a frigid wind blew down from the peaks. I sat by a big rock to keep warm.

From here the rest of the climb to the glacier was rocky, long, and very steep so we decided that we were close enough to see what we wanted. A strong impression of the glacier was that it looked very dirty on top as though it had accumulated much dirt. The huge deep icy crags along its edge were a sky-blue color. This enormous river of ice certainly stood out against the pure white snow and blackish gray cliffs around it.

On the way down two Argentine sailors talked to me; and although I was a little afraid of them, they turned out to be gentlemen. They have been as far north as Jacksonville, Florida, where they were surprised at the nature of the racial problems so different from their previous impressions that the blacks had absolutely no rights. They pointed out to me a wind called the Susana which blows very strongly for 15 minutes every hour. (Above in the valley we could also see the channel dotted with small islands and thru the binoculars a very distant farmhouse on the other side.)

One of the places where we went to buy food was an American style supermarket. We ran into John K. there and some of the South African mountain climbers' expedition.

I became extremely lethargic while staying at the Club and almost depressed. The company was good, and the mountain scenery and sunsets we could see from the double-pane windows were beautiful, yet something bothered me very much (I don't know what). I was unable to gather my energies for moving yet found myself lying awake late after others had gone to sleep.

I managed to scratch out a few feelings in cards and letters but certainly couldn't concentrate enough to write here.

USHUAIA - FEB. 20, 1973

I was cold last night and had all the clothes I own on while curled up in my flimsy sleeping bag. After we got our gear arranged on the floor last night, we went to the flicks and saw an English version of a Walt Disney animal film, called *Ring of Bright Water*, a story about a man and an otter. The second film was about the Rolling Stones at the Altamont Free Concert. Not bad, but not good! Good music though!

This morning, I went to the beach and bought king crab for forty cents. We had a heck of a tasty breakfast. We had some bread and cheese with it.

There are six other travelers sleeping up here on the 2nd floor of this building. All are Americans except a girl from Ireland and a couple of Argentines. One of the Americans was a student at Harvard, who had a $4,000 scholarship to do his Ph.D., but said that wasn't the kind of life he wanted and had stuck his thumb out for the road.

What a beautiful evening! There are nine of us from various parts of the world, cooking on their little gas stoves: soups, curry, rice, and tea. Long hair, nylon jackets, stocking hats, a guitar strumming in the background, and a neon light add an accent of warmth in the center of this cold concrete room. Backpacks: nylon, canvas, and leather, line the walls along with rolled up sleeping bags the colors of orange, blue, red, and light blue. All have a constant factor: well used. A flashlight here and a can of powdered milk over there. Socks hanging on a makeshift clothesline, people talking in small groups or reading a time-worn novel or just writing a letter. Stories are passing around the room and people are getting to know each other as if we were long lost friends.

USHUAIA - FEB. 20, 1973

On Sunday we hiked to an iridescent green, 100-foot-tall glacier wedged between a crumbly, jagged mountaintop high above this village. The force and power of this sluggish giant could wipe out the entire town of Ushuaia in half a minute.

Jane G., who has done a great deal of study in botany and anthropology, was with us along with her husband Mike. Both are all-around good people. Jane, from her seacoast heritage, showed us how to cook our pink king crab that I bought from an old fisherman who was picking hundreds of them out of the tangles of his net. Jane also showed us the edible blue "Calafate Berries" which grow on large spiney bushes. She also showed us the Rain Berry which hides remarkably close to the ground on open hillsides. The Rain Berry looks like a Red Raspberry. Jane and Mike are interesting, both being very much into basic life having a knowledge of many worldly things such as the moon's effect on weather, the collecting and naming of plants, and cooking seafood.

We walked down to the gymnasium today to splash our stinking bodies under hot, yes, hot water. Nice!

It's very difficult to bring my mind around to living on Argentina pesos now, especially when prices are so high here; and the value of the dollar is going down. The best exchange rate I could get here was 10 to 1. Before it was about 11.50 to 1 or more.

On the way back from the gym, I strolled through the little cemetery down the street. I was welcomed by lonely, black, wooden crosses that are as much a part of cemeteries as flowers. There were wonderful warm, orange-colored poppies and spring-like, pure white daisies growing from the soil. There were several large, ugly as usual, mausoleums with chained doors that lead to the inner sanctum stuffed with mountains of gross plastic flowers. The strange thing was the wooden, brass-handled coffins stacked on concrete shelves with mountains of plastic wreaths on top. Just the coffin on the shelves, a picture of the deceased framed on the wall, and the cross on the altar seemed out of place at first. I hate plastic flowers.

FEB. 21, 1973—**D.C.**

We finally made it out of town to the Tierra del Fuego National Park. A Polish Canadian (New Brunswick) family in their VW camper picked us up. First we went to a small inlet Bahia Lapataia and put our things on the porch of a locked wooden house which we were told was once a mussel packing plant now moved. We saw that the house was slightly furnished inside with bare wooden beds and a few saddles; but since it was very windy, cold, and rainy and the barns and corrals showed no signs of recent farm life, we decided to stay on the porch and see what happened. A grassy front yard stretched down to a small creek. We could see the inlet and rugged mountains around us. We were told that Chile was only 2 kilometers away.

Not long after Terry came back with some firewood, a park ranger came and told us that it was private property, that we would have to leave. Fortunately, the Canadians hadn't gone from their picnic yet and we caught them just as they were preparing to leave. They took us to Lago Roca where they parked to camp, and we went to set up inside a metal shelter where a lone, young Argentine, Edwardo Goldman, was already hanging his Brazilian hammock and making a fire.

Soon it began to rain and continued all afternoon and night. Although the smoke from the new fire we built inside choked us and burned our eyes, it was worth it to have the warmth and the opportunity to cook something. We sat around it on the low log benches all day and talked. Edwardo seemed a strange young man at first, but we soon grew accustomed and began to like his very expressive way of talking and facial mannerisms. We became used to his soft voice, his almost servile passiveness. When it was bedtime, we set up our tent inside the shelter in order not to take it apart for the ground cover. We knew we would be warmer inside it also.

PARQUE NACIONAL (NATIONAL PARK), TIERRA DEL FUEGO - FEB. 22, 1973

We caught a ride to this forested park with a family who had driven from Canada to here in their VW Bus. The father Adam C., a professor at the University of New Brunswick, Canada, has been teaching for a few months in Brasilia, Brazil. Their son Peter is a 15-year-old who the ladies at the tourist information office thought was a girl because of his young face and high voice.

Anyway, we're camping about 4 kms from the Chilean border on Lago Roca set high in the mountains that cascade sharply and steeply to the water's edge. From a distance, the dense tree cover on these mountain sides appears as if covered with a high-quality green carpet. Every inch of these mountain sides is covered with trees.

It's been raining lightly almost all the time we've been here, but that hasn't bothered us because we've made our home in a small Quonset hut shelter with a Porteño (person from Buenos Aires) named Eduardo. He's an easy-going guy with long wavy hair hanging on his shoulders in ringlets. We've pitched our tent in this hut and kept our fire going all day. Eduardo sleeps in a hammock and got quite cold, but Danelle and I are very snug in the tent. The hut helped keep the wind from cutting through us. It's very cozy in here, and I feel like this is our own cabin beside the lake. The only problem is that it does not have any doors left. They have been used for firewood long ago. The wild cottontails come nibbling right up to our door along with the sparrows all around. This is a perfect camping site with dead wood a-plenty and grass everywhere as if it was a front lawn. The rabbits keep it freshly mowed. Wild Calafate Berries are in season and are waiting to be picked. They are a good supplement to our diet of cheese sandwiches and soup.

Tourists from organized groups have been flocking in by the busloads, debussing, wandering around, snapping a photo here and there; then seemingly within minutes, a guide with an amplified megaphone shouts out calling all people in bus #32 to come back to load up and head for the hostel. It was odd for us, after traveling for over a year across South America, to see people arriving neatly by boat over a very short period. It seemed like an odd way to see the world.

I've been talking to an American guy and his English friend. Travel stories were flying while we sat huddled around the glowing fire, drinking maté (tea). Good times!

They made a sign with the date on it to hold standing in front of their camper. They plan to send it to all their pessimistic friends who were afraid for them driving across "savage" South America. Then they took a photo of Danelle and I holding the same sign.

We are huddled around our warm fire cooking a soup in a large can that we brought from Ushuaia. It's boiling rapidly. I know it's going to be a tasty dish with potatoes and shellfish picked fresh from the Beagle Canal in a cream-of-vegetable soup mix. Five more minutes and it's ours. The night has closed around us, and the candle is flickering its faint light on the pages of my journal. The coals are glowing red, the cold is on my back, and I have a warm feeling in my stomach, hands, and heart. The whole arching room of this Quonset hut is filled with a hazy smoke further accenting our central fire and this warm friendly atmosphere. Que bien! (How nice).

FEB. 22, 1973—**D.C.**

We were awakened very early by the loud voices of excursion tourists who exclaimed how nice the shelter was, how it had tent inside, how a man was sleeping in a "Paraguayan" hammock. Various bus loads came to the lake during the day. The buses even had loudspeakers to call the wandering tourists when it was time to leave. These were very imposing sounds in the moss-floored woods.

Outside many rabbits nibbled on the grass near the hut. Once when I walked out to the lake, there were 8 of them who hopped away flashing their white tails. The abundant Calafate berries growing on thorny bushes are in season and have a good grape-like taste. I didn't eat many though since they have so many seeds and render little. There is a wooded mountain behind the shelter, and the green lake and the snow-capped hills around it are in front of us. Tonight, the lake was extremely still. After sunset, a brilliant luminous gray shone where the light from the sky was not blocked out by the dark reflections of the mountains. Later the clouds and the stars could be seen clearly reflected by the water. In the grass, tiny rocks or shells shined in the dark. Looking at the ground was like seeing another sky.

We used the cans given to us in Ushuaia to do some cooking. Edwardo was given some mussels (mejillones) by an English and American guy (Bob and Dave) who turned out to be acquaintances of ours. We cooked mussels in their own water until they opened. We took out the bite-sized flesh from the open shells and pulled out a small sprig of algae that grew on some of them. Later we put this shellfish with potatoes and macaroni to make a nice soup. The Canadians left today. Since they had Terry take some pictures of them with their polaroid camera in front of their van holding a big Tierra del Fuego sign they had made, they also took two pictures of us and gave us each one. Peter, 15, the only son sat with us a while and talked in Portuguese with Eduardo who once spent 5 months in Brazil. Adam, the father, recently spent a semester as a visiting professor (of surveying and map making) at the university in Brasilia. Bob and Dave came for a visit and bought their maté cup. We tried their maté with milk which was very good. Our talk was mostly about traveling people who had been robbed and where and Dave's trips in India and Nepal. I decided that Eduardo reminded me of Tiny Tim, the American muscian known for his 1968 song "Tiptoe Through the Tulips" with his long curls which are not crinkly; but his quiet, almost effeminate voice and gestures and his big, hooked nose with the flattened end somehow reminded me of the faint image I have of the singer.

USHUAIA - FEB. 23, 1973

Today we began our long trek back to the USA. We are on the rebound. Bahía Lapatía is as far as the road goes. We are about 3,124 km from Buenos Aires and at the southernmost end of Argentine National Highway #3. I feel like I'm riding a yoyo with a long string, and I've just started rolling back up to the hand that threw me down to this part of the world. We visited with the Americans that were on the Chilean ship with us since they are all camping at this park too: John K., Mary D., Lyle M., and Dutchman Robert S. We are seeing "everybody we ever knew" repeatedly. This is a small place with few roads and no public transportation, so our paths cross often.

We said goodbye to our Tiny-Tim-looking friend named Eduardo Goldman and hit the road. We caught a ride to Ushuaia where we jumped in the hot showers as soon as we arrived at the gymnasium. Was that ever a great feeling! We're sleeping in the gym tonight instead of the Club Andino. It is warmer.

FEB. 23, 1973—D.C.

We decided to leave today, so I made a short visit to Dave's and Bob's campsite. A few tents, automobiles and campfires were scattered among the trees with reason. The woods looked very inviting with their pale green light, mossy clearings and very slowly deteriorating, wet logs. Bob was sitting beside a smoky fire laid between bricks. The site was well settled with bits of furniture and miscellaneous pieces of chapa to protect the fire. Since these guys are planning to stay for a while, they gathered what they needed from the area. Dave had gone to town to buy more food and mail letters.

Bob and I talked a while about our maladjustments, so to speak, in the US. As I so often try to do when this conversation develops, I pulled out memories of groups of people, the groups alike in many ways but living what they thought to be conflicting images. The members of each group not only would not accept, socially or humanly, members of other groups but often would not accept members of their own group who wanted to associate frequently with anyone outside the group. A person (or group) might find another's philosophy or practice intolerable even though he had practiced the same at a different time, even as little as 2 weeks before. America's young people seem to be desperately evolving from one identity to another, searching yet frequently scorning whatever is different from them now. For me, the need to be strongly individual, yet tolerant of the differences of everyone else, was a constant social problem. I often saw myself as a link between 2 groups. By my acceptance of both, I somehow hoped my acquaintances on each side would openly admire the good qualities of the other and drop their varying degrees of hostility. As a result, I usually was rejected by both, or by frustrated efforts, left lonely and isolated, turning gradually inward to depend on my own inner resources to compensate for my social inadequacies. On and on it has gone until I hardly ever find myself comfortable with anyone.

When Edwardo passed by and looked embarrassed at seeing me sitting next to Bob, I remembered that Terry had told him that we were married. Certainly, in this culture and probably in ours as well, it wouldn't be acceptable for a married woman to visit another man's camp alone and sit so close beside him.

On the road I ran into Dutch Robert, Kansas Lyle, Mary, and John and told them where Terry was, so they were keeping warm beside our fire when I came in. We saw them again later at the gymnasium where we had gone for a hot shower. We ended up sleeping there because of the warmth and comfort (we even had beds to sleep in).

We had coffee, bread, and dulce de leche that was offered to us by some very nice Argentine travelers, Silvia, and Florencia. Silvia later gave us her address in Buenos Aires. The eyes of the man who was traveling with Florencia looked very familiar. He told me he lived only a few blocks from Plaza Francia. Handkerchiefs were stuck on the bathroom walls to dry, and clothes hung over the heater fan. I was given maté [tea] and told again that to say "gracias" in Argentina means you don't want any or are finished.

John K. cooked a big pot of vegetable soup which we gladly shared. The Argentines went outside and cooked an asado to which Terry was invited, but I wasn't. I sat on the bed and wrote a letter to the people in Los Olivos [Panamá]. I was strongly drawn back to them and recognized again how superficial my knowledge of their way of daily life was. They had given so much to me; and yet, with all the silly unfinished projects and my clinging to privacy, I never really gave enough of myself. Again, as always, it was very difficult to write as I recalled the activities of the season and wondered about the various images they must have had of the "gringa." Their way of doing things and their humanity is so much more meaningful to me now that I don't see them in the light of my work responsibilities. When the lights were turned out, I wrote on by a candle flame. Nearby on a mattress on the floor, John and Mary were reading also by candlelight and seemed to be appreciating the warmth of this steamy girls' dressing room as much as I was.

BORDER OF CHILE AND ARGENTINA - FEB. 25, 1973

We arrived here last night after difficult hitching from Ushuaia. Our sixth ride took us across the ten-mile "no man's land" from Argentina to Chile. Mary and Danelle climbed into the cab of the big truck; and John, Lyle and I hopped on the small platform directly behind the cab with all the gear under us. There we were, hauling balls, jamming it, tooling it, plowing through the night's blackness. Wind was whipping us all around, but we were kings on our thrones, owning the world but owning nothing. I couldn't have felt better.

As usual we were greeted by Chilean hospitality, only this time it was the border guards who opened their hearts to us five raggedy vagabonds appearing out of the night. After hearing that we had tents and sleeping bags, the guards offered us a room in one of the vacant, wooden, laborer's houses on this old estancia (ranch). There is nothing here now except the long narrow buildings, sided and roofed with corrugated metal sheets. This used to be a ranch full of people and life, but now it is a ghost on the prairie. The silent, hollow windows stare at you from all directions. Wild geese flap their wings in the wind as if washing them in the crisp breezes. Sheep, recently sheered, spook easily as I walk down the dusty gravel road. These scattered buildings are the remains of a prosperous ranch but, after being taken over by the State, now lie in ruin except for the main house in the center of all the buildings, now the "Carabinero's" border guard station.

The room the guards gave us for the night was empty and had a clean wooden floor. The windows were boarded up, giving us protection from the cutting wind whistling across the prairie. We settled into this little room with a central candle dimly lighting our figures, watching John prepare potatoes, onions, garlic, and hot dogs served under cheese. Danelle and Mary were talking about intestinal worms and their symptoms, and Lyle was cutting jokes. I was peeling potatoes and John was slicing onions. It was a satisfying meal, and the room provided a warm place to sleep. Who else but Chileans would lend a helping hand to strangers in the night?

An icy wind and glowing sun greeted us as we straggled out of that bare room. The golden prairie and open sky, shaggy but rounded hills, reminded me again of parts of Montana and Wyoming. We certainly are stuck here. There just is no traffic at all at this isolated frontier border station. I don't know when we'll get a ride across this desolate back country.

In Ushuaia, we were living on 25 cents a day, and we've still got quite a lot of food left; so, it will probably average out less than that. We still haven't had to pay for a place to sleep since we left Buenos Aires, thanks to our pup tent and goodness of strangers.

WAITING FOR A FERRY TO THE MAINLAND - FEB. 25, 1973

After hanging around the border station all day long, we caught a ride all the way to the ferry which took us to the mainland of Argentina. The driver of a tour bus that just arrived at the border with a load of tourists, told us that he'd take us back across the Straits. Now we're waiting for the tide to rise, so the ferry can sail. We were able to finish cooking our soup of bacon, carrots, carrot tops, garlic, onion, and noodles. John, as before was the soup chef last night and night before. When we asked him why he liked to cook, he said, "It's the Jewishness in me." Anyway, he puts together outstanding stews. John even scrounged and haggled with the neighbors for the freshly picked carrots from their gardens and the chunks of pork. He's not Kosher.

I have been riding in an Opel station wagon driven by an 18-year-old Chilean named Alán H. whose grandmother is from the Falkland islands. He also drove tourists to the border along with the bus. As we rolled the dusty gravel roads, we passed wild, llama-like animals called guanacos and hundreds of wild geese. The bands of sheep roaming and grazing on this windy plain reminded me of photos of prisoners with their heads sheared. They looked and must have felt cold having been recently sheared.

I was amazed to see barking dogs chained to small, corrugated, metal dog houses beside each cattle guard which crossed the road. This system must make cattle guards a little more efficient, but what a shitty life for a dog! It may have to go days without food and water, helplessly chained by his neck to the doghouse. With nothing to do but bark at passing vehicles and pee endlessly on the corner of its house, its only job is to chase away a few curious sheep that may try to jump over the cattle guard.

As darkness fell over this part of Tierra del Fuego, I could see the seemingly endless reflections of natural-gas flares glowing orange in the clouds. Fires were everywhere. This all seemed symbolic of the many fires the Indians once kept burning in their boats and across this land of fire, Tierra del Fuego, many moons ago. Early explorers saw these warming fires in considerable numbers and thus named this wild island. I find it appropriate to leave in the darkness, for this will be a memory of times well spent and well gained these past 10 days on this island.

FEB. 24-27, 1973—**D.C.**

Since I'm developing a chest cold and Terry an earache, we decided to take advantage of our shelter in a classroom of the Salesian Mission School of Río Gallegos and take a day's rest. We certainly need the rest after the past 3 days it took us to hitch from Ushuaia to here.

Our first day on the road was a game of leapfrog with Lyle, John, and Mary. We would pass them, then they would pass us. They would bounce by with a speedy ride which we were sure would take them all the way and reduce the competition which I sensed in the air no matter how hard I fought it. But when our next ride came, we either passed them or found them already sitting where we were let off. Once we all got a ride together, but the small pick-up had a flat and had to turn back.

By the time night came, we were all stuck at the Argentine side of the border waiting for a ride to take us across the 10 kms. stretch of land to the Chilean border station. We weren't allowed to walk it even if we had wanted to. The guards were noticeably unfriendly and tried to talk a few passing drivers into getting us out of their hair, so to speak. Finally, John convinced a reluctant truck driver to load all females in front and all our packs and males in back (standing) and take us over to the Chilean side.

As we had expected the Carabineros were quite friendly, hospitable, and pointed out camping space and 2 doors of empty rooms in a long barracks where we might sleep. With the help of the frigid wind, we quickly chose indoors and picked the larger and cleaner room. We spread our sleeping bags around this wooden square, and John and Mary put their can-sized gas stove in the center. John cooked a dish for us all from the cheese and wieners he was given at an Argentine estancia today, threw in potatoes, onion, and garlic. The candles hadn't burned down yet when we were into our sleeping bags.

I recalled the impressions of the day: the familiarity of the scenery, the names of estancias with the close-set groups of chapa buildings sitting near the road and high snow fences, moss-draped log fences, wire fences with mossy wooden gates, small winding rivers gently pushing through soft clay valleys of marshy grass which slightly overhang the banks. We had hopes of getting a ride to Río Gallegos with a man in a big red car who had picked up John and Mary the first day, saying he would be going the next. However, when we went into the border station, we were told that he had already passed thru. We paid for getting up late.

We waited at the station all day, out of the wind but restless. We shyly asked the drivers who passed thru, but they were usually crowded. At lunch we went back to the room to cook and eat but soon found out from a furious woman accompanied by children that this was Air Force property, the responsibility of her husband who was absent, and completely outside the authorization of the carabineros. We were off, not wanting to cause any problems.

The day drug on. I spoke briefly with a young gaucho, who was waiting with an older gaucho to finish by short wave radio some red tape necessary for shipping a load of Argentine sheep thru the stretch of Chilean territory which divides the Argentine Mainland from her section of Tierra del Fuego. This young man told me that 5 months ago they had come from the Buenos Aires province because all the land on the pampa was taken up. They chose not to go to the hot, unfamiliar Chaco Territory. His relaxed, light-brown eyes never left mine as he talked. As hard as I tried to return this favor, I couldn't and had to uneasily look away. For my tastes he was not an exceptionally handsome young man. He was tall and strongly built, light skinned as to appear of pure European descent. Short, light-brown hair curled out around the edges of his black beret. He was typically dressed in boots, bloomer pants, dark sweater over white shirt and brightly colored print scarf. His Patagonian gaucho image along with his calm gaze made him so attractive to me that, when he talked of the loneliness of life on the estancia, which had he asked me, I would have gone home with him to stay and keep him company. I recognized this desire as my distinct symptom of road weariness. I had had the same feeling about campesino Native men I saw on trucks in Perú when day after day of travel was bringing my fatigue to the breaking point. I later heard that the estancia he named, Menéndez-Betti, was one of the many owned by the Menéndez-Betti family who had practically exterminated the Indians to gain ownership of nearly the whole of Patagonia.

Fortunately, John K.'s cocky, take-maximum-advantage attitude didn't cause me the ugly scene it could have. In a goal-seeking friendliness he used with the border guard, he managed to get himself a drink of pisco which supposedly was to be in exchange for convincing me to go in and talk with the guard. The guard had taken sexual interest in me upon learning from John that I was not Terry's woman. Such a situation we usually avoid by pretending to be married. All this finally ended (so I understand) in the guard's asking John whether, since I wouldn't do it for love, would I do it for money, like 500 escudos ($1.75). I was angry about being the object of such a foolish conversation which for a Latin border guard perhaps is normal but for John was purely selfish stupidity. But at least this carabinero was not aggressive enough to approach me himself, so no problem resulted.

In the evening, an excursion bus drove in, unloaded its tourists onto another bus, and prepared to return to Punta Arenas. Since Lyle wanted to go there, he talked with the driver, who it turned out would be going via Punta Delgada and would take us all to the ferry. We had a very long, comfortable ride sitting on pullman-type seats looking out the tall, wide, glass windows at prairies, fires, and herds of guanaco. At the oil company town

Cerro Sombrero, we had a long stop which gave a chance to observe the atmosphere of the 10-year-old site of pastel tin roofs, A-shaped church, glassed in gymnasium of three arches, colored squares and rectangles decorating the walls of the movie house. The streets were quiet; everyone seemed to be occupied indoors watching television, even in the casino and billiard room. Before we left the bus was filled with young workmen with small traveling bags. Some were laughing and joking all through the trip, even thru the several hours we sat waiting for the ferry in the middle of the night. I slept well in the seat despite the noise, feeling secure since the driver had offered to let us stay on across the straits to the border-Punta Arenas crossroads.

Once left off, John, Mary, Terry, and I (Lyle had gone on with the bus) set up our tents beside the road and slept a few short hours before the strong morning wind flapping the edges of the tent woke us. Before starting to hitch, we went to spend our remaining escudos at the nearby hostería (inn). The inn was a 2-story, wooden house with a long bare wooden hall onto which opened a big kitchen with wood stove and heavy, long, wooden table where we haggled over the exorbitantly priced half kilo of cheese and bread; it had an undecorated bar room and table-clothed dining room, where we drank tea at four times the usual price. The connected, glassed-in porch looked to be a pleasant place where one might read, chat, or write letters; but we dared not imagine what the price might be of such an isolated but importantly situated inn. Terry and I sat behind a bush to block off the cold dusty wind and ran up the ditch bank to hitch every time a car passed. An 11 km. ride gave us only a slight advantage of being past another exit; and besides, it picked up John and Mary who were a little further down the road. There were the 4 of us together again, this time using a country health center near an asentamiento [settlement] to shelter us from the wind. We waited here almost all day watching the few reluctant tourist cars go by and searching for the almost invisible vehicles coming along a distant road to the ferry crossing.

When we asked the people inside for hot water to make our coffee, they instead invited us indoors, sat us down at a little white table near an examining table and served us hot coffee with milk, bread, and butter. The doctor comes to this center about once a week. In the meantime, the live-in nurses take care of any emergency. An old crank telephone on the wall by the table keeps them in touch with Punta Arenas just in case.

Terry and I were finally taken as far as the Monte Aymond border station where the prairie has been broken by volcanic activity and sheep graze between black lava stones. The Banco Central has a tiny one-room building in which it carries on its dreaded business of changing foreign currency at the thieving official rates. The border officials continued a meeting inside for an hour or so, while lines of cars formed on either side of the roadblocks, and the receiving room filled with people. We asked a few for lifts, but the ones with the most room insisted most strongly that they were full. Later some young people questioned us; and although their car was in fact full, they offered to take one of us if the other could find a lift. By the time the grouchy officials appeared, we were set up for a lift to Río Gallegos where we would meet.

I crowded into one small car with two young couples from Buenos Aires. Of these four, two were psychoanalysts, one a doctor and the 4th, Pepe the driver, both a doctor and a psychoanalyst. My pack was laid across three of us in the back seat. Lively conversation about life in the US compared to life in Argentina was constant until we saw the lights of Río Gallegos.

We located the car Terry was in, and both drove us to the Salesian Mission School where we were eventually received by a thin, freckled priest who chatted unhurriedly with us as though to study our characters before showing us a place to lay our sleeping bags. A long-haired Argentine hitchhiker brought the register, a small school notebook where the travelers printed their names, addresses, destinations (I put Manizales, Colombia) and comments. We searched thru the book for familiar names and found most of the people we had met, run into, or heard of in Ushuaia including Nick and brother, Joe and Rita, David, Nigel and Elaine, Henry and Dierdra, Edwardo, Pancho, Norberto, Dave, Jim W., and Kathy but no trace of Nito, Jim, or Edder. We were shown an almost empty classroom with wooden floor, blue nonfunctioning radiators and blue-trimmed windows.

Here Terry and I and the two couples we rode here with, spread our sleeping bags. We were invited to eat supper with these people; and, although they have been camping, the meal was as Argentine style as if it would have been in their home kitchen, with 3 courses and tea. Beatriz, Pepe's wife, gave us their phone number in Buenos Aires, so we might call and go for coffee sometime. A few Argentines have come in and out, conversing, bringing medicine and hot tea and again leaving us their phone numbers in B.A.

Terry has made the acquaintance of an overly talkative Mendozan, about 35 years old, who has done a lot of bumming around South America and the U.S. and is in the process of doing more. He often talks uselessly, just to be practicing his English, and talks very loudly, a rather nerve-racking habit. This evening a number of young men sitting on the reading-table chairs are grouped around him as he sits on the floor like an old guru with his disciples. We can hear him although we are shut off in another room. Now and then a priest comes by to ask how we are doing or to introduce us to some mission visitors. We have been most appreciative of our day out of the cutting cold Patagonia winds.

FEB. 28, 1973—D.C.

From *Narcissus and Goldmund:* "It is not our purpose to become each other; it is to recognize each other, to learn to see the other and honor him for what he is, each the other's opposite and complement."

RIO GALLEGOS, ARGENTINA - FEB. 27, 1973

After crossing the Straits of Magellan on the ferry and traveling the 16 kms to the intersection, I looked at my watch and found it was 3:30 in the morning. This was the place where we spent several hours hitching a couple of weeks ago. Lyle went on to Punta Arenas and "John, the former surfer," "Mary the belly dancer" and "Danelle the wanderer" and "I the searcher" set up our tents in the gentle breezes of darkness. Danelle pulled out a handful of dried apricots and there we were. The next thing I knew, the sky was gray. The wind was tugging and pulling at our tent, and a new day had arrived bringing the worst hitching we have ever experienced. Fortunately, there was a hosteria (roadside tavern) at the same intersection where we were able to spend our remaining escudos on bread and cheese. Then we jumped out into the gale-like prairie winds to begin hitch hiking. Danelle and I hunkered down behind the minimal shelter of a bush while John and Mary waited second in line down the dusty road. After a long hour we caught a ride which took us all of 11 kms to another intersection but a little closer to the border.

So, there we waited, freezing cold, windblown, and dusty, waiting desperately, searching the freezing horizon for any sign of dust that could be kicked up by a car, truck, or anything. We didn't have shelter; but after about five hours in the knifing cold, the people in the health clinic invited us in for an "Once." Of course, they were Chileans showing Chilean hospitality. Six or seven hours passed, and finally Danelle and Mary got a slick ranchero to stop. The guys inside agreed to take me and Danelle to the border 30 kms away. Mary and John were left behind.

At the Chilean border we were able to get rides the remaining 60 kms to Rio Gallegos, Danelle in one car and I in another. Isn't it strange how people who do not have room aways make room for one more and those with room never have enough space?

We slept on the wooden floor in the classroom of a Catholic school in this windy city. We have decided to stay here today resting, for Danelle, after the last few weeks in the wind and cold, has come down with a chest cold. She is resting well now. The sun is filtering through the windows of this high ceiling classroom, but the wind never lets up. Thanks to our tent and good people, we still haven't had to pay for a night's lodging since leaving Buenos Aires. The constant dirt, dust and continuous cold make it impossible to wash our cloths and keep them clean. We must wear everything we have just to keep warm.

BARILOCH, ARGENTINA - MAR. 8, 1973

Nine hard-traveled days have passed since my last entry, and a lengthy story has unfolded. The most memorable fact about this past week is that we were unexpectedly awarded the hitch-of-all-time, a 1,700 km ride from Rio Bote to Bariloche.

We traveled across the heart of Patagonia's vast stretches of sheep grazing land on gravel roads that were bouncing, winding, endless, and dusty. Far flung estancias (ranch houses) were rare. In most places there were no towns. Only the larger estancias are marked on the map, and in places, a lonely, roadside hotel. It doesn't take long to know you are "far from nowhere." River crossings are by ferries instead of bridges. The ferries accommodate two vehicles at a time and are guided across the river's current with heavy ropes and the operator's strong arms.

Getting out of Rio Gallegos was a hassle. We received several short rides which eventually took us to the intersection leading to Lago Argentina in the Andes Mountains. A typical Italian-Argentinean truck driver took us the remaining 50 kms to the intersection. He was pot-bellied, had every other tooth missing in the front of his mouth, and was really trying to put the make on Danelle. Yuk! He showed us the .22 caliber rifle he kept behind him tucked under the blanket on his bed. At one point the guy pulled out a can of underarm deodorant spray and handed it to Danelle. She gave me a glancing look and later told me she could not figure out why the guy handed her the can: for her to know that he used it and didn't stink, or whether he thought she should use it. She handed the can back to him and said she didn't use that stuff.

The truck driver was going all the way to Buenos Aires, 2,636 kms, a four-day trip. Even as slow as he was going, it sure was tempting to hang in there with him, especially after thinking of the hitching hassle, especially for Danelle in her weakened condition.

Due to the driver's oddness, we decided it was best for us to say adios (goodbye) and climb out of his cab at the intersection. We hunkered down out of the knifing wind and waited about half an hour before we were picked up by a young guy in a pickup truck. We talked of cowboys and jobs on ranches in the USA as we bounced across the flat yellow prairie to La Esperanza where he dropped us off.

Fortunately, the weather was sunny and warm with no wind because we waited and waited there in the open as few cars and trucks went by. All were full or not going very far. I was content sitting there reading my history book of Latin America and Danelle reading the classic, *Narcissus and Goldmund.* We were enjoying the afternoon and not in a big hurry to get anyplace down the road where there might not be anything at all, not even a bush to shelter us if the wind kicked up.

Well, we waited, and waited and six hours slid by and not a ride. We still were not perturbed until 4:00 PM when the wind came streaking across these wide-open flats and started ripping through us. La Esperanza means hope, but we were feeling down. There was an expensive hotel, a gas station, and a police station there and nothing more. Hope was all we could do. Danelle and I were sitting on my rolled up sleeping bag, backs to the wind, knees drawn up and heads tucked between our crossed arms resting on top of our knobby knees, just as if we were a couple of Peruvian or Bolivian Natives huddled against the cold.

Finally, just before dark, a truck driver stopped and said he was going to Rio Bote, 122 kms north, which would leave us close to our immediate destination. There we were, saved by another Italian-Argentinean truck driver. His was very suspicious, as all truck drivers here seemed to be. He asked me twice before we even got in the truck if I had a gun and if I was going to rob him. I assured him that I did not have a gun and had no such intentions of robbing him. I told him I was a peace-loving man and even "crisscrossed my heart and hoped to die" to assure him I did not have bad intentions. This was enough for him to relax and let us climb into his cab. Getting out of that numbing wind was a welcome relief. However, climbing into the cab was a real surprise: total disorganization, paper, and trash everywhere, a half-eaten salami on the bed where we sat, and an open-topped, half-full coke bottle propped up in the corner of the bed with his dirty pillow. That was quite a contrast to all the other buttoned-down truck drivers we normally see on the road. He said his name was Victoriano. He was a first-class clown if there ever was one. Every move he made was a performance, as was his face and the whistles between sentences. It was hard to stop laughing, as he was extremely funny for the first half hour. As with other Italian truckdrivers, Victoriano's conversations and statements were filled with sexual inuendo, as if sex were an obsession with him. I knew it was coming when he finally broke out the story that former President Perón had three testicles and a 35 cm (14 inch) long penis. He said Perón killed his wife Eva with his dick and that she did not die from cancer as everyone thinks.

In the blackness of the star-studded night, we finally pulled into an estancia where our driver was to pick up a load of wool in the morning. Victoriano rummaged around under his seat and produced three loose tea bags and scraps of paper. We heated water on his butane stove while sitting parked in his cab and had hot tea, and, of course, cheese sandwiches.

The wind was still howling outside, so Danelle and I made our beds on the floor of the empty truck box. Sheltered from the wind by the side walls of the truck box, truck's huge tarp under us and our tent spread over us, I laid there quite warm staring upward into the starry night. Shooting stars were crossing the sky, and I couldn't help but feel as if they were a good omen.

In the morning Victoriano brought the first words of the lucky omen. He said, "You are lucky. I must drive to Calafate with the jefe." While the old gauchos were physically loading the huge bales of wool into the truck bed, we were invited to breakfast in the kitchen of the beautifully located estancia. Bread with strawberry jam and butter, and coffee "con leche" started the day off right. The young girl who waited on us was the daughter of the cook. We had a magnificent view of the widening valley as it spread out for miles and miles below the estancia. The yellow grass transitioned into the blues and purples of the ridge line beyond. This was not the first time I was reminded of Montana.

The kitchen had a wood-burning stove and a large table covered with an oil cloth. All the hired hands were friends from neighboring estancias who came to help to shear the sheep. They were fed and housed by the estancia. The cook said they always eat meat and not much else, meat and bread.

When we arrived at Rio Bote, we were standing in the back of the truck dressed for the cold with stocking hats, gloves, ponchos, long johns, pants, shirts, sweaters, and the rest of our clothing. That is when it happened, our "MIRACLE." The entire cosmic universe seemed to blend into one at that instant. Danelle said that all our bad hitching and time delays must have been for one reason, so we would be at that spot, Rio Bote, at that moment and time.

We met Silvio and Jane M., a couple our age from Buenos Aires. They had slept overnight at that "small dent in the road" and were just getting ready to leave when Silvio started talking to our truck driver, Victoriano, who for no reason but fate, was stopped there. When Silvio saw us in the back of that truck, he told us we could go with him, for he also was going to Calafate. That was 40 kms away, but closer to our destination, Lago Argentina, where the Moreno Glacier lay waiting for us to visit. Little did we know, this was going to be the "ride of all rides."

We climbed into Silvio's Fiat station wagon after saying goodbye to Victoriano and learned they also were going to Calafate and the Perito Moreno Glacier, so one less problem to face, that of hitching to the glacier and back. They invited us to go with them.

I really did not know what to expect as we neared the glacier. I had seen glaciers as a youth but always from a great distance, like the one above Ushuaia. As we neared the glacier, we rounded a bend; and through the trees we saw an expansive mountain valley with a magnificent ice mass wedged between the stone mountain sides. We hurried on to get closer to this stealthy, mysterious giant. Finally, we were standing face to face with a tremendous ice wall slowly creeping down the valley. Its 240-foot-tall, massive wall of iridescent ice ranging in color from white to dark blue, radiating ever-changing hues between jagged crevices and melting holes. Sharp explosions, sounding like rifle cracks and mortar fire, cut through the air as giant slabs of ice snapped off high above, falling into the azure-colored water below.

I was taken by this force of nature and was left wondering what other wonders of the world I would be fortunate to experience. A blind person, who could not see this giant, could hear the awesomeness of this slow-crawling giant. I was especially moved by the jagged, craggy top of the glacier which bore the dirt-stained scars of movement over the past thousand years. (A month ago, five people were killed. They had been standing at the water's edge alongside a tower wall of ice when a huge slab of ice fell. The ensuing wave of water had lapped them up.)

After walking around viewing the glacier from the hillside across the narrow bay from the glacier, we ate lunch on a spongy area of yellow and brown leaves. I was appalled at the total disrespect Silvio and Jane had for nature by throwing their cigarette wrappers on the ground, leaving their food bags and other trash on the ground, and walking off with a clear conscience, especially after being strongly affected by the awe-inspiring glacier they had just witnessed. As they walked to the car, I hurriedly picked up after them, leaving the spot as we found it.

On our way back to Calafate they decided that we should go with them up the route along the base of the Andes mountains instead of the boring route along the Eastern coast of the country. Fantastic, HERE WAS OUR MIRACLE. The next day, they would take us 806 kms to Perito Moreno, a whopping distance for gravel roads. We are two of the happiest people in the world. Silvio let us off at the Calafate campground where they would meet us the next morning at 7:00 am to begin our journey north.

And who should we find at the campground but our old friend the soup maker, surfer John, and his belly dancer, oboe player Mary, binocular-carrying Nigel, warm and friendly Elaine, weird Henry, and his Irish girlfriend. All are friends from Tierra del Fuego. Also, there was a middle-aged, emaciated, always-talking guy who we met while sleeping at the Catholic School in Rio Gallegos. John, of course, began to whip up a vegetable stew. It is strange to keep seeing these people repeatedly on the road.

Our long trek north was under way. River crossings were done on small, two-car ferries. A cable was strung across the river, and from it the ferries held tightly as the swift current tugged each ferry with its load across the river naturally. Two spare tires and windshield protectors are necessary for all who travel these rough roads. Even a full gas tank can help. Dust, unbelievable dust, is a constant companion. Scattered estancias, with their names marked on the map, and roads are all there is manmade out here on this great expanse.

When we came to a town, it was small, with one street, and a few houses made of mud and logs. They could have been in New Mexico. All men wear typical gaucho clothes of baggy pants tucked into calf-high boots, a colorful sash, shirt, old suit jacket, neck scarf, and a hat with small brim. The corner general store is an item of necessity. It has its central, pot-bellied stove and ubiquitous grain bins and sells everything, cloths, soap, canned foods, fresh onions, wine, tools, leather, etc.

After camping a night at Perito Moreno, we drove back 80 kms to see the 9,000-year-old cave paintings. At the site we climbed steeply down a high-walled canyon with a fresh clear water stream at its base. Green grass grew right to the water's edge while purple-flowered thistles waved in the sunny breeze. It was a magnificent setting reminiscent of parts of the Grand Canyon in Arizona. As I stood by the small stream I could see the mouth of the cave high along the face of the perpendicular rock wall. We climbed the steep, loose shale hill to get to "Cueva de las Manos" (Cave of the Hands). The cave is named for the hundreds of handprints stenciled on the walls. This wall art is one of the most important prehistoric Stone Age sites in South America.

In the cave and on the walls outside the cave, were the marks of what I thought was aerosol spray paint sprayed over the painters' hands with outstretched fingers. It was like the spatter painting we did as children to record the shape of a leaf, a flower, or our hands. These ancient people did it with natural pigments: colored red ochre, black, yellow, and brown. Carefully painted herds of wild guanacos running across the stone walls were especially interesting. While the guanacos were running, human stick figures were surrounding them, waving their arms full of motion as if to be rounding them up. One of the prints was done with an ostrich foot. What an interesting and full day this was! I found an old stone scraper near the cave, and I felt like a rich man. I buried it where I found it.

Both rear shock absorbers were so tortured on those rocky roads that they were completely useless. Silvio took the car to the garage the next morning to see about them. Danelle and I were worried that would be the end of our trip, stuck again in the middle of nowhere. Silvio came back within a half hour and said that we would continue and that the garage mechanic said the more weight in the car the better.

Feeling extremely happy, we were on the road again pushing to make 534 kms to Esquel. During the entire trip from Rio Gallegos to Esquel, we kept seeing herds of wild ostriches, or ñandu, as the gauchos call them. They take off running, wiggling their funny shaped bodies, as they stride along. Wild jackrabbits, guanacos, foxes, armadillos, horses, and flamingos are among the animals one sees every day in the Patagonia.

Sleepy villages in fertile valleys below wild bench-land, grand sunsets, constantly changing clouds, and strong yellow and brown colors make memorable setting of this part of the continent.

At Esquel, we met an American couple who had driven down in their VW van. Their motor was broken, and they were waiting until after Carnival to get it fixed. John was from California and Carol was from East Texas.

We went to the national park near there and saw more rugged mountains and deep blue lakes. Best of all, we stopped at a waterfall that seemed to put us in a good frame of mind. It's something one can spend hours watching. I climbed to the top of it to see what the stream looked like before it crashed to the rocks below. I was impressed by its diminutive size. It was smaller than I imagined.

Danelle and I splurged that night. We bought two huge steak dinners for $1.00 apiece. Included with the meal was bread, salad, soup, wine, chorizo, T-bone steak, two fried eggs and tea. We deserved that after all those days of cheese and lunch meat sandwiches. That was a fitting meal for us two raggedy, dusty, worn-out travelers.

Our days with Silvio and Jane were very warm, for these two people were very open and interesting beings. We conversed about politics, the Vietnam war, churches, and the Jewish religion. Both Silvio and Jane, now our good friends, are intelligent and interesting to talk to. At one point in a heated discussion, Silvio stopped the car, told his wife to drive and climbed into her seat so he could really jump into the argument. We were talking about the American military in Vietnam. He was really riled up.

They have given us not only a 1,700 km ride through the roughest part of their scenic country but have even extended an invitation for us to stay at their home in Buenos Aires. Jane speaks Hebrew and Silvio's hobby is studying UFO's and their relationship with the Mayans, Aztecs, and Incas.

Finally, Silvio and I changed the shock absorbers while in Esquel and drove the remaining short distance to the ski resort town of Bariloche. This town is high in the Andes with gift shops, stores selling chocolates and tourists. The town plaza is the oldest and best part of town with many rustic stone and log buildings. The old post office, municipal building, and museum are excellent examples of Swiss alpine-style architecture. The tall clock tower has wood-carved figures of an Indian, a missionary, a conquistador, and a colonialist which appear in a small door below the large clock. At 12:00 noon the clock door opens, and the procession of the four figures begin their rotation as if dancing around the edge of a disc. The clock is disappointing; but the plaza and its multicolored flowers overlooking the blue glacial Lake Nahuel Huapi, the towering Andes Mountains, cloudless sky and floating clouds are impressive.

One day we paid $3.00 apiece and took a tour of the area. The boat took us to Arrayanes National Park, where the strange forest of orange-colored trees, twisted and winding, project a fabled feeling of a wonderland, where the boat captain said Walt Disney chose to film the movie Bambi. Our boat then took us to Victoria Island where there is a forest experimental station. They planted every type of tree from around the world that can grow in this mountain environment.

One of the strange experiments is the number of giant Sequoias planted within 5 feet of each other. The ranger said within 40 years they will be joined together as a sort of tree wall. It would be interesting to see them then. We have overdosed on mountain and lake scenes, so the tour didn't come off as strong as it could have. We have just seen too many lakes and mountains.

MARCH 8, 1973—**D.C.**

We were extremely happy to see Silvio and Jane come honking up to the campground where we sat on our packs waiting for them. We were to realize that day that our good luck would extend further than we had ever dreamed. Besides offering us so much help, Silvio and Jane were very open to our friendship and were wonderful people to know and accompany. We were afraid that we would have to get out because of our extra weight when the hydraulic shock absorbers were broken by rocks and drained, but the mechanics told Silvio that on the contrary, the more weight the better!

For the next 4 days we accompanied them, bumping along 1600 kilometers of serruchos [ruts in the road] and flying gravel which inspires the use of windshield screens which are such a common sight in Southern Argentina. We passed vast, seemingly unfenced expanses of prairie, long mesas of yellow grass clumps. In some areas plants were not growing and rocks occupied the pale ground surface. Hills, some with bizarrely shaped, rock outcroppings, varied the scene along with the comparatively green river valleys, where among planted rows of poplar, willow, and other trees, could be seen the chapa, brick, or stone buildings of estancias and one-street towns. Our maps of Argentina fill in this area's spaces (like Tierra del Fuego) with the names of roadside inns and estancias, and even those are very far apart. The evening shadows of sage clumps, canyons, dust, thin flattened clouds, still and deep grays on hot pink sky get my admiring attention. Guanacos were almost as common a sight as the frightened sheep. They would lope away from the road to a safe distance, where they could stand and curiously watch the car go by. Just as frequently we came upon flocks of gray ostriches (ñandu as the gauchos say) who ran desperately, their tail feathers flopping and swinging. Thousands of small, white-breasted birds exploded into a rapid, zig-zagging flight, all flashing their white undersides together in code. Once or twice small foxes crossed our path. Two flamingos stood in a small pond we passed.

Then after several days of travel through this desolate sheep country, I reacted excitedly at seeing Hereford cattle near Esquel. In the area of Lago Viedma, the car had to be taken across river by ferry at 3 separate places. These free, state-owned ferries are connected to cables and operate by the push of the current. Some maneuvering is done when the operators use their bat-like notched poles to hook, push and pull away from the cable. These ferries take one or two cars at a time and go into operation as soon as a vehicle arrives.

MARCH 11, 1973—D.C.

Again my days have been so occupied with traveling and my corresponding lack of writing concentration that I have let the time rapidly pass without recording its small circle of events that whirl around us. But since we are lying in the tent all day to keep out of the drizzling rain, I have the opportunity to retrace the steps which brought us from Río Gallegos to the forested edge of Lago Espejo, which is located on the Road of Seven Lakes near San Carlos de Bariloche, a distance of about 2,000 kilometers. Though it is not so difficult to remember these events and their order, this dry, late recording seems to make it impossible to record the scenes with the vividness they deserve.

There was (Feb. 28) the first middle-aged Italian-type, truck driver with the rifle under his blanket for protection against hitch-hiking robbers. He freshly demanded my attention by constantly tapping my arm or whereever he happened to hit with the back of his hand as he talked. His almost bitter questioning and conversing was the type that often leads to a scornful, indirect, then direct, sexual proposition. He even once handed me a flowery can of underarm deodorant. I wasn't sure whether he was trying to demonstrate his own desirability by showing that he used it or trying to improve my desirability by offering it for my use. At any rate I was counteracting all the advances I could and didn't hesitate to tell him that I never put on the stuff. I was certainly glad that we were getting off at a nearby crossroads to Lake Argentina and wouldn't be tempted to continue with him on his 4-day-and-night trip to Buenos Aires.

At another site we waited all afternoon huddling close in our ponchos to modify the bite of the blasts of wind. Pillars of clouds rose from the horizon piling up into the 180 degrees sky dome. We were picked up here by a boisterous, jolly truck driver who made us promise that we weren't carrying arms and wouldn't rob him before he would let us in. We moved aside salami and loaves of bread so we could sit on his disorderly cab bed. This time Terry sat on the inside and had to absorb the sounds of this lonely man who had scarcely talked to anyone for 3 days. At the top of his voice the driver sang bawdy songs, told jokes like how is an ambulance like a bra—they both pick up the fallen—spoke of how Perón had 3 testicles and a 42-cm. long penis which eventually killed his wife Eva whom he had tamed from the life of a pornographic film star, pretended he didn't know where he was, made dirty signs, and talked about how the people on the estancias spent their winters "planting" (sembrando) babies. One of the few interesting and believable things he explained was the use of the house-shaped boxes we saw at the estancia gates. Mail, food, etc. was left there to be taken to or brought from town as ordered by note or telephone from a regular, trustworthy errand truck that travels these roads between towns. Our driver's horn was broken (thank God!), so he whistled loudly at every sheep and rabbit.

As sunset drew near, the flat landscape changed to hills; we could see snowy peaks again on the horizon. It was night when we went down a steep hill and turned sharply into the Estancia María where the truck was to pick up a load of wool bales. Victoriano invited us to come with him to the estancia and sleep in the back of his empty truck instead of putting us out along the road to set up our tent in the dark however we might. We jumped at the chance to go because we had long been wanting to see something of estancia life in these areas. Victoriano was very uneasy that the estanciero [rancher] might discover he had two hitchhikers with him, so he had to say we were his neighbors in Buenos Aires. He refused his supper at the still-lighted kitchen saying he had friends in the truck he wanted to have tea with. He sat with us in the cab and heated water for our lemon in a little kettle on his small tank stove and talked to us as we ate our bread and cheese. Although there was a thick tarp under us and our tent spread open over our sleeping bags, I slept very lightly. With every creak of the truck, I would wake up and be a while looking at the clear brilliant rainbow of the Milky Way which arched above us. Since we are usually sleeping inside the tent, it was a special occasion for us to be able to look out at the stars from our beds.

MARCH 12, 1973—D.C.

I was astounded by the beauty of what I saw when I got up in the morning and looked over the edge of the high, truck bed. The few brick structures of the estancia sat in a semi-circle of rounded, gray-green, gold-trimmed hills flowing out to a wide yellow valley where a road and a thin river disappeared into the shadows of barren, dark-blue ridges. Near the closed barn the bales of wool waited to be assessed and loaded. A rickety 20's pickup was parked near and soon would have to be moved so that the truck trailer could be backed up to the loading embankment. Smoke coming from the stovepipe chimney indicated activity in the main house, and before long the workers were appearing from behind the kitchen door.

Victoriano informed us that we were lucky that he would have to make an unexpected trip to Calafate to take the ranch boss to get some necessary papers, and we would be able to go with him if we would ride in the truck box. He also threw in the tease that the rocking of the truck box had awakened him in the night. What had we been doing to make it rock so much? (We had felt some rocking ourselves but thought it was his turning over in bed!) Anyway, as we waited to leave and hesitantly stood watching the preparations for loading, the graying boss who had on a black Andalusian felt hat, a colorful pink and green faja [hand-woven belt] wrapped around the waist of his gathered pants, and black alparagatas (rope-soled cloth sandals), told us to go to the kitchen for coffee.

We were well received there by a mature, simply dressed teenage girl and her mother who were busy cooking, washing dishes, and making bread at the cabinet below a long glass window which offered a view of the valley. I questioned them about their life at the estancia so as to compare it with my experiences on ranches in the U.S. It sounded similar in many ways, the bread-making, the men's strong preference for an unvaried diet of potatoes, bread, and lots of meat (even for breakfast here), the loneliness alleviated occasionally by friendships on neighboring estancias, and the cooking for extra men when some special work required extra hands (only here most are friends from neighboring estancias). In this kitchen the big, iron, wood-burning stove has advanced in usefulness by the addition of a water heating system, a step our technological advancement mostly skipped.

Questions about the long winter are again answered with emphasis on the amount of snow. These people were surprised to see that one of Victoriano's "amigos" was a female and that I had slept out in the truck box. Very obviously they would have been happy to give us supper and a place to sleep indoors; but since we had to follow up on the story Victoriano had given them, we said we had recently immigrated to B.A. from the U.S. and were his neighbors. We had coffee and plenty of jam and bread; and while Terry was out trying to take a picture of the loading, I was offered a *Gente [People]* magazine to read, the in-crowd, Porteña society magazine with articles about movie stars and other artists, fashion, and beauty contests.

As we rode along in the back of the truck, we had to stand on the huge spare tires in order to look out at the passing scene of yellow grass clumps and distant snow peaks. The truck stopped at a hotel near a river, a place called Río Bote. Before we knew it, Victoriano was opening the steel box door and introducing us to a young Argentine tourist couple, Silvio, and Jane, who had agreed to give us a ride the rest of the distance to Calafate. So Victoriano, the vulgar, boisterous truck driver delivered us to the care of this sophisticated young man and woman with one last tease that since we didn't have the money to pay him for the trip, that I should stay with him.

Silvio and Jane rearranged their luggage and set up the back seat which lays down to form a bed in their small station wagon. We soon realized that our good luck extended much further than we had imagined. They also would take us to the Glacier Moreno at Lago Argentina stopping along the way so we could speak to every acquaintance we saw including Dutch Robert, the Swiss woman, the Mendozan, Henry, Dierdra, and Norberto.

We stopped so both Silvio and Terry could take pictures of our first spectacular view of the huge, jagged, glacier peaks that ascended gradually into the sierra where the pure white snow so blended with the color of the sky as to make the miles of blue ice and snow appear to stretch out eternally into space. At the end of the road Silvio parked the car with others, and we walked down the hillside to get closer views where we began to realize the enormity of this glacier not only in expanse but in height and force. Jagged pale blue, 100-200 ft. high pillars of ice fused, some erect, some curved with deep blue chasms between them. Sharp delicately balanced chunks of ice of varying sizes sit precariously above on the slowly melting top surface and eventually fall crackling like a gun shot, smashing into the lake creating waves (which have at times been large enough to carry to their deaths tourists standing too near the lake's edge), then floating as bizarre-shaped icebergs at the feet of mother glacier.

The small leaves of the trees near the rocky lake shore were in fall colors. We sat on the leaf-covered forest floor with Silvio and Jane for a lunch of fiambres (lunch meat), cheese with bread and Orange Crush. The conversation was very pleasant, interesting, and relaxed, about movies, books, life in our countries, travel.

By the time we were back at the campground at Calafate where we had a noisy and story-filled reunion with John, Mary, Nigel and Elaine, Silvio had offered to take us north along the cordillera to the town Perito Morena, a very long distance and agreed to pick us up early in the morning at the campground. We had been planning to return along the more boring but more traveled Atlantic Coast road but with much talk and this lift, Silvio convinced us easily to try the mountain route.

Later as we talkatively were shared supper with John and Mary, I paid for always kidding Terry about his habitual dropping of food on the ground. I spilled a whole pot of macaroni and asparagus soup, [I was totally mortified and disappointed!], the second course. Dogs peed on the K.'s rucksack. Elaine gave us a little, old, rusty alcohol-burning wick stove from Colombia made of a tin can and other scraps. It was so worn and so appropriately matching our gear and down-and-out appearance that we elatedly accepted it and showed it off as though we had been given a beautiful work of art. We slept lightly, waking almost every hour to check the time because whatever we did, we were determined not to miss this unbelievably lucky ride for early morning.

MARCH 23, 1973—D.C.

A characteristic Terrance Brown quotation "Such a small world, but so grand!"

[This is Danelle's last journal entry.]

PUERTO MADRYN, ARGENTINA - MAR. 16, 1973

Here we are again, sitting in the sand on the side of a sandy beach road on the other side of the continent. Also hitching here are John, Mary, and Lyle. Strange how we keep running into each other. We all arrived in town about the same time and, by happenstance, met in front of the bread store. Just like that! They had traveled up the Atlantic coast, and we had come up through the mountains. It sure was good to see them. We had not seen Lyle since we separated at 3:00 AM just after leaving Tierra de Fuego. We last saw John and Mary at the campground in Calafate where John cooked us a big stew. Well, yesterday, he did it again. At noon, we had a big stew of lamb, potatoes, squash, carrots, seasoning, cabbage and other goodies like onion and garlic, all cooked on his little gas stove, barely strong enough to support the big pot.

We were huddled on the dirt floor of the Catholic church's garage, thanks to the Father. He was a kind man. Last night we were put up in a grade school where the kids live while attending school. The cooks let John have full rein of the kitchen with its huge central stove. With all that room, big pans, cutting board, etc., he went wild cooking up a king-sized meal and roasted lamb "asado." We were stuffed and had a mountain of dishes to do, but it was truly worth it. We even had a bed to sleep in and a shower to bathe in. It was raining outside.

We share our good fortune with the bad, for they both come hand in hand. Just after leaving Bariloche to camp in the seven lakes district just north of there, we spent a day and a half lying horizontal in our little pup tent waiting out a constant downpour. We were on a beautiful glassy lake called Lago Espejo (Mirror Lake); it was nice, warm, and sunny when we arrived with great hope of warm, relaxed camping.

I washed my clothes and body in the lake and just barely got them dry when the wind came up. I scouted out a more sheltered place, and there we struck our tent. There we lay, horizontal and damp. If we sat up, we would touch the slanting pup tent roof with our shoulders or back and cause the water to run through. We lay there reading, writing, sleeping, and even cooking soup on our little alcohol stove. We ate cheese and pate de foie gras (duck or goose liver) sandwiches, raw carrots, and an Argentine candy named Mantecol which we have grown to enjoy. It is a semi-soft nougat made from peanut butter and tastes somewhat like a Baby Ruth candy bar.

On the morning of the third day Danelle went to a nearby house and asked if she could buy some bread. The lady sold her a very hard home-baked loaf and a package of crackers which was our total food supply plus a little jar of cherry jam that Michelle gave us. The man of the house told her that because it rained all night, it probably wouldn't begin raining again until noon. We decided to pack and head for the road where we waited and waited in the rain which did not let up. It seems like every time we go camping for fun, rest, and relaxation, it storms, rains and thunders.

There we were, sitting at a once-dusty crossroad huddled under a piece of black construction plastic pulled tightly around our shoulders. We scrunched like that for three hours. Two cars passed and did not notice us. They probably thought we were construction material stacked along the road's edge covered with plastic, like sacks of cement or something.

Suddenly there came a car, and it stopped. I still had rain dripping off my nose. The driver said he was going to San Martin and to hop in. He said, "Do you have many things?" I enthusiastically said no and hopped in. He was a good guy and said he usually never picks up hitchhikers, but with us stuck out there in the mountains, he could not pass us by. He took us to San Martín, Junín, and out of the mountains to Neuquén, halfway across Argentina. He even took us to a campsite on the edge of town. He was a fine, fine man.

Next morning, I thought I was back in Saigon hitching on the smoggy, noisy, crowded road that goes through town. I had a strange feeling when we arrived in that town the night before. We entered a strip, like in any town USA, with glassy store fronts lit from the inside, neon signs, a carnival all ablaze, and Bobby Vee singing one of his classic songs on the car radio. It was a strange experience to be in a big, hustling, noisy, smoggy town again where we must look four or five times in both directions before crossing the street. Danelle and I felt, and probably looked, like mountain people just out of the wilderness.

We did a lot of waiting along the road the next day; but after several shorties, we snagged two big ones, both jewels. We were "kings of the road," riding in the back of pickup trucks tooling down the road. I was sitting on huge boulders in the bed of the first truck; and in the second, I was huddled under my poncho. The wind was whipping my hair and face, and black ribbon of road was rapidly passing under the zinging tires. The gypsy-like guy who picked us up was a butcher who raced cars. We covered 451 kms traveling an average of 120 kms per hour. Hauling balls, he pushed that pickup truck along the open stretches of new asphalt. He took us within six kms from our destination, the intersection of the road.

The butcher had his wife and two little kids in the front with him while Danelle and I and his puppy shared the back. When night came, we put Danelle's sleeping bag over our legs and pulled the butcher's bloody, stinky tarp over the top of us to keep off the driving wind and rain.

We pitched our tent at that intersection and slept beside the road as always, cars or no cars zinging by. We caught a quick ride to Puerto Madryn the next morning; and that's when we met John, Mary, and Lyle for the seventh time.

I am surprised with our good fortune. Ever since Maggie gave Danelle that silver ring with special symbols, we have been recognizing it's worth. Maggie did say she would help us. I guess we would have gotten to all the places without it, but the improbable rides we've gotten to help make our lives a little easier are impressive. Maggie gave the silver ring to Danelle after finding Danelle was worried about getting on the Chilean boat heading South. She said "It is a ring of good luck. It has negative and positive vibrations in the form of horizontal lines, but several stars cut its way into the lines to cross both the negative and positive forces." With it we got our boat ride to Punta Arenas and good hitching to and from Ushuaia and Calafate and from Bariloche to Puerto Madryn, all in a brief period of time. Strange things, beautiful feeling!

We are camped nestled beside a sand dune on an Atlantic beach called Puerto Pirámedes where there is a sea lion reserve 10 kms to the north where the sea lions are protected. It is a nice feeling to see such graceful animals in their native habitat. This reserve was created three years ago. Until that time, these beautiful animals were hunted ruthlessly in this area. Older sea lions still remember this, making it dangerous for humans to go near them. I watched them from a hillside listening to their barking, yells, and groans. They are very sluggish on land; but in the sea, look out!

John's out cooking spaghetti for all of us while Lyle, Danelle and I sit in our cozy little tent, candle flickering in the middle, where we eat our cheese sandwiches and raw carrots. It is a comfortable warm feeling in here.

PUERTO PIRAMIDES - MAR. 17, 1973

What a pleasant, clean beach this is with no oil slicks, clear blue ocean, and no people. A small town of 80 people is nearby. The water was down about 12 feet because the tide was out. Circling the bay are jutting sandstone projections extending to the sea. The sea lion reserve is within view and thousands of black shells completely cover the sandstone abutments. Endless small clam or mussel shells are glued to the sandy cliffs. This is a beautiful place. Now we are sitting around a borrowed table. John is cooking spaghetti sauce. We are talking about how to make money in Buenos Aires as we are nestled among the sand dunes. Mary wants to belly dance in Plaza Francia instead of sleezy clubs to make money. Now we are talking about being constipated. Mary says she's been constipated for weeks.

The guy who owns the table let us use his propane stove and gave us wine. Now we are half drunk, feeling good like a family reunited once again for the seventh time. It was a good sunset. Now we are talking about having to pee in the early morning, moaning about having to crawl out into the cold from warm sleeping bags. John said he was going to whip up an easy dessert. This is a nice evening. Hugo, a guy from Buenos Aires, just rushed up with a pan of fried minnows and salmon. What a friendly gesture! It will be nice when I can be in a

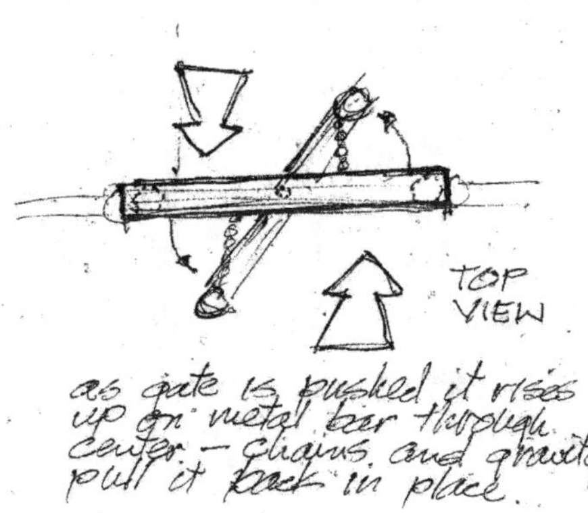

situation where I can treat people like they treat me here in South America.

John's cleaning up now, and Lyle's reading Danelle's diary. Mary's eating bread and Danelle's talking. John's stirring the pudding. It's going around in a circle being shared by everyone. It's going to be one beautiful, moony night. Lyle eats everything and anything. Good stories, good people! We tried to hitch out of here this morning but had no luck, so we stayed this day.

PUERTO MADRYN - MAR. 18, 1973

First thing this morning, we hitched a ride to see the sea elephants and sea lions. Eduardo and Hebe picked us up and sped down the road. Just before we caught the ride, Danelle and I were able to wash up a little and get a big drink of fresh water in the Argentine Automobile Club (ACA) gas station.

Eduardo drove fast, and I feared for our lives; but what could I do? We were on our way to the Elefanteria (Sea lion reserve), a long way from nowhere. After driving across 70 kms of mostly flat, sage-brush country, where nothing but birds, guanacos, ostriches, and sheep roamed, we finally arrived. And to my amazement there were the huge, rolling-with-blubber, sea elephants. They just lay all stretched out in the sand. At times, a hand-like front flipper would scoop up the sand and heave it over its back or it would scratch its face or side. We were able to see these animals much closer than the others in Pirámedes. Huge male sea lions with lion-like faces and necks with long fur had their families gathered around them as they lounged near the crashing waves. The young sea lions frolicked in the edge of the ocean.

We then walked to the place where thousands of sun-bleached bones lay on the beach. After watching live sea lions, it was a strange sight to see this multitude of bones of massacred ones. They had been killed by the thousands for their skins and blubber for oil. How insane! White bones littered the beach for over a mile. We found ancient jaw bones and pried out two huge teeth for a remembrance.

After this place we circled the whole peninsula, stopping to see more sea lions lounging in the sun far below on a rocky cove. Sandstone cliffs dropped straight down to the sanctuary, offering them ideal protection. The turquoise-green water, misty background, white and red cliffs, and sunny sky left warm impressions.

We pushed on to Punta Delgada, a narrow point with a lighthouse. There we climbed up to the top floor of the lighthouse to look at the lamp. I had no idea the lighthouse lamps were so complicated. Setting on a mercury-guided, precision base were huge, curved-glass prisms, illuminating gas light thousands of times. I've wanted to climb the winding stairs of a lighthouse since I was about 10 years old.

The trip back to Puerto Pirámedes was striking with undulating prairie, purplish-blue salt lakes, open sky, and mud puddle roads. We immediately caught a ride back to Puerto Madryn where we are now camped. Our tent is pitched on the roaring beach under a full moon. We ate cheese sandwiches and crackers with jelly, an apple, and some candy. I'm ready for bed. Tomorrow we are going to the bakery and then head for Buenos Aires.

80 KMS SOUTH OF BAHIA BLANCA - MAR. 19, 1973

Danelle and I just pitched our tent on the soft, fine, sandy soil of a barrow ditch beside the gasoline tanker we've been riding in all day. I spent most of the day stretched out on the driver's bed which made an otherwise slow, boring ride enjoyable. I even read a few pages in my book, *The Source* by James Mitchener, as we crawled along. Danelle can neither sleep nor read in a vehicle. We weren't planning on hitching with truck drivers; but when he stopped and said, "Vamanos" (let's go), we jumped in. This is a tranquil spot, even if it is beside the main highway. Cows are mooing in the background while a fog, wet and fresh is moving in. Frogs are adding to the music but the occasional car streaking by adds to the symphony of nature like crashing cymbals.

We ran into John, Mary, and Lyle again this morning as we were hitching out of Puerto Madryn. They were sleeping at the school and had a big meal all made up, thinking we had come. Such as it is!

BUENOS AIRES-ONE MORE TIME - 21 MAR. 21, 1973

After traveling hard for three months to the day, we finally returned to this huge, bustling city. It was a nice feeling to finally be back. We both need a rest after these thousands of kilometers we have put between us and the 21st of December, when we set off on our adventure to the wild lands of the Patagonia.

We looked odd and out of place in our traveling rags while we were walking through ever-moving traffic. We had tasted it in Bariloche for the first time, and now we're in it deeply. Carrying our gear on buses, traveling from one part of this city to Silvio and Jane's apartment, was an inimitable experience. One bus driver was unfriendly, people stared and gawked, and a caretaker told us to go away when he found us sitting on the front steps of his fancy high-rise apartment building. We told him we were waiting for Silvio and Jane who are expecting us. He said it wouldn't look good for us to be sitting on the steps nor waiting in the lobby. So here we are, leaning against a humble building across the street waiting for our friends to arrive.

We have passed through poor neighborhoods of Buenos Aires where people live in shacks among factories. I saw nothing like the slums of other cities this size, but these are poor people. It seems like all the barrios of B.A. are like the other small towns of this country. Sidewalks are made of rough, broken, clay tiles about 8 inches square. The streets are lined with short, round trees which are severely pruned in the Fall to keep their round form. The leaves are large and are the same general shape of a maple leaf. Buildings on the corners are always cut at a 45-degree angle to aid the view of drivers as they enter the intersection. This must be a national building code, for few buildings escape this rule, and those that do are very old. The houses are small and neat. Some, like those in Spain, have exterior walls that rise from the edge of the sidewalk; others, like the English, sit back a short distance to allow for a small plot of grass and flowers with a hedge or a simple low fence built across the front at the edge of the sidewalk. Large houses have higher walls along the property edge, painted steel fences, and hedges. The sweet fragrance of flowers fills the air and radiates from these knobby trees.

The ice cream vendors and the sausage, fruit, vegetable, and cheese shops vie for business on busy intersections. The small confiterias (shops), that sell wine, soda, coffee, and tea, provide small tables with chairs for customers who want to talk and pass time. Choice tables are always on the sidewalk where young girls walk wearing this year's styles, mama and the kids wanting this and that, and oh, the flavor of those ice creams. There is the shaggy bum standing glued in one spot listening to music blaring from the loudspeaker in front of the candy and cigarette shops. Everybody strolls by peering at the brightly lit window displays or just stroll around the block.

We did not get very far yesterday because most of the day was spent hitching along the long black highway. The afternoon we spent waiting around in the car of a friendly, clean-cut businessman who made his sales in the city of Coronel Dorrego. The day wasn't totally wasted since our driver bought us four sizeable smoked-ham-and-cheese sandwiches, a large beer for me, and, not one, but two Pepsi Colas for Danelle. One sandwich and the drinks filled us, so we took the other two along for supper. He also bought us a sweet-tasting bunch of grapes and, later down the road, a tea and several Alfajores, a very sweet bisque-like pastry with dulce de leche inside. He must have thought we were starving to death.

He dropped us off on the outskirts of Tres Arroyos with another traveling salesman who took us to Necochea where we pitched our little pup tent for the last night. These last couple of days have been warm enough for Danelle to take off her poncho and bulky sweater and let her hair down. This helps getting rides as she says, "At least they know one of us is a woman."

Our tent was still damp from the night's mist when we packed up after sleeping along the side of the road. When we unrolled the tent on the beach at Necochea, sand was stuck to everything: the mosquito net, the tent top, and both beneath and on the tent floor. It was hopeless; sand kept falling in our faces the entire night. The next day, after getting to the edge of town on a city bus, we waited with great patience while reading our books. I am reading *First Circle* by Solzhenitsyn. At times I get so wrapped up in my book that I forget to stick my thumb in the air as a car drives by.

After this long wait of sitting on my rolled up sleeping bag and Danelle on her pack, a guy pulls up and whisks us off to Buenos Aires, just like that. So, we were good as home. We were in this 35-year-old Yugoslavian immigrant's car cruising along the hardtop. I groped along the edge of the seat. When I felt a seat belt, my spirits sprang up. I felt better being strapped in while speeding down the road because I was riding shotgun. Danelle liked to ride in the back seat to keep the driver from having strange ideas and because she did not enjoy marathon conversations. I did. It did wonders for my Spanish.

We drove through Miramar and Mar de Plata, two beautiful beach resort towns of the highest caliber. The driver told us that Mar de Plata has the largest gambling casino in the world. I was impressed by seeing great expanses of green, manicured grass and round trees growing to the edge of the cliffs which fall to the breaking waves of the ocean below. Mar de Plata is a large, clean, and exciting city. From these cliffs thousands of people appear like ants walking along the beach. An airplane, trailing jets of smoke, towed a banner advertising NIVEA hand cream. Huge old English, half-timbered houses sit on the slopes above the main beach. The high-rise apartments and hotels begin at the edge of the ocean. There is a definite relaxed-dress requirement here as compared to Buenos Aires. Even old men walk into stores without shirts on. The Argentines like to compare Mar de Plata to Miami Beach.

BUENOS AIRES - MAR, 23, 1973

After waiting for Silvio and Jane until 10:00 PM, we called Dan Figgins, the young American friend of ours who works in the US Embassy. He said, "Come on over!," and that is where we are now.

Yesterday I went to the US Embassy and picked up forty-two letters and four packages. I felt like a king. That is a three-inch stack of letters. It took me five minutes just to open them all.

BUENOS AIRES - APR. 2, 1973

Oh, this beautiful city and all its excitement! So much is going on that I just don't know how I will get everything done before I leave. I have been having an enjoyable time lounging in Dan's big mansion with these good people. The first night we got here, they handed us a tray of huge brownies supreme which sent me soaring. It's been nice seeing all our old friends, especially Oscar (friend who gave us the pup tent). The weather has been perfect with a lot of sun and not too much humidity. The trees are still flowering, and grass is green as ever.

I met a beautiful young lady named Nazaria (Zari) L. who has helped make my stay in Buenos Aires memorable. Last night, as I was accompanying her to her apartment (girls only), our spirits interconnected. So, I asked her if she knew of a place where we could spend some private time together. She knew of an alojamiento (accommodation) near her place, so off we went. The guy at the desk asked me if I wanted two hours or the entire night, so I said two hours. He handed the key to room 505 and I paid him $2.50. We tangled in each other's arms and legs for two short hours. There were blue lights on the wall at the head of the bed, a radio, a huge wall mirror on the wall beside the bed, and a clean bathroom. I have heard about these places in Latin America but never thought I'd get a chance to experience one. Alojamiento Brooklyn on Junín 759 is quite a fancy place.

BUENOS AIRES - APR. 6, 1973

Dan is a good guy for opening his home to us. It is an enjoyable experience to live here with all these different people who are here, there, and everywhere, then all come together for supper. There's Vox Dei (Voice of God), Willey, who is a member of a well-known rock and roll group in Argentina; and Canadian Willy who traveled down here by land with the hope of living in Argentina. It is strange to know someone wanting to leave Canada. There's Chris who is waiting for his wife to drive their VW bug down here from the States with Crazy Barry. There is Scott, who is Dan's two-year-old son; and of course, Dan who is a diplomat in the US Embassy; and Blanca, a beautiful, warm, loving girl who spends her nights with Dan when she is not rooming with Zari. Chris is a quiet, talented man who plays the guitar and dulcimer well and makes excellent detailed jewelry.

We are all learning in this situation. Dan is a very intelligent man struggling with a career in the State Department but wants to grow into education which his wife has been into all along. At some point he will get it together. I think his mind would be better off in the creative teaching field, not only for himself, but for the kids who will learn under him. He has much to offer.

We are having a surprise birthday party for Blanca tonight. It should be an enjoyable time. She is turning twenty-one.

I am coming down with a something. My shoulders ache, and my neck glands are swollen. It has been raining all night and all morning. I have a few things to do but don't know if I will get them done.

Danelle's decided to go with me to Uruguay; but then she's going to come back to help take care of Nito, who will soon be getting out of the hospital. He has hepatitis. She said she is not ready to leave yet and is meeting some fine people here, so she's staying in Buenos Aires a while longer.

One of the guys she met is a Chicano from Los Angeles who was in Vietnam in 1966, '67 and '68. He drove convoy trucks and one time ran over a mine that knocked him out of his truck and wounded his arm. He received a Purple Heart Medal but was disappointed because the truck that was blown up was brand-new; and after the incident, all they gave him was an "old crate." He said he always had two wall lockers full of candy, cigarettes, etc. to sell on the black market because he had five ration cards instead of one. He said he traded a box of ice cream to an officer for a jeep, so he had his own wheels to get around to make black market deals. Understandably he was a sergeant who got thrown out of the Army with a dishonorable discharge while back on a post in the States. These are interesting stories. He said he got out of Nam when it started becoming modernized with everybody watching movies every night, sleeping in buildings instead of tents, refrigerators in most every room, etc. "You know, like on TV."

TIGRE, ARGENTINA - APR. 10, 1973

I have finally gotten it together to leave Buenos Aires and head for Brazil. It has been comfortable living here, but I must move on to Rio de Janeiro. I am crossing the Rio Plata on a small boat that goes to Caramelo, Uruguay, from Tigre. We're motoring along in a canal now which appears like a liquid road with houses lining both sides. It's very lush and green with trees and shrubbery growing down to the water's edge. Reeds sway back and forth as the waves of brown water lap against them. The $4.50 boat ride takes about four hours to reach Uruguay.

These houses lining the rivers are English-style houses of the early 1900s and appear cozy, comfortable, and ornate. They are vacation houses. Each one has a dock and a name sign, and it's not unusual to see people waiting on them for the river taxis.

Night before last Zari and I went to the Brooklyn Alojamiento again because it was going to be our last night together. I have enjoyed her company. My life has grown richer through our short, sensual relationship.

Yesterday I mailed the last of my packages to the States. It feels good to get rid of all that stuff. I am getting my traveling gear down to the bare minimum, and I still have too many things. These last couple of days I have visited the sites of Buenos Aires that I knew before traveling to Chile. It was nice to pass by all these familiar places and buildings one more time: Banco de Londres (Bank of London), Plaza de Mayo (Central Park), Casa Rosada (Pink House), El Edificio del Ejercito (Military Building), 9 de Julio (July 9), my old office, the works.

Danelle left for Uruguay yesterday morning with Rick, her new friend. I am supposed to meet them in Caramelo, Uruguay when the boat arrives.

MONTEVIDEO, URUGUAY - APR. 11, 1973

Danelle met me after I passed through customs into Uruguay, said goodbye, and hitched out to Paraguay. She and Rick caught a ride with a truck driver. I've been waiting here for about three hours and nothing, except a promise from a guy who said he'd be coming back about 6:30 PM. I am already very lonely and miss Danelle.

The guy did return; and a 17-year-old Chilean hitchhiker named Hernán and I were on the road for Montevideo. I feel anxious being with him. He has no money and is even begging from me as well as everyone he sees. He expected me to buy him a cafe con leche (coffee with milk). I am sharing my food with him. Both our rides today were with well-meaning people, but Hernán would get into great, heated, political discussions, so heated that one of the drivers wanted to put us out. Hernan was begging cigarettes from truckdrivers and gas station attendants. He scored some sandwiches from a restaurant where I was looking for a telephone number. I wanted to separate and get rid of him. He made me nervous. When we got to the center of town, I told him I was going to split and call a friend, a guy who gave me his address on the boat from Argentina. He lives with his family, and I did not want to invite Hernan for fear of intruding on my invitation. Hernán was forceful and expected me to ask if he could also stay with my friend. "Qué peso!" (What a heavy scene!) My friend had no number, so that solved that; but we were on the street with nowhere to sleep.

About that time, a small man named Rubén came up and started talking to us; and I asked him if he had a floor on which we could sleep. After a little indecision due to his being afraid, naturally, he said he'd put us up. We hopped a bus and are now sitting around a table in a funky house that looks like a gaucho's house in the campo. It has a brick floor, burlap-covered walls painted white which is mostly worn off, leather reins, plastic bags, a bicycle frame, dried branch with leaves, a towel, and a smudged black-bottom pot both hanging on the tattered burlap wall. A bare light bulb hung from the center of the tiny room which was cluttered with oilcloth-draped tables. A new refrigerator stands in the corner. Through a low doorway is the bedroom with two beds and saddles. I feel as if an old gaucho lives here. No, it is Rubén's house, and he is a little different or lonely.

MONTEVIDEO - APR. 12, 1973

We slept until 1:30 in the afternoon and gathered our things and headed for the center of town. I told Hernan we were splitting up and gave him enough money to get a bus out of town. I got off the bus about halfway to the Center, and Hernan went on. It was a relief to get rid of him. He was starting to become dependent on me and planning to stick with me all the way to Brazil.

I looked for the address of my friend Tomás but could not find it nor remember it. So, I bought some bread and a couple of pears and headed back to Rubén's house. He'd told me when I left this morning that I could come back if I wanted or if I couldn't find my friend, so I am back. There are eleven dogs of assorted sizes, chickens and a pig all running around outside. It's a real concert when they all get to raising hell in the night. I would really hate to be a robber coming to this house.

My cold is running its full course now. For the first few days I did not feel good. Now the swelling in my neck glands is down, and my throat is comfortable, but my sinuses are draining. I still feel a little run down.

Uruguay looks much like Argentina but appears to be not as advanced. Most of the cars I see are of the 1920s. The campo (fields) along the roads appear to be farmed more intensely than in Argentina. The police are edgy, and people in general are tense. There has been a great amount of urban guerrilla activity by the Tupamaros, an organization striving to overthrow the government, like in Cuba.

I was able to get a view of the center of Montevideo last night. They have a well-lit center with multiple neon lights and flashy signs lining the streets. The buildings are low and unimpressive. I was, however, impressed by the simplicity of the government house on the main plaza.

MONTEVIDEO - APR. 13, 1973

I have been hitching for four hours trying to get out of this city. All I want to do is go 100 kms to Punta del Este where I'm supposed to meet Danelle and Rick. I am really feeling down, not getting anywhere, and don't know what I will do.

I finally got a ride an hour later with a young truck driver hauling Coca Cola. He's spent five years in the States, so his English is very good. I figured I'd get to Punta del Este on time after all, but we got a flat tire about halfway. This day has really been a mess and a great disappointment. I'm still going to the Post Office in Punta del Este to see if Danelle and Rick are still waiting. If not, I'll go to the camping area and look for them.

The truck driver is a friendly, jovial, rotund guy and says he likes to help people. He gave me a Coke from the back of his truck, and my spirits were back up. They always are when I am tooling down the road.

PUNTA DEL ESTE, URUGUAY - APR. 14, 1973

After waiting five hours to get a 100 km ride, I figured I might arrive in time to meet with Danelle and Rick; but we had that flat tire, and the truck driver "had to talk" with a guy driving another Coke truck who intercepted us a little farther down the road. I finally made it to the post office at 8:00 PM, two hours late. A lady selling magazines said Danelle had been there and had asked if she had seen me. Danelle left no word.

I went searching along the beach for Danelle, but all I found were large boulders and two policemen. It was getting late, so I bought a chorizo sandwich, made dulce de leche, and tried to find a place to sleep cheap. I checked with the jail, but all the jail cells were occupied. I went to a church and could rouse no one, so I found a small concrete slab on the side of the church and rolled out my sleeping bag. Before I knew it, a tiny puppy showed up. I had to put up with him all night. At first I thought he might be covered with fleas, but we played a while. I let him sleep on the foot of my sleeping bag. He woke me up a couple of times in the night; but I slept well, even though laying on hard concrete.

It seems like drinking maté is the national drink of choice. People drink maté through their metal straws even while waiting for buses to work. The taxi driver, who rolled by in a beat-up old car, was drinking maté through his straw. The round gourd with a small opening on the top for the straw helps keep the steaming drink from spilling.

I never thought I would feel so down traveling as I have been these last couple of days. I miss Danelle. I feel lost without her, and I feel awful. I'm also getting tight on money; and, without a traveling friend, I am alone for the first time on this long trip. Usually, I meet someone on the road to travel with but not now. I tried relieving this feeling by playing my Peruvian flute, but now I'm watching pigs mating in the pasture across the road. The male pig is funny. He looks like his eyes are closed while he is mounting the female. The cars just keep passing by full of people and luggage; they don't even have room on the roof for luggage. Now the pigs are separated, and the female is wiggling her tail and ears.

The Uruguayan countryside is what Argentina must have looked like fifty years ago, wild-west gaucho country. Grass grows everywhere and there is so much luscious, green vegetation that it is monotonous for the lack of a color change.

Well, I did it. Nothing but full cars passed me for five hours. It got too much for me, so I spent my last $2.00 of Uruguayan money on a bus ticket to the border. I don't know what I will find at the border, but I hope it will be better hitching in Brazil.

The last three or four days made me feel like I've been sitting under constant pressure of an anvil on my head. Maybe it's because I want to get to Rio or because I want to go home. It sure has been heavy. I'm in the bus station on the Brazilian side of the border now. I feel a little bit better after washing my hands and face which were sticky and dirty. At this point, security is in buying a bus ticket, which is an act that only delays the insecurity of what is ahead.

CHUY, BRAZIL, AND CHUI, URUGUAY - APR. 14, 1973

I arrived here about 8:30 PM. I finally got out of Uruguay. The hitchhiking across Uruguay was terrible. We passed good-looking country while on the bus to the border. Rolling hills and multiple stands of trees, mostly Eucalyptus and Pine trees, spread across the countryside. I am seated on the floor just inside the bus door because all the seats were sold before the bus even arrived at the bus stop. I wanted to see the countryside and couldn't do it standing, so I asked the driver if I could sit on the steps beside him. I told him it was the only time I'd get to see Uruguay, so he consented.

Most impressive are the expanses of golden yellow prairies with scattered palm trees. There always appear to be just enough palms so one wouldn't have to ask, "How come those few palm trees are still standing, and why haven't they been cut down too?" The palm trees were in scattered clumps.

It's raining, so I've had to find lodging indoors. The hotel prices were all sky-high, at least for me. The first one wanted $1.50 a night. I couldn't afford that price; so, on my way to the police station, I found another one, where, after some hard bargaining, got the clerk to let me pay 50 cents to sleep on the floor in one of the rooms. Not bad! Good guy! Tomorrow I will try hitching to Brazil. It is obvious I am nearing the end of my funds.

It did not take me long to understand that Uruguayans are simply cautious of stopping for hitch hikers. With my long hair, beard, and hard-traveled appearance, I must appear to them to be a Tupamaro Guerrilla, a Marxist-Leninist, urban guerrilla group using aggressive efforts to undermine the establishment.

TORRES, BRAZIL - APR. 15, 1973

As usual all these troubled times must have been for a reason. Everything fell into place this morning, beginning when I opened my eyes. It rained terribly hard last night, so I was glad I was sleeping inside. I carefully peeled the sheets and blankets off the bed and slept in my sleeping bag on the mattress. I had a good sleep and remade the bed in the morning.

I ate three slices of rich, brown bread with dulce de leche, washed my hair, sharpened my knives, and got a young guy with a motorcycle to take me 4 kms to the border. The border officials wouldn't let me fill out a tourist card until I had a way to cross the border other than by hitchhiking. There I was, feeling like I hit a wall. I wandered out the door in utter disbelief with the thought of what do. That was the first time I had a problem at the border since entering Belize over a year ago. It was like being stabbed; and to make it worse, I couldn't understand a word he said because he was speaking Portuguese. I was shocked. I could buy a bus ticket but didn't want to spend the money. The people in line behind me noticed my predicament and said I could go with them for a little way, at least to get me across the border. Fantastic! That "little way," turned out to be a ten-hour trip of 720 kms. I'm sleeping in their car tonight and will go with them tomorrow 400 kms to Curitiba where I turn off to travel to Foz du Iguazu. ¡Qué suerte! (How lucky!)

This noon we stopped at a restaurant where I ate and ate and ate until I was stuffed. It was an all-you-can-eat menu. I ate lettuce, tomatoes, potato salad, spaghetti, rice, pork, chorizo, kidney, beef, heart, chicken, pineapple, coffee, and beer, all for $2.50. Incredible! These wonderful people paid for my meal. All the meat was roasted on a spit in small chunks, and the waiter never stopped coming around with the different steaming-hot varieties and carved-off pieces onto my plate. It got to where it was torture to have him keep offering us more, more, more, all we could eat, and then more. These people are wonderful. Two Argentine families, "como no!" (Of course)!

TORRES, BRAZIL - APR. 16, 1973

I learned nice traits while traveling with Danelle. She always simplified everything. She would often say, "Just let it be. It will work out." Sometimes when we would be in a situation where I thought there was a need for a white lie or a question injected to secure something needed, like looking for a place to sleep; or convincing the driver to just take us to such and such a town a little farther down the road. She helped me realize how I was forcing myself on others. She says, "Just don't say anything, just let it happen. We'll see where things are when we get there." I used to get myself into a sweat trying to keep something going when it was already going by itself.

Like yesterday, when these kind people offered to take me across the border just a little way down the road, my mind was already working at how I could get them to take me to the next town or farther. Yet I traveled all day with them without encouraging them. Stop, let it flow! What happens, happens! Once I was in the car and rolling along the asphalt everything was flowing. Like Danelle says, "let it be," and everything worked out all right. I shouldn't have even worried about it. However, traveling alone is a strange experience, and I am having trouble getting used to it.

The friendly family I was traveling with let me off a few hundred kilometers before Curitiba, so I started hitching. Three rides got me to Curitiba. My last ride was with José, a young Brazilian who has helped me tremendously. He changed $20.00 for me, took me to his apartment to meet his roommates, and took me out to eat at a magnificent restaurant, like the one I ate in yesterday with its mountain of food, only here we had more high-class entrees such as mariscos (shellfish), asparagus, everything a stomach could want and more. Then came the carne (meat); it's incredible! What a good guy! He also told me to look him up when I return if I have time.

I bought a $6.00 ticket on a bus to Foz do Iguazu (Iguazu Waterfalls), so I can travel all night and not have to pay for lodging. It's 676 kms and will save me three days of hitching.

Hitching in Brazil isn't bad. It's a heck of a lot better than Uruguay. Besides that, I'm eating good. My second ride bought me a glass of wine, two apples, a jar of palm hearts and five empanadas.

It's amazing how many Volkswagens are on the road here. I appears that 60 to 70% of all cars are VWs in all sizes and shapes. The tropical scenery is green, green, green! The air carries a scent of fresh flowers.

FOZ DO IGUAZU, BRAZIL - APR. 17, 1973

My luck is coming back now that I am not in Uruguay. The all-night bus ride went well. I slept good for riding in the back seat. We had a blowout this morning, but it didn't take long for the driver and helper to change the tire. I checked my things into a baggage room at the bus station and caught a bus for the famous waterfalls, Foz do Iguazu (Iguazu Waterfalls), an expansive, sprawling waterfall complex along the order of Niagara Falls, but with many more falls spread across a broad distance. The bus ride cost 4 cruzeiros, or about 65 cents. One of the impressive things is that we could walk up to the falls, over them, and around them. They are in a beautiful tropical setting with lush green forest.

I met a Swiss guy named Woody, who has a VW bug. He will take me with him to Asuncion, Paraguay, tomorrow since he must go there as well. That saves me a $2.00 bus ride. He's driven his little Beetle to all the places I've been on this trip, and the car still runs well. That is incredible, after driving across Bolivia, the Patagonia, and Tierra de Fuego. He's been living in this little car for so long he refers it as "he."

I just cut my hair a little shorter. It's devilishly hot and humid here. That's a strange change from Tierra del Fuego.

I was saddened this noon to find the rich brown bread I bought in Punta del Este was moldy and soggy. I was looking forward to having a snack with that rich staff of life. It was the best bread I'd ever tasted. I ate it anyway.

ASSUNCIÓN, PARAGUAY - APR. 18, 1973

I slept well in the "shotgun seat" of Woody's VW. It rained all night and was hot and sticky because we had to have the windows up. Earlier in the evening Woody boiled rice and put an orange in it to give it flavor. The next morning, he fried what was left for breakfast, and we hit the road for Asuncion. I had a very refreshing bath in the river after the sun went down.

The 305 km drive to Asunción was through wet, rainy jungle. Many distinctly impoverished people were walking in the rain along one of the two paved roads in the country.

We are staying at Steve Jarett's house. I studied Spanish with him in Antigua, Guatemala, a year ago. He's an interesting guy, an engineer, but now collaborates with people in the United Nations UNICEF program. Like me he's a traveler and has an interest in art. The artwork he produces is very good for someone who hasn't studied art.

Last night Steve took us to a big restaurant and treated us to some Paraguayan delights. Live music was played by one of the best Paraguayan folk groups. The harp player was extraordinary. The two guitarists sang as beautifully as the harpist played, and with good harmony. It was a rich, rewarding evening.

Woody and I just had supper. I put a package of dehydrated Minestrone soup and rice in a pan, added a couple of bouillon cubes, let it boil 20 minutes, and ate it with buttered bread. I enjoy eating bread, especially with butter or some spread on it.

ASSUNCIÓN, PARAGUAY - APR. 21, 1973

This Paraguayan capital has a population of 380,000 and appears similar to a capital city of one of our smaller states in the US. The streets are paved, and orange trees line the streets in the city center. Occasionally I see someone jumping to snag one of the low-hanging oranges. Asunción is small. An eight-to-ten-block walk encompasses the important tourist sites of the city: the port, Capitol, plazas, monuments, the main shopping street, and the Hotel Guaraní, which to my surprise, is pictured on the five-Guarani paper money. It is unique to have a hotel's image on paper money. It's a small town of mostly one and two-story buildings. It's a convenient size to control for the Colorado (colored red) political party, that of President Alfredo Stroessner, the dictator who has ruled the country with an iron fist for 25 years. There is little crime here, and that goes for vandalism as well. I was amazed to see a large bronze statue of a Spanish conquistador with sword in hand and a dangling sword sheath at his waist, neither of which have been damaged or bent. Even the spurs with revolving rowels have not been stolen or damaged.

Uruguay has had various dictator presidents. One of them, Francisco Solano López, declared war against Brazil, Argentina, and Uruguay in 1864-70 and was the deadliest interstate war in Latin American history. I was told that the war resulted in over 400,000 deaths; three-quarters of them were Paraguayan (60 percent of Paraguay's population). After the war there were about 25,000 males left. Today the population of Paraguay is the same as it was before the war. Paraguay was forced to cede disputed territory to Brazil and Argentina.

Lately I've seen a mongrel, wirehaired dog roaming the streets of the Center. He looks good. I'd like to have him; or I should say, I'd like to have his companionship.

There are no traffic lights in Paraguay, not one, not even in the capital. They have young women in gray uniforms standing at intersections directing traffic. This country's capital is simply a rural town.

CURITIBA, BRAZIL - APR. 25, 1973

They have peculiar pine trees called a Paraná Pine in this part of Brazil. The branches all curve upward and the needles form a flat top. I was informed that this is not a true pine tree, and it is an endangered species found in Southeastern Brazil and adjacent areas of Paraguay and Uruguay. It is odd that I did not see these distinctive trees in either of those two countries.

Woody and I just finished a trip across Paraguay and southern Brazil, about 1,000 kms. We rode all night and today. A young Paraguayan and his father bought Woody's 1965 VW for $600. They came with us to Foz do Iguazu, where they removed Woody's license plates and put theirs on. They took off all the accessories on the outside and bought a can of marine paint to cover the reflective surface Woody put on the top of the car. It's in pretty good shape considering Woody put on 50,000 kms on it in Latin America. The Paraguayans had to disguise the car to get back into Paraguay without getting caught and having to pay the outrageous taxes.

Woody lucked out there. I hope the Paraguayans got back into Paraguay. Woody also sold his transistor radio and typewriter for $60, the same as he paid for them. We went first to the pawn shop, but the store owner didn't offer a decent price. A lady, standing outside

FORTE SANTANA
FLORIANÔPOLIS, SANTA CATARINA
BRASIL

the window while we were talking to the owner, motioned that she wanted to buy them; so, we went outside. Soon a crowd gathered and the whole scene almost turned into an auction. Soon after that, a guy came up and said he'd take both without much hassle on the price. He was a man with money. We had to follow him out to a rich neighborhood to get the money. He had a good-looking daughter. The guy even showed interest in buying Woody's car and said he would get the stamp (buy the car) for Woody's carnet (car papers). Oh yah, Woody sold his tent to a Peace Corps volunteer for $30.

When Woody and I arrived in Curitiba, we took a taxi to Jose's house. He is the young guy who gave me a ride a week earlier, treated me so well, and invited me to stay at his place when I returned. It was great to have a place to stay, for we were both exhausted from not having slept much the night before. We had been traveling for nearly 20 hours. The next day Jose took me to the intersection north of town and Woody south, for we were hitching in opposite directions. I was finally on a direct route to Rio, and I felt good. The thought of lovely Jan was on my mind.

After hitching for half an hour, I caught a ride to Sao Paulo with a friendly, middle-aged guy in a VW van. That hitch saved me the price of a $4.00 bus ticket. The guy even took me across that huge, modern city to the other side where I began to hitch again. There I was standing on a double-laned freeway, crowded with thousands of smog-belching trucks and cars. I endured an hour of constant hitching in this exhaust-pipe atmosphere. It was terrible. I felt like my face was attached to the end of an exhaust pipe. I was having to hold my hitching arm up with my other one because of the constant traffic flow and nobody slowing. My eyes were burning, my brain was fogged, and I said, "That's it! I'm taking a bus."

About that time, I caught a ride with a young guy going about 100 kms up the road. He spoke a little English, and I was happy to be out of that exhaust pipe. I was back with people again, and even the short distance of 100 kms would make it a $1.00 less expensive to catch a bus the rest of the way to Rio. I really wanted to get there. I had even wanted to travel on the bus all night. Instead, I stayed at this guy's house and caught the early morning bus to Rio, feeling good.

BETWEEN SAO PAULO AND RIO DE JANEIRO - APR. 27, 1973

Woody and I have parted company, and now I really felt bummed out riding on that bus today. No personal contact with people. I saw the scenery but don't feel I know it, the people, their language, or this country. The coldness wrapped around me. I want to get my thumb out and begin hitchhiking to feel this country.

Buses are so impersonal. I'm on a bus sitting beside an older lady who calmly sits with a blue bag held secure in her lap with crossed arms. Rolling green hills pass by along this neatly manicured road. The bathroom at this bus station looked like it could have been in a banquet hall with people wearing tuxedos: marble-lined, wall-long mirrors, oval-shaped sinks set in marble, marble floor, and pink balls of soap hanging by chains above each sink. All this in a bus station! Imagine that!

RIO DE JANEIRO, BRAZIL - APR. 30, 1973

I am constantly amazed at how, by just letting things happen as Danelle said, they aways turn out right. I felt very good about arriving in Rio, to Jan S.'s house, and in her arms again. It has been a year and five months since I last saw her on the moonlit beach in Acapulco, Mexico, and again in Mexico City. When we first met, we felt a mutual, spontaneous togetherness; growing affection; stimulating touch and intense excitement.

Jan is in the Peace Corps in Rio. This is one of the last places of my journey. Both she and I had wanted to get together again, and that we did. It was a wonderful weekend of love and affection. Oh, how she can make me feel good! We spent Saturday afternoon walking on Ipanema Beach, a place of sun, surfers, and young bronze bodies.

Jan was having an interview with a newspaper reporter in the house in front of her apartment; and suddenly she was back, crying, saying, "Terry, I just found out that my father died, and I'm going to be flying home as soon as someone from the Peace Corps office comes and takes me to the airport." Wham! Just like that, her life and mine changed. About an hour later her former boyfriend, but still admirer and also a Peace Corps volunteer, arrived in a Peace Corps vehicle and whisked her off.

First she was here, and now she's gone. I'm alone in her house, and she won't be back for at least two weeks. Our first night together drew very strong emotions from both of us. I really felt close to her but still so far apart. Maybe it was because we both knew I would be leaving soon and maybe never seeing each other again.

I decided to leave before she returns. I cannot take the loneliness, and it will be easier that way. Peter, her ex-lover, still loves her; and she feels the world for him but not strong enough to still be living with him. I sort of felt like a second steering wheel.

Jan is gone, and I will soon be home. At this point in my travels, I am drawn to home as if a magnet is pulling me. I really don't feel like spending time seeing Rio, nothing here for me now. My family needs me, and I want to be at our upcoming high-school reunion. I felt good with Jan, but something just wasn't right, too temporary; and we knew it. Hard to explain! I have deep feelings for her.

I'm going to fly home, probably through Brasilia, instead of boating up the Amazon River to Colombia as I originally had planned. I'm looking forward to the quick flight. I want to be with my family again.

RIO DE JANEIRO - MAY 1, 1973

Last night I woke up cold. It was a chilly night. Jan was gone. I missed her, missed being beside her. I don't know what time it was, but the insect repellent spiral was still burning, and I was shivering. I used her blanket that was on top of her suitcase and my sweater. All I really needed was to be able to roll over beside Jan. I enjoyed being with her. I felt lost after she left. I guess because everything happened so fast, I was glad that her Peace Corps friend and admirer was the one to take her to the airport.

I'm sitting in her house, in her environs wanting to have her here with me. I feel a warm closeness to her. I think that will be a feeling that will be with me for quite a while. There is a ladybug crawling across the table now. When I think of ladybugs, I think of butterflies.

Today I went with John and Gigi, the Peace Corps couple who live in the front house on the same property. I like them. John is working in air-pollution control downtown, and Gigi is working with children in an orphanage for the children of people with leprosy. Jan works there too.

On the way to the beach, we saw several Macumba-worship left-overs [an Afro-Brazilian religion] scattered around. The first one we noticed was a bizarre scene alongside the main street. In the middle of a dirt road intersection a large cross was formed by two-foot-wide strips of black cloth. All around the edges of the cloth was the wax of melted red candles. On the horizontal cross-piece were two clay bowls with grizzly charred remains of sacrificed chickens in each one. Empty beer bottles and offerings of cigars were also displayed on the cloth cross. This was a strange symbol to an odd god [Orisha] or demon. A little farther down the road were the remains of another fiery offering but not so gruesome. Cigars were arranged in a radial form around a melted candle. The cigars were charred on the ends. Strange things!

The girls on these Brazilian beaches are very sexy looking in their bikinis which are high cut on the sides. The hip is exposed, and the narrow front panel plunges down and passes between their legs and is nothing but a string in the crack of their ass. These bikinis seem to be a constant hassle, for these luscious-looking girls are always checking and adjusting parts of their bikini, checking to see if some body part is sticking out or not covered. That fragile piece of cloth always seems to slide around. They love it and the guys do too.

RIO DE JANEIRO - MAY 3, 1973

I like the idea of being able to pick fruit off the ground, or if ripe, off the tree and then spontaneously eat it. I just used a couple of fallen oranges off Jan's tree to make an ice-cold orange juice with a little honey added. There are bananas growing from the large, thick-trunked trees, but they are not ready to eat.

Rio is a fascinating city of seemingly uninhibited people who are often jiving, making music of some sort, singing, and clapping hands on the side of the city bus, as they ride to the Ipanema or Copacabana beach. They walk with a rhythm as they window-shop in the center of town surrounded by high-rise buildings. Clothes, or should I say, the minimal amount of clothing one wears, seems to be of no significance.

Weather and climate dictate the amount of clothing people wear, and here it is hot and tropical. A man in a suit may be walking along with a man in swimming suit. It does not seem to matter if a man wears a shirt or not, is barefoot, or wears shorts around town. It couldn't be a better paradise for girls. Anything goes except nudity. It's strange how a place can flaunt the human body almost to the limits but then have a government ban on such magazines as *Playboy*.

The new architecture here is sleek and elegant. It's beautiful and bold. Most of the older buildings are plain, and the tiny colonial buildings are dwarfed by the towering giants surrounding them.

RIO DE JANEIRO - MAY 4, 1973

I was wakened this morning to the sound of a pounding jungle rain. It was pouring. It's nice to let nature take care of my day. I've been reading all morning and finished about half a book that I started when I woke up. It is a diary written by a woman who spent over 10 years living day by day in utter poverty in one of Sao Paulo's slums.

At noon I got to cooking. I enjoyed that. Put a cup of rice into a pot with a couple of onions and a wilted carrot. After about 15 minutes, I added a package of dehydrated chicken and rice soup mix and had a scrumptious meal topped off with bread and butter.

It's interesting that out of all the tapes Jan has for her cassette player, I find myself listening only to folk music of Bob Dylan, Ian and Silvia, and Cat Stevens, sometimes to Bach and the Beatles.

I think I will repair Jan's chair today, the one I sat on and broke the other day. One of the legs had a weakening worm hole that caused it to snap when I sat on it. I think I will draw a picture too. Galbreath, Jan's little dog, is playing with his only toy, an old belt. She's a clever dog. It's fun to watch her frolic and roll.

It's been raining at least twelve hours now. That should do a lot to get rid of the air pollution.

RIO DE JANEIRO - MAY 6, 1973

Last night, I met my Brazilian friends, Joao, and Hugo, who I first met in Chile. Hugo was the guy who got shot. They took me for a nighttime ride along most of Rio's beaches; then we drove up to the top of Corcovado where the towering statue of Christ watches over Rio with outstretched arms. It was a memorable scene up there. The immense statue glowed from brilliant light shining on it and appeared to be lit from within the figure itself. It was glowing white in the night with clouds drifting past and around his giant feet. Very weird! The glimmering view of Rio from up there is memorable. It's a different dimension to see a city from such a lofty point. The city and vehicle lights curving around the black voids of high hills and ocean made the entire setting an exciting experience. I could even hear the pulsing city below as the clouds swirled around me.

It appears most of the cars in Brazil are less than five years old, and the vast numbers of them are shocking. The Volkswagen Beetle is by far the most popular. It looks like eight out of ten vehicles are VW's. These people are really trying hard to copy the life of people in the USA.

The bus drivers seem to be very relaxed to rules. People can sit on the bus entry stairs or on the railings by the driver. I've even seen little kids sit on the front window ledge with the bus driver not getting nervous. Sometimes rules just aren't human. They know that. That would never be tolerated on buses in the Andean Republics.

I noticed how the Sheraton Hotel and a few other large hotels are being constructed on the beach far out from the main city center. They are trying to lure people out of the city.

I went to see a "Hippy Fair" and spent a few hours walking around. It was interesting to see the variety of craft items being displayed and sold are the same as you see in Buenos Aires. This fair is in a park called Orino and is a block away from Ipanema Beach. Artists, leather workers, jewelry makers, and other craftspeople display their goods. Sandals were the popular item for sale. I bought six bead necklaces for 80 cents each. They will be nice gifts.

Then I took a bus to Ipanema Beach again but couldn't get anything out of the experience. I had a headache. Now I feel like I'm getting a chest cold which is strange because I usually get a cold about once a year, and I just had one a month ago.

It's unusual to think that after this long stimulating journey of a year and a half, I'm going to just end it easily by hopping on a plane and fly to Mexico. I have $384 left and a ticket to Mexico on Pan Am Airlines will cost $314 of it. The airline allows passengers to stop over twice, so I chose to stop in Brasilia and Guatemala. That leaves me with $70 to get from Mexico City to Lubbock, Texas, which shouldn't be any problem; I will hitchhike. It felt strange to sign off a stack of travelers checks and decimate the wad of money I was frugally guarding for a year and a half.

Best of all, I will be able to make it to my 10-year high-school reunion at the end of June. I will be with my brother which I look forward to. If I didn't have such close ties with my family, I would buy a ticket to Africa instead of the USA, work awhile, and then move on.

FLYING TO BRASILIA - MAY 8, 1973

It's happening fast now. I'm on the plane streaking over the clouds watching the Brazilian countryside below. It's beautiful to look over the tops of these clouds, which I've always enjoyed. I like seeing clouds better from above. Everything is a new and exciting experience. Flying is another way of seeing our world but does seem like sort of an easy copout after all these months on the road and find myself in the easy seat just like that.

It looks like everybody is considered first class on this plane. The stewards just came by, serving all who want them, mixed drinks, or beer. Me, I'm sipping down gin and tonic and munching cocktail snacks. Fat city! Now they are serving dinner. This is too much. It's beautiful.

It was a meal and a half: steak, French green beans, rich with vegetables, palmitos (palm hearts), bread and crackers with butter and cheese, a tasty pastry, and, wouldn't you know it, wine. Now they are bringing coffee. I haven't had a steak in a long time.

When I landed at the Brasilia Airport, I checked my "bags," grabbed my camera and stuck my thumb out for the city. And, wouldn't you know it, somebody must be looking out for me. Things couldn't have worked out better. I caught a ride.

BRASILIA - MAY 9, 1973

Yesterday I caught a ride to the city about as fast as snapping my fingers. Hugo and Marcia stopped for me. Marcia is a beautiful woman who speaks English and works for Varig Airlines. Hugo is her friend. From then on my stay in Brasilia was complete. I first went to their

"Super Block," and up to their apartment where they offered me a glass of water. What a nice basic gesture! These Brazilians aren't insulted by drinking water instead of Coca-Cola, Fanta, or other soft drinks. Many other Latin American countries wouldn't think of offering water to a guest.

We then drove in their car on a sightseeing trip of the city center of this 13-year-old city designed by Oscar Niemeyer, considered to be one of the key figures in the development of "modern architecture." Brasília is an expansive city of completely new "modern" buildings. It has grand open green space between buildings and wide boulevards, unlike the stacked up building and narrow streets in most Latin American capitals. It was great traveling in a car for this reason. My tour through the House of Representative and Senate complex was interesting. I was surprised to see the floors in both public buildings were heavily covered with carpet. The House has gray carpet and the Senate had deep purple carpet, wall to wall and on the walls. Both have ample seating for the public.

Outdoor sculpture adorns all areas of the city, especially the Center. A trip up the elevator to the observatory on the TV tower, where one could see the overall city layout, was distinctive. I enjoyed visiting a new creatively designed, modern city.

Marcia's two brothers speak fluent English. It was interesting conversing with them. All three spent at least a half a year in the States, and all crave fried chicken. Luis wants to open a Kentucky Fried Chicken place in Brasilia and wants me to send him a complete list of the foods sold in a Colonel Sanders restaurant and a recipe for Kentucky Fried Chicken.

These four young people live with their family in Super Block 308, Block 3, Apartment 107, one of the thousands of Le Corbusier-type of high-rise housing units on legs. Nearly the total population lives in these apartments that are all self-sufficient. All are units complete with stores, barbershops, and shops of all types. The Rayol family quite enjoys living in the blocks and has no complaints except that the Blocks are too far apart. They never get to know people in other blocks. There are 50 families in their block.

Last night Marcia and I went out driving. She wanted to show me the night club area where all the young people party on Saturday nights. She is just learning to drive so she asked me to drive. It felt odd to be driving the car along the light-studded freeways of Brasilia. I was in the saddle. It was a pleasant experience. Nice lady!

Darn it, I lost my pen! Now I must use this pencil. Checking in for my flight this morning was a sobering experience. First they hit me up for $3 for a Guatemalan visa, then they grabbed $3.50 for an airport tax. So, what I thought was going to be a reasonable $314 plane ticket to Mexico rapidly increased. These extras, plus $1 airport tax in Rio, brought the price up to $20 from the original fee. So now I have $54 to my name counting the $10 that Jan gave me. I am at the end of my money which is a sobering experience.

Thanks to the Rayol family I learned a great deal in a brief time in Brasilia. I never had to pay outlandish hotel fees. There are no cut-rate hotels in Brasilia because they are all new.

We just passed 35,000 feet over Bogotá, Colombia. It was strange to see such a tumultuous city from the sterile environs of up here looking down. The craggy green Andes are clear below us and look like an impossible, or at least, difficult mountains to cross. The clouds are beautifully soft looking.

Immediately after takeoff the stew. asked if I wanted a drink. I remembered yesterday's flight on Varig and said rum with coke which was promptly provided. I broke the seal on the small bottle of rum and poured in the coke and took a sip. Then the stewardess came by and said, "That will be $1 please." I nearly choked. For me, a dollar doesn't come that easy. I said, "Sorry I can't pay for that." So, she said, "Then you will have to give it back." She gave me a free coke instead.

I found my pen. Everything is going fast now. I am riding for the first time in a 747 plane. It's huge and looks like it could carry thirty elephants lying on their sides in a line. Nine seats across and two aisles and a lot of pretty "stews." Two hours more and I will be in Guatemala. I guess this trip must end sometime. It might as well be now.

The first-class section and the upstairs lounge is off limits to us standard-fare folks, so I went to see how the first-class bathrooms looked. They were designed with warm colors, well-lighted, clever design, and the bathroom water is extra blue.

We ate tasty sandwiches en route: one beef and others ham and cheese with lots of meat. Pan Am does not give the quality of service that the Brazilian Airline Varig provides.

ANTIGUA, GUATEMALA - MAY 9, 1973

I finally returned to Guatemala after my long journey in South America. Last night I was sleeping in Brasilia; now I'm sleeping in the Okrassa house in Antigua. When the 747 landed, I took a taxi to the center where I caught a bus to Antigua. It was the last bus, and I

Arco de Sta. Catalina Antigua

thought the short taxi ride would cost about the price of a $1 hotel or less. I was shocked to the bone when the cabbie told me $2. I said it can't be. It was. What a rip-off! It doesn't really matter because I'm here with my Okrassa family, and they are wonderful. They welcomed me with open arms, gave me a bowl of black beans, a scrambled egg, fried bananas, and hot milk. Just like old times! It sure is good to be here.

I have not seen Danelle since we parted in Montevideo, Uruguay; and I don't know when I will see her again.

ANTIGUA - MAY 10, 1973

Oh, how warm and friendly this family is! I feel like I'm home with three meals a day and a lot of black beans. I missed these people, Antigua, and the food they eat. It's natural, fresh, basic and without strong spices or chemicals. I can taste the unusual flavors and feel the textures in my mouth.

I'm sleeping on a bed with a straw mattress in the same room as before, the living room, with its concrete floor shiny from much waxing. Four huge pictures with early European nature scenes hang precariously on the four walls and almost touch the ceiling made of tongue-and-groove pine boards. A year ago, when I was sick and laid-up in bed in this room, we had an earth tremor that shook the whole house. I thought my body was just going into a nervous twitch; but when I saw one of those huge four-by-four-foot pictures dancing over my head, I knew it wasn't me that was twitching. The entire town was moving. All I could think of was, what if that thing fell on me? The walls are three feet thick and are painted a light green color but different than the light institutional green. A locked book cabinet sits diagonally across one corner. A television-and-stereo cabinet lines two walls; a huge handmade, solid wood table occupies the center of the room. A bare 25-watt bulb dangles above the heavy table.

ANTIGUA - MAY 15, 1973

I am becoming interested in taking Mary B.'s job of Student Coordinator for the American college students who come here for the work-study program. Should I decide to take the responsibility of the program, and should the Experiment in International Living want me, I would, under intense pressure, set this program on its feet and not make it so hardcore gringo oriented. There is a lot more to living with Indian families then the emotional experiences obtained by such an encounter. Just the question of whether we should even be here bares great thought.

Yesterday we had pickled pigs' feet for dinner. I never thought I'd be subjected to eating that. I know I could try anything; but when Elena grabbed my plate and started piling the feet on, my stomach dropped. When I started eating one, I found, to my amazement, that there was not meat on them at all. They were all fat. So, there I was with the entire family eating around the little knuckle bones and spitting them out sparkling white, and I was truly having trouble on the first one. They tasted all right, but the thought of eating all that fat ruined it for me. Somebody mentioned how quiet I was. After I finished eating, my pile of knuckle bones wasn't very clean, but I could not help it. I remembered how my grandfather liked pickled pigs' feet; but every time I picked up part of the pig foot and found it was a pointed toe, I couldn't eat it.

I vividly remember the time I was in Mexico taking a dump in a dry riverbed behind a clump of bushes. I had just finished pulling up my pants when I heard rustling in the bushes behind me. I turned around just in time to see a pig jump out and gobble up the pile of human waste I had just left. It even ate the paper. What a revolting scene! I don't guess pickled pig's feet will ever be my favorite.

Don Roberto, 68 years old, still plays the zither expertly. It's a delight to hear him play this instrument which his father brought from

Germany. He played the Blue Danube tonight, and it was enlightening. He also plays the mandolin, piano, and a little guitar.

The sandals I made when I was 21 years old are still going strong. The soles are made from automobile tire tread. About every three years I must replace the leather straps, and I've already replaced them twice. Now I'm putting on my third set. I bought the leather straps from Don Luis, the old man who makes anything out of leather. The six long straps cost me 70 cents. Don Luis says his machete cases cost about $3.25. His leather sheaths demonstrate considerable skill. Maybe I will buy a machete and have him make a sheath for me.

The cats still fight on the roof, and the racket they make on the corrugated metal roof sheets is terrible. Now they have zopilotes, a large black buzzard, bouncing around, practicing landings, and just plain making noise. When they move, their hard claws scrape loudly against the metal. What a strange menagerie!

ANTIGUA - MAY 16, 1973

I finished crafting my sandals this morning and placed them in the water tank to soak the leather, and I've been wearing them all day to break them in. It feels good to know that I will be able to go another three years with them.

I just had a strange experience while strolling through the market. I saw dangling in front of my face, a six-inch-long, green and blue lizard. Someone with a morbid sense of humor had strung him up by the neck and left him kicking. When I found him, he kicked only when I touched him to verify if he was dead. I looked around to see what the people would do if I made a move towards him. The scene didn't look too hostile, so I reached up and untied him and freed him. I put him under a counter; but when I left, I saw little kids throwing corn kernels at him. Now I'm thinking I should have brought him home and tried to revive him. He was in bad shape.

SAN JACINTO, GUATEMALA - MAY 17, 1973

I'm propped against a cornstalk wall of this Mayan family's house where I've been staying all day. The 14-year-old girl sitting in front of me weaving is stunningly beautiful. Her name is Maria C., and she looks at me the same way I look at her in amazement of beauty. She probably thinks I look odd with my beard.

Wendy, a young American, has been living with this family for over a year. The family speaks Cakchiquel, a Mayan language, and live in poverty conditions. This noon we sat in the kitchen while eating. The kitchen is a small building separate from the sleeping building. The main family - parents and small children - and Wendy sleep in the sleeping room where dried corn hangs over the rafters. The young daughter and her husband sleep in the kitchen. Both buildings have cornstalk walls and red tile roofs. A fire, or at least the coals, are always burning in the corner on the floor of the kitchen surrounded by clay pots of beans, atole (corn drink), coffee, and rice and water. Supported over the fire by three round rocks is a comal, a large clay disc which is used for toasting the daily staple of tortillas.

We ate a crumbly white cheese with a little peppery sauce on the tortillas for lunch. Kids and all! Being a male, I was offered a tiny chair to sit on. The seat was only about ten inches off the ground, like a kid's chair. The women sat on the dirt floor with their legs doubled under them. I think they had it better off down there low to the ground. I was sitting perched on my little chair by the doorway, and all the smoke was going right into my face and eyes. We drank pinole, a hot drink made of roasted yellow corn with cinnamon, pimiento gordo and a little sugar. The corn is finely ground on a stone metate.

The men and the mama dog just returned from the fields, and the two hungry pups are now having their meal. The girls are now building up the fire for supper. The man also brought a load of firewood on his back.

The sleeping room is larger than the kitchen and has a dirt floor. There are two plank beds without mattresses. Just a reed mat on the boards makes the bed. A rope, strung along the wall with clothes draped over it, serves as the closet for their meager clothing.

The women wear their typical costumes of bulky, delicately woven blouses called a huipiles tucked into long skirts that fall to their ankles. The skirt is held tightly around their waist by a long, multi-colored band called a faja. They are resplendent in color.

A transistor, battery-powered radio is their only modern convenience other than a coal-heated vintage iron for clothing. Wendy says their combs are made of plastic. I haven't seen any other thing here made of plastic except a few plastic bags and a large plastic sheet or two hung on the interior of the walls by the beds to protect them from wind and rain. The women constantly listen to the blaring Ranchero (country) music on the radio as they work around the house and weave with their backstrap looms.

Wendy slept in her sleeping bag on a woven reed mat on the dirt floor and offered me her board bed. Custom dictated that I sleep on the bed off the floor. In the corner opposite the parent's bed, sleep the two little boys on the dirt floor with a dirty blanket full of holes. I had a constant battle with fleas. They were terrible, and everybody was bothered all night by them. My shirt in which I was sleeping was multi-spotted with blood indicating where I had been bitten.

I told my family in Antigua that I hoped I didn't have fleas; and they said, "You do." If I do, it's going to be a hell of a job getting rid of them. Almost everybody in that family also had head lice and took turns searching each other's hair and scalp for them. Wendy says sometimes they sit four or five in a row searching the head of the person in front of them of those bothersome insects.

Our noon meal was tortillas, always tortillas, cheese, and a sweet, hot drink like molasses made from panela (pure, dried, sugar cane juice).

As I climbed the hill leaving that Mayan family, I knew I had had an unequalled experience and learned a great deal about poor Mayan farming families in a brief period of time. Other observations are when the kids get cranky and mad, they usually begin to run their hands through their hair as if they were slowly messing it up or scratching their heads and letting out a drowning whine. If they aren't given enough food or aren't served in their own plate, the whining begins immediately. This morning one of the little boys wouldn't wash his hands, so his mother wouldn't let him eat until he did. He sat there whining and being a pest until everyone was almost finished eating and then slipped out of the kitchen, when no one was paying attention, to not lose face. When he came back in with wet hands, his mother asked him if he had only washed one hand or both hands.

Household water is collected from a stream and carried by the women in large, round, clay jugs, usually on their heads. The women take along their babies who are snugly held against their backs most of the day, especially when the mother is away from the house. A large tzute (shawl) is used to carry the baby as if in a hammock supported by the mother's shoulder.

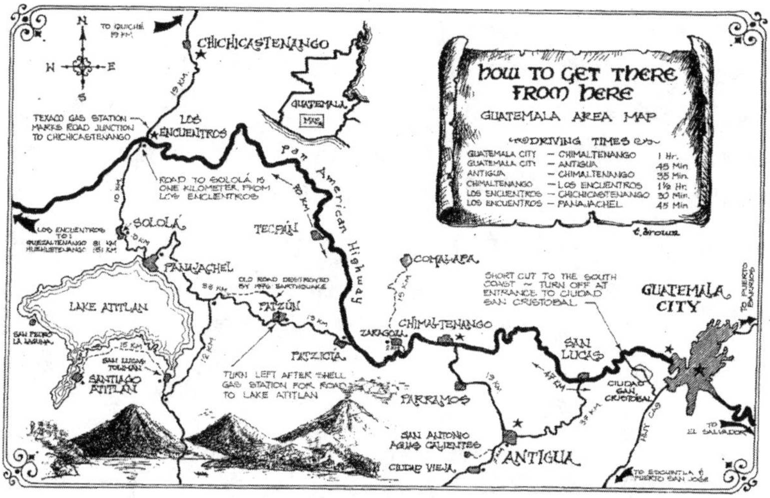

The boys spend much of their days, when not in school, roaming in groups of three or four searching for birds to shoot with their slingshots. Their slingshots are strange looking for us North Americans because they either have a ridiculously small crotch or none. The rock is skillfully projected over the top of the slingshot instead of through the crotch.

Their "bathroom" was in the woods to the right above their house. There was a trail up to the bathroom area where most of the family went. They just drop it anywhere up there and use corncobs instead of paper. It is said that sometimes they can get two years out of a cob. Hmmm! If it is used one year and found the next, they can use it again.

Bathing is done in the river about once a week or so. One day when we were walking to the river, we came to a large pool. The little boys, who joined us, stripped, and dove in. It looked fresh and inviting, so I joined them. Wendy wanted to come in also; but that wasn't an accepted custom, meaning those little boys weren't supposed to see her or any woman naked until they were married.

ANTIGUA - MAY 20, 1973

Before I stayed with the Mayan family, Wendy and I spent the evening together at her friends' house in Chimaltenango. When we were studying Spanish together over a year ago, we used to study together in my room at the Okrassa's. Afterwards I would walk her to her house. Those were the good times, and that other night made up for lost time together. I enjoy being with her, for she is extremely sensitive and sensual.

Last Saturday I had the fortune to be asked by the directors of the Proyecto Lingüístico Francisco Marroquín (PLFM) to work for them. What a wonderful feeling to know they have confidence in me. They said that I had plenty of experience in Latin America and collaborated well with people. I feel honored.

One of the PLFM's policies is to have short hair, so I got a couple of mirrors and my scissors; and after an hour I had a decent short haircut.

This project is one of the best development projects in Latin America. Its philosophy is to place the decision-making into the hands of the communities with trained Mayan people from their own villages working with professional Mayan linguists. There is Bob G., who created and manages the project; Jo F., a Peace Corps volunteer categorizing the Mayan languages and working in administration; and Tony J., a British volunteer, serving as the director of the PLFM. Now I have been added to the staff as the student coordinator and Peace Corps trainer in the PLFM Spanish School.

The Canadian government did a study on all the Spanish schools in Latin America and found the PLFM to be the best school and least expensive. Besides the Spanish school, the PLFM engages in writing the dictionaries, grammars, and alphabets of twenty-some Mayan languages spoken in Guatemala.

I was going to travel to Texas with plenty of time to spare, but now I won't be leaving here until the 23rd of June. The school pays for my room and board plus $40.00 for the five-weeks work, and I will be working my butt off. We have a lot to do. With this $40.00 I might be able to fly directly from Mexico City to Lubbock where my brother is. We'll see. I am pleased with how all this has turned out.

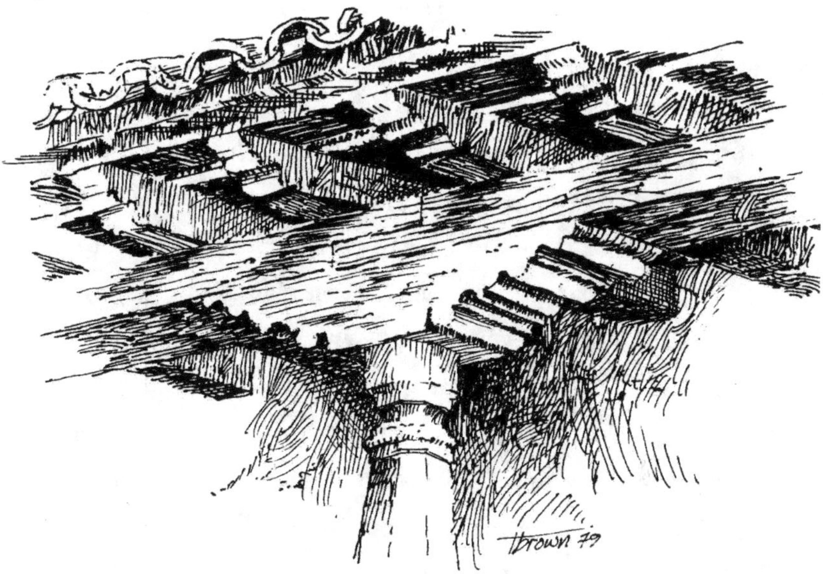

ANTIGUA - MAY 2, 1973

Bob, Tony, Jo's mother, and Will N., one of our Peace Corps linguists, and I went to the Gran Tasca Restaurant again tonight. Bob especially likes eating here because of its friendly environment, the food tastes great and is reasonably priced, and the students don't know about it.

The PLFM is growing fast and has a future, a good one. It's interesting how after negotiating and thinking about taking over Mary's job as coordinator of the Americans who come here for the work-study program, I'm offered this job with the PLFM to be their student coordinator for the Spanish School from which I graduated a year and half ago.

I just remembered how the skinny, starving dogs of San Jacinto get so little to eat that they eat human fecal material. Wendy told me they gobble it up while it's still steaming. I thought, dogs? I knew about the pigs in Mexico, but dogs? The strange thing about this is that the dogs are these people's companions and house guards, yet they get nothing but disrespect and bruising kicks. They always come sneaking into the kitchen looking for crumbs and try to get to the baby's food when he is distracted. They usually succeed. They get kicked, hit, and chased out of the kitchen but keep coming back.

Bob just gave me four shirts, old ones, which were a little worn or stained. They were starched and packaged neatly. He said he didn't need them. I've been switching between wearing two shirts for so long now that it feels strange to suddenly triple that amount. Now, I'm going to have to make daily decisions, which shirt I want to wear each day. That decision used to be made for me by a natural process called dirt. I wore the clean one while I washed the dirty one. I feel rich with these four sparkling dress shirts. I still have two pairs of pants, but they are in decent shape and have no patches.

ANTIGUA - MAY 26, 1973

I am an architect graduate, designer, sculptor, leather worker, wood carver, plumber, a fixer, artist, and a lover of people. I like being me, and I want to know and learn more.

Last night I met Wendy in Chichicastenango, and we made passionate love most of the night. I have been waiting all week long with desire to see her again. It was nice indeed.

I was talking to Tony at his place next door, referred to as the "bunkhouse," about literature. On the way home, I passed the Madura Bar. Sprawled on the sidewalk in front was a young man passed out, face down in the dirt. He had barely made it out the door. Music was drifting out of the doorway, and everybody was going about their business as if this guy lying there was an everyday occurrence. It probably is. If not there, it's somewhere else.

ANTIGUA - MAY 27, 1973

I have been enjoying the thought of being with my family after so much time away. I have even applied to enroll in a university, but now I have a vivid picture of my service to the Mayan people in Guatemala. Working with the PLFM is a terrific opportunity for me to perfect my Spanish, train volunteers to work in Latin America, collaborate with Guatemalans and help Mayans improve their lives. I'm getting excited about this work. Perhaps I would not stay in Montana once I got there. I thought I had my life figured out. Now it has changed. I feel good about overseeing, fixing up, and remodeling our new classroom building. It's of the old Spanish style with red tile roofs and adobe walls with smooth plaster. It's in terrible condition so we have a lot to do. I will be designing, hiring a foreman, carpenters, and laborers, and managing the work.

It's strange to know that I am still on my way home from this long trip; just sidetracked. If my family ties were not so strong, I wouldn't even try to go back to the States, especially now that I have this new job. But I must go back! I want very much to see my parents and high school friends.

ANTIGUA - MAY 30, 1973

I just returned home from a long day. I am dog-tired. I drove our jeep to Guatemala City and had to hassle and wait around for three hours to get five boxes of books from customs. What a waste of time! I'm firmly convinced the poorer the country, the more forms, and signatures they must have for anything, especially with government "red tape." I also had to pick up supplies. When I was at the Aduana (customs), I couldn't help but feel sorry for those miserable people working their lives away in that huge warehouse painted institutional green. All the employees wore gray uniforms. Improper lighting or not enough sleep damage their eyes. They looked like machines. Their personalities are just blah. At noon, the women selling food to the employees sold me lunch for 40 cents. I had a delicious meal of beans and pork with rice, tortillas, lemonade, and a mango. When everyone finished eating, the lady's daughter packed up everything - dishes and all - in a large basket and raised it to her head and off they walked. Tomorrow they will be back and the next day and the next.

When I returned to Antigua, I checked the work of my carpenters, unloaded the books from Guatemala City, and worked with Tony, making notes of everything I need to do tomorrow while he and Jo are in the city. I also learned how to use the ditto machine which was an interesting process. I feel good about my job: doing administration work, buying paint for the carpenters, solving personal student problems, etc.

ANTIGUA - MAY 31, 1973

I was wakened by an earth tremor about 11:00 PM last night. I was sleepy but I remember the walls and picture frames dancing and swaying. Earthquakes and tremors are not new here. An earthquake severely damaged this city in 1717 and again 1773. After that last quake, the Spanish authorities decided then to not rebuild their small capital city and moved the capital to present-day Guatemala City. Since then,

people have been rebuilding. Antigua is now known for its Spanish Colonial buildings, cobblestone streets, charm, and mild weather.

ANTIGUA - JUN. 2, 1973

Yesterday was unusual. After a hectic morning of getting everything ready for the new students who are scheduled to arrive next week, I rushed off in a taxi to Guatemala City to pick up a new student arriving at the airport. The information on her said her plane arrives at 3:40 PM from Miami. I arrived at 3:30 PM but didn't find her. The customs slips showed she had arrived a half hour earlier. I had her paged on the intercom to make sure she wasn't waiting somewhere in the airport to no avail. So, I headed back empty-handed to Antigua and sure enough, she paid a taxi $12.00 to bring her here and was waiting for me when I arrived. I paid $5.00 for my taxi round trip. She is a nice young lady with spunk. Tony was worried that my old taxi had driven off a cliff or something drastic.

One of the students invited me out to eat last night along with his French girlfriend and had a young lady arranged for me as well, a tall blond. We went to Ciudad Vieja (Old Town) and had chateaubriand and shish kabobs for $3.00 a plate, a mountain of food.

When I received the bill, I was shocked. The food cost about $15.00, and the bottle of wine cost $9.00. One puny bottle! We did some hard talking and refused to pay it, so they lowered the price to $4.50 for the bottle. The thieves!

Then we drove to Guatemala City and headed for a discotheque. The music was so loud we all had to stuff toilet paper in our ears to make it bearable. Like most Latin American discotheques, a handful of people were dancing inside; and a flock of pseudo-hippy, teeny-boppers were hanging around outside. I smelled the odor of grass as I walked toward the entrance.

Late in the evening, four suited 40-year-old-looking guys entered and sat down on the cushions where my sweater was. I went to retrieve it, and they asked in broken English what I was looking for. It was hard to hear, but one guy on the end of the bench had a 45-caliber pistol in his hand. He happened to be the one sitting on my sweater. That was strange. We danced to one more song then left. It was a full day.

ANTIGUA - JUN. 3, 1973

I woke up this morning to the sound of exploding firecrackers. A whole string of them were going off next door. It's common here to begin someone's birthday with a big bang right in front of their door.

This town is so alive yet so tranquil. Exploding firecrackers first thing in the morning to celebrate a birthday, a solitary minstrel singing to anyone and everyone who passes, a drunk lying on the sidewalk too drunk to get up, music floating out the door into the cobblestone street from a ten-man marimba group playing in a fancy restaurant, and horses and wagons rattle down the stone streets; all add color to people's lives. Bells from the many churches ring throughout the day to mark time and church functions.

The other day, when I went to the Parque Central (central plaza), I noticed a small herd of goats huddled against the wall across the street from the leather shop. A woman was milking them and selling milk by the glassful. She milked the goats right into the glass handed to her by the maid of the house.

Fuente en Parque Colonial Antigua, Guat.

COBÁN, GUATEMALA - JUN. 5, 1973

Juan Yool, a Mayan linguist working with the PLFM, and I have been traveling by bus for nine hours today. Both he and I thought the trip would only take three or four hours. Little did we know the bus was going to stop at every village along the way.

It was good to get out of town and on the road again. At noon, when we stopped at a road intersection, we were rushed by groups of girls selling mangos, "comida-al-instante" (fast food), coconut milk still in the coconut, and cashews. Juan and I each ate a couple of stuffed chiles with tortillas. We added a couple of freshly opened coconuts to drink, and there was one hell of a meal which cost 30 cents each.

We passed through country with tile roofed houses similar in appearance to rural Mexican houses. The atmosphere was arid, verging on desert conditions. Then we began climbing to the lush forests where the houses changed to thatched roofs. The countryside was green, and it rains often. The women's huipiles in this mountain area are lighter in weight than in cold parts of the country. They are simple, colored blouses of sheet-like material with a yoke of embroidered flowers circling the neck. A few of the older women wear a hand-woven huipil with a continuous pattern over the entire huipil.

We are staying in a nice, clean pension (hotel) for $2.50 per person which includes breakfast and supper. The super had my favorite pieces of chicken in tomato sauce, rice with tomatoes, sweet boiled plátanos (cooking bananas), black beans, French bread, coffee, and cookies.

COBÁN - JUN. 6, 1973

When I woke up about 5:30 AM, I was racked with gas pains and a sudden urge to let my bowels go. I couldn't hold it any longer, so I clumsily jumped up, put my pants on and jammed my feet into my boots and hurried to the john. The first stall had to do. I couldn't make it any farther. I yanked the door open, and I found a woman grabbing for the door with a surprised look on her face. I excused myself, for I had already unbuckled and unbuttoned my pants on the run. All I could do was stand cross-legged and strain like a weightlifter until she came out. I almost exploded when I finally got to the toilet.

Juan is playing his harmonica while I'm writing by candlelight. For some reason, there is no electricity here at night. It's kind of poetic. I showed Juan a couple of licks on the harmonica, especially how to tongue it and get a rhythm along with the melody. He really got a kick out of that. His harmonica is a gift from one of his students who he was teaching Cakchiquel, his indigenous Mesoamerican language.

We visited the Benedictine Fathers this morning and solicited their help finding a house to rent and Mayan instructors for our summer linguistics program. They have been very helpful. Obviously, they felt threatened by us being there. After all, we were in their territory trying to set up another school and looking for teachers. Unfortunately, they feel like they would be competing with us instead of collaborating with us. It's sad that they should feel threatened.

When Juan and I went to visit the governor, he was sitting in an easy chair in his large office reading a newspaper. As we entered, he stood up, huge and towering over me, greeted me with a handshake that "lifted me off my feet." That was strange. He pulled me to the sofa beside him and asked me to sit down, all the while shaking my hand. He caught me off balance. I wasn't expecting him to pull me. Very strange! After listening to our story, he told us to see the Minister of Education, who turned out to be a very friendly man who is going to see about getting the chairs and tables we need to borrow for a couple of months.

COBÁN - JUN. 7, 1973

Everything has been unfolding rapidly today. We convinced a school to let us borrow 12 chairs and a nearby club to let us borrow 6 tables. The Minister of Education loaned us a blackboard. We rented a house with five rooms and a bath for $50 a month, not bad considering the other two houses we looked at were asking $80 a month; the house we rented had larger rooms.

We even have a Mayan Q'eqchi' language teacher. Our first is an intelligent young lady and should be a terrific addition to our staff. We spent an interesting afternoon talking to her sister and mother in their dirt floor house. They are poor in wealth but rich in life.

Cobán only has five blocks of paved streets. The remainder are constructed of crudely laid rocks that torture the barefooted Native Mayan who use them. It seems like every other person I've seen barefoot had a bandaged foot or badly stubbed toe. This is a very rural community of adobe buildings, rugged stone, and gravel streets, and no electricity at night. The new electrical plant was constructed poorly and is falling apart, so the town has limited-to-no electricity. The streets at night are only illuminated by the moon or a passing car's headlights. It's been a full day.

COBÁN - JUN. 8, 1973

First thing this morning after our breakfast of cream of rice, ranch style eggs, black beans, juice, coffee, and rolls, we jumped a bus for Chamelco to visit Padre (Priest) Estéban H, a noted linguist on Q'eqchi,' the Mayan language of this area. He says he speaks 13 languages and dialects and says his strongest language is Q'eqchi'. He has already written a grammar and is now working on a dictionary.

Padre Estéban was standing, leaning against the wooden railing of his balcony, and talking to Mayan natives, when we arrived. We knew he was there because his VW was parked under the balcony. He greeted us cordially and invited us into his cluttered quarters. We sat on wooden chairs with foam rubber pads. His bed was a cot-type affair near one wall. Around the corner from his bed, and in front of us, hung his black clerical robes. He was a man of about 60 wearing black trousers, white shirt, and always a black beret covering his bald head in an unfancy manner.

His desk was a market table, unpainted and directly in front of the only window. There was a high, six-foot-wide bookshelf beside the desk piled with papers. On the other side of the room was a harp waiting for the delicate fingers of whoever wanted to play it.

We had an intense, but short conversation with this great linguist. He's smart and knows it. Strong in his ideas and culturally sensitive to native Mayan ways of life. It was the most linguistically oriented conversation I have ever had. Padre Estéban is completely dedicated to his work and, I guess, to God as well. He's lived here for fifteen years. He said the Mayans, in contrast to Western thinking, work not for the sake of gaining more wealth but to gain more to be able to give more away. What a wonderful philosophy!

It was strange to have to up and leave his presence. The bus was leaving, and the next one would leave in four hours. We didn't have time. When we were running to catch the bus, I turned my head; there he was, leaning on the same railing of his balcony as if he hadn't even moved or as we hadn't even been there. He gave us an education which we will never forget. Both of us have been affected by this well-meaning spiritual man.

We got the run-around on the tables we were going to be loaned, so I went on a trip to see the nuns who work and live in front of our school and kindly asked if they had any tables we could borrow. They said they were hard up but had four tables with short legs; and if we wanted to put extensions on the legs, they were ours. Sister Mary V, a friendly woman from Illinois, pulled a tape measure out of her pocket; and from her shop, a saw, hammer, hatchet, and machete, plus wood to add extensions on the table legs. So, there I was, extending the table legs. Those legs hardly even wobbled when I finished. I brought the tables up to a standard height of 30 inches.

Juan found two more Mayans who wanted to teach for us, so we now have a total of three. We need three more. The two new ones, two young ladies and one guy, will be good because they already have experience teaching Q'eqchi'. They are members of a Mayan Cultural Association which is helping to realize their importance in the world.

I am returning to Antigua on the 6:15 AM bus tomorrow. Juan will stay a couple more days to finish. I have too many things to do before Monday. It's not difficult writing by candlelight except when the candle flutters, which bothers my eyes.

It feels strange for me to have the aptitude to just come into a strange country town with rough, rocky streets, and mostly Mayan Natives who speak Q'eqchi,' and set up all the necessary requirements and equipment for a cultural or educational institution. I like it.

ANTIGUA - JUN. 11, 1973

It's raining now. Don Roberto and I went to Jim B.'s house tonight with our musical instruments. Jim is studying Spanish in the PLFM and is a noted trimaran boat designer. Everybody there contributed to the music. Jim played the autoharp while his wife sang along. His friend sang a canticle and acted out a short play. Excellent job! Then Don Roberto played his Sitara exceptionally well and ended up playing a beautiful rendition of the Blue Danube. Those three or four beers loosened him up. He was in fine form. I played the guitar and sang a few songs; and Jim's son, Steve, sang a couple of beautiful songs with the autoharp. It was at this gathering where I was introduced to Mark

H. who built a thirty-seven-foot plywood and fiberglass ocean-going trimaran (designed by Jim Brown) and sailed it 40,000 miles around the world. That tough little boat sailed safely through four hurricanes.

I sure do like it here, but it's going to be good to see my family again.

ANTIGUA - JUN. 14, 1973

Nancy N., a new student, came over to visit tonight. She is a tall, brown-haired woman about 21 years old. She's hauntingly beautiful and has an aura of grace and interest about her. She is very sensitive and intelligent and is simply a good person. I'd like to get to know her better. It's nice to be in the company of a person like her after all this time in Latin America.

ANTIGUA - JUN. 15, 1973

Here is the paradox. Nancy has been on my mind most of the day. I want to get to know her better, but there seems to be a barrier between us. Maybe it's my position in the PLFM, and she is a student. The feelings between us aren't as open as I would like them to be. Nevertheless, she is a wonderful person, beautiful and fresh as a flowery meadow.

I woke up late yesterday morning and ate breakfast of French bread, fried plátanos, and black beans, always black beans. I even had a greasy fried egg. All this went down my gullet in about a minute. I just concentrated on eating fast and orderly. I was off like a flash and really didn't feel rushed.

In the late afternoon I always begin thinking about supper, which is always black beans, French bread, coffee, and sometimes fried plátanos or tamales.

I enjoy eating in the smoke smudged, white-walled kitchen. A bare light bulb casts a glow over a cluttered, but neat kitchen. Plastic cups hang in a row on cup hooks. Elena cooks meals on two propane gas stoves. The old charcoal-burning pit which Elena used to cook with before, fell apart from long use. Now she cooks her beans on the charcoal-burning forge in the shop in the back of the house. It's cozy in this kitchen.

Recently, we've been having a steady diet of soup for lunch. Usually, the soup consists of a green leafy plant called Barro that grows along the streams. It is picked and boiled with a few tomatoes. We've had other plants cooked the same way, but they have different names. The wonderful taste of these soups sure beats dumping vegetables out of a can. It's so natural.

ANTIGUA - JUN. 19, 1973

The PLFM has a hair length requirement which I am required to enforce. Being a barber, I am also the official hair cutter. I hate having to ask someone to cut his hair, but it's necessary. This is a conservative culture, and we Gringos are visitors in this strict town. In an organization like ours with thirty or more Gringos around, it is important to present an appearance acceptable to the local population. The entire program could have a monkey wrench thrown into the works with freaky, long-haired people around. It wouldn't be difficult to be branded as a hippy hangout where people do weird things and smoke dope.

Even the young Guatemalans wear their hair relatively short and excellent quality clothing. Anyway, I'm getting good at cutting hair with scissors. I had two students this morning ask me to cut their hair. This is a subject I really hate to hassle with. They either cut their hair, or they don't study here. Studying in Guatemala is a heck of a change from the liberal universities up North where one can do as they please. We just expect men to wear short hair and no shorts. Most anything else goes. We foreigners are in just too delicate a situation to keep pushing ourselves around in Latin America. We can't take the chance that one long-haired guy in the program could ruin the last five years of work our linguists have been doing.

On the sidewalk near the market was a small herd of goats. It was the same herd I saw previously. Some were lying down, and some were standing but not as tightly huddled as a flock of sheep would be. One of the goats had a rope tied around her neck. She was being milked. The streams of milk were filling a glass which the owner would sell. That's as fresh as it gets.

Finely crafted bronze door knockers adorn heavy wooden doors on nearly every house. This one was particularly interesting because of its depiction of a lion.

This is the day of the Antigua Market which is held in the ruin of a convent refectory. It's thick plastered, brick walls are still decorated with religious figures of saints and angels. Mayan women in their colorful traje (dress) sit on the ground with their legs doubled just behind their wares. The have baskets full of carrots, onions, chiles, tomatoes, exotic varieties of fruits, and even tortillas made in the early morning. Charcoal, cloth, drinking glasses and pottery are common sights in the market. Women from the town, or mostly their maids,

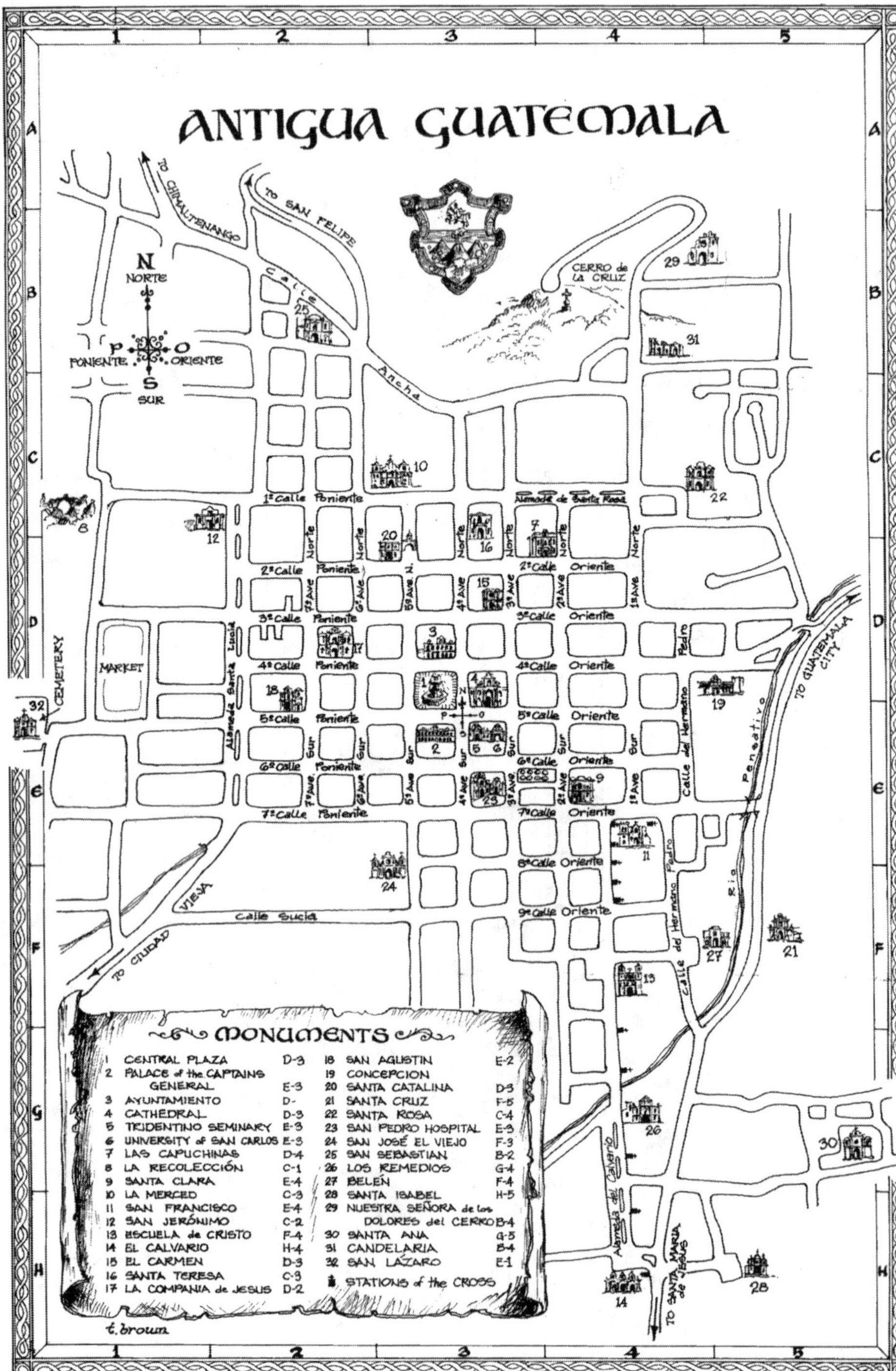
ANTIGUA GUATEMALA
TO CHIMALTENANGO
TO SAN FELIPE
CERRO de LA CRUZ
N NORTE
P PONIENTE
O ORIENTE
S SUR
Calle Ancha
1ª Calle Poniente
2ª Calle Poniente
3ª Calle Poniente
4ª Calle Poniente
5ª Calle Poniente
6ª Calle Poniente
7ª Calle Poniente
2ª Calle Oriente
3ª Calle Oriente
4ª Calle Oriente
5ª Calle Oriente
6ª Calle Oriente
7ª Calle Oriente
8ª Calle Oriente
9ª Calle Oriente
Alameda de Santa Rosa
Alameda Santa Lucia
Calle del Hermano Pedro
Rio Pensativo
TO GUATEMALA CITY
MARKET
CEMETERY
Calle Sucia
VIEJA
TO CIUDAD
Alameda del Calvario
TO SANTA MARIA de JESUS
MONUMENTS
1 CENTRAL PLAZA D-3
2 PALACE of the CAPTAINS GENERAL E-3
3 AYUNTAMIENTO D-
4 CATHEDRAL D-3
5 TRIDENTINO SEMINARY E-3
6 UNIVERSITY of SAN CARLOS E-3
7 LAS CAPUCHINAS D-4
8 LA RECOLECCIÓN C-1
9 SANTA CLARA E-4
10 LA MERCED C-3
11 SAN FRANCISCO E-4
12 SAN JERÓNIMO C-2
13 ESCUELA de CRISTO F-4
14 EL CALVARIO H-4
15 EL CARMEN D-3
16 SANTA TERESA C-3
17 LA COMPANIA de JESUS D-2
18 SAN AGUSTIN E-2
19 CONCEPCION
20 SANTA CATALINA D-3
21 SANTA CRUZ F-5
22 SANTA ROSA C-4
23 SAN PEDRO HOSPITAL E-3
24 SAN JOSÉ EL VIEJO F-3
25 SAN SEBASTIAN B-2
26 LOS REMEDIOS G-4
27 BELÉN F-4
28 SANTA ISABEL H-5
29 NUESTRA SEÑORA de los DOLORES del CERRO B-4
30 SANTA ANA G-5
31 CANDELARIA B-4
32 SAN LÁZARO E-1
STATIONS of the CROSS
t. brown

do the shopping and are professionals in the market. They know the prices of everything and haggle to the last cent. The customers walk slowly along the narrow aisles; and, if they stop, they get pushed from behind by impatient people. One simply must get out of their way.

In the corners of the market, people can buy inexpensive meals of boiled rice with carrots and pepián (spicy chicken sauce with vegetables and spices) and a piece of meat with a deep brown sauce called mole. People simply look over the steaming cauldrons to find something that suits their taste and choose. Eating is done on metal plates on oilcloth-covered tables with benches. It's an interesting down-to-earth scene.

ANTIGUA - JUN. 18, 1973

Bob G. returned from New York City Saturday; so, we spent all day Sunday talking about everything, including my life for the next year or so. The PLFM directors decided to reimburse me for the remainder of my $56.00 ticket to Texas and my return flight to Guatemala from Montana. In return, will work with Tony, Bob and Jo for the next year

and a half after a one-month vacation from June 22 to July 21. I will receive a $5.00-a-month raise which brings me up to $85.00 a month salary. I will be collaborating with a Guatemalan teacher setting up a new Spanish School in town of Huehuetenango in the Cuchumatán Mountains near the border with Mexico. That should be an interesting experience.

I have been tossing around the idea of joining the Peace Corps, asking to be assigned to the PLFM, and drawing $125.00 a month salary instead of the $85.00, then having $75.00 a month automatically put aside for a readjustment allowance.

ANTIGUA -JUN. 19, 1973

Every day in Antigua there is a symphony of ringing bells from different churches. Just now La Merced church was playing magnificent little bells, medium bells, and large bells. First there was the slow rumbling from the bold-sounding, large bells; next the little bells, then all of them peeling all at once as if the most festive day had begun. It was beautiful.

A poor man without shoes was curled up on a stone bench under shelter from the cold, damp rain. He was apparently trying to sleep, for he had a square of white cloth over his face. A disabled Mayan woman, stricken with polio and now wearing a leg brace was crutching her way into the church. The voluminous white, interior of the church seemed spotless because of its bright color. I don't know why the grand peeling of the bells was brought to life because the church had only three people in it. Maybe it was for them, or maybe because it was a beautiful thing to do for the people of Antigua.

HOUSTON BOUND - JUN. 22, 1973

My extensive journey is ending. I am cruising along at 28,000 feet in a Pan Am 707 jet, and that is as fancy an end to this trip as I could ever imagine. I never thought I would be flying back to the States, not with only $50.00 in my pocket. But here I am feeling comfortable in this luxurious airplane. We are beginning our decent to Mexico City where we have a short stopover.

We are coming in for a landing, and I am looking at everything out the window. Everything looked to be straight and orderly except for the contour of the earth. These strange lines (ditches) curved their way along the edges of the fields, flowing as if they were taken off a topographic map etched on the ground. The guy sitting next to me said they were rice fields, and I imagine the ditches were following the contours of the ground. That is common sense. In the USA, especially in the West, rectilinear fields and roads laid out in a grid.

On landing at the four-year-old Houston International Airport, I was surprised at how sterile looking the airport was. People paid millions of dollars to design this plain looking building. It does, however, have nice details. I feel that these past few years have wizened me far beyond anything I have ever learned in the University.

Passing through customs was extremely easy. The lady did not even open my bags. She only wanted to see my passport. I saw a guy open his wallet to pay for a plane ticket and saw a slew of credit cards. No money, just cards. That was strange to see.

I just walked through the metal detector and the machine BEEPED. The lady made me take off my pouch and walk through again. BEEP! THERE IT WAS AGAIN. I then took off my belt with a large metal buckle and finally made it through. I thought they were going to make me strip. That's all right though; it sure stops people carrying weapons on board.

I went to the bathroom and pulled open the toilet stall door and was surprised that there was no charge to enter the stall. I pulled out a tissue seat cover and punched the perforated hole out of it and laid it over the seat. Just as I was sitting down, I noticed I had put it on the seat backwards and could not rotate it because the flap was dangling in the water. These modern problems! On the wall was written the most absurd, gross story by a "17-year-old." When I walked out of the john, a guy standing on the scales was cursing because he did not have a penny to put into the machine to weigh himself. Men were walking by in white shoes and shoes with high heels. Both appeared to be odd styles, and I felt a little out of place wearing my old combat boots.

The latest in airport public transportation systems connecting these sterile complexes is uninviting as well. The train to various terminals is rough riding, breaks down and is slow. A waste of money! Sixty million dollars down the drain! Most of the telephones here don't work and gobble up the dimes at the same time. I think they should just blow up the entire building complex and start over. The interior is nice but nothing special.

I called Morris, my twin brother. It was good to hear him; and wow, I even talked to his oldest son. I'd only known him as an infant, so this was unique. It will be wonderful to get to Lubbock to see him.

I can't concentrate in this huge sterile terminal; too much is happening at once. Motion, the constant drone of noise, crowds of people, and a cacophony of color, light, and energy bothers me. I feel like I'm sitting in an electric dynamo. It's too much to take in. I want to get where it's quiet and no jabbering from the overhead intercom and the bustling crowds. I'M HAVING CULTURE SHOCK! However, I am immensely pleased to be back in the USA, but I have a lot of adjusting to do. I have been on the go in Latin America for a year and seven months plus the ten months I served in the Vietnam war; I've been through a lot; and the tough traveling with Danelle to the Patagonia and back took a lot out of me. I look forward to visiting my brother and his family in Texas and my parents in Montana. I also look forward to attending my 10-year high school reunion in Hardin, Montana, and returning to Guatemala to work with the PLFM. That will be a new chapter in my life.

During this epic adventure, I frequently offered travel information and recommendations to other hitchhiker's and travelers. After my return to Guatemala, I began illustrating a hitchhiker guidebook. The following illustrations are the beginning of a never published booklet.

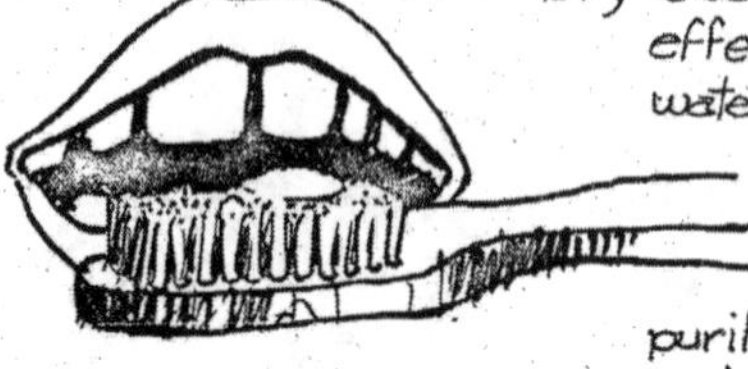

Dry Cleaning Your Teeth — You can effectively brush your teeth without using water simply by using your own saliva and and a smaller amount of toothpaste than they show on the T.V. ads. Many times you will be caught without purified water or have no water at all. It's just a psychological adjustment thats all.

This small item may prove to be your best friend. You will always need one if you sleep in cheap hotels. The padlocks furnished by the management to lock your rooms are flimsy and they may have an extra key. Do yourself a favor and carry your own.

While on the road it is generally better to stay overnight in a small town than the big city. Numerous hassles await you in all big cities such as getting in, & getting out. Carrying a pack on a crowded bus, that is if you can get on, can be a bad experience.

A knife of any type is always handy. If it's a very unique or unusual knife, a customs agent may decide he'd like to have it. A plain hunting knife that's not too large and any type of pocket knife except a large switchblade can be carried without problems.

■ If you don't keep your knife sharp it's worthless. A whetstone and a knife are inseparable.

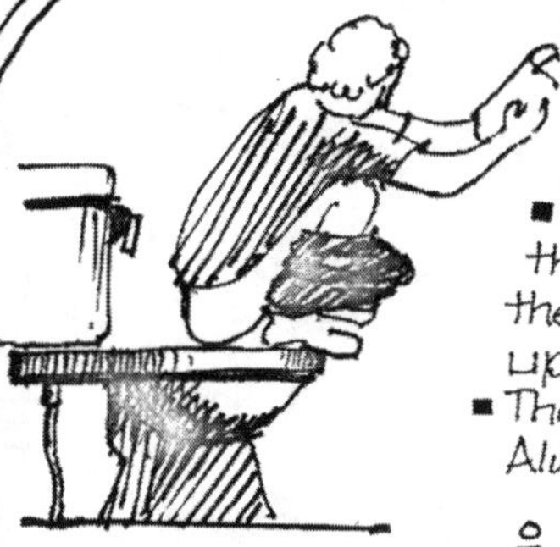

- While traveling on a low budget you will probably be sleeping in cheap hotels — places that do not have toilet seats.
- It may be a good idea to practice this position at home before hitting the road. Be careful when climbing up.
- They don't furnish toilet paper either. Always carry your own.

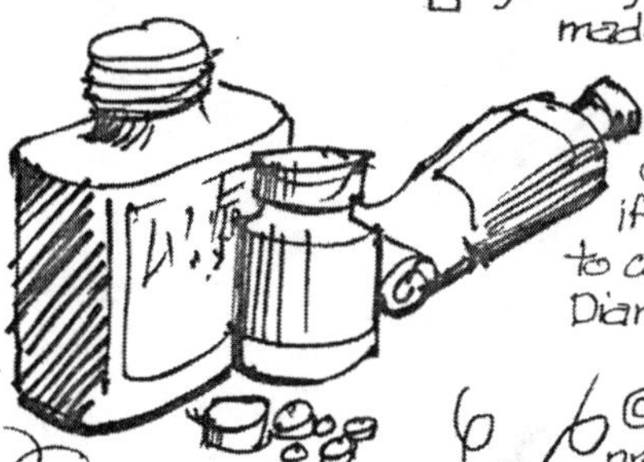

If you buy medicines and other articles made in the country you're in you save money ■ A 75¢ bottle of diarrhea medicine can go for as high as $3.50 if it's imported. ■ It's a good idea to carry diarrhea medicine at all times. Diarrhea can attack at any time.

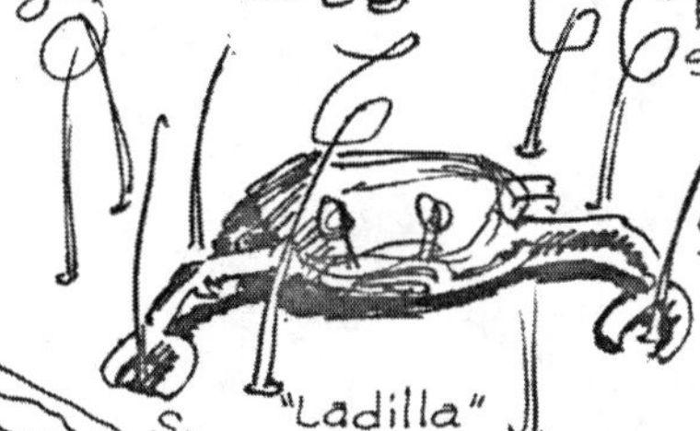

"Ladilla"
Spanish word for crab

Crabs — they itch like hell and prefer to live in pubic hair but sometimes go to the pits & eye lashes. The crab's cousin, the louse, reserves the head and their other cousin, the cootie claims the body. They are bummers. Do them in with

- Shaving
- Kerosene (2 applications 10 days apart)
- DDT powder (on body and clothes)
- Medicine from druggist

10 ft. of rope is a sure friend.

Good for tying packs on trucks, setting up tents, a clothes line and many other numerous uses that pop-up at unexpected times. Of course one can do without it but it is one of the few posessions that hasinnumerous value to the traveler.

- The Slip Knot is an easy to tie knot with many uses. It's just an overhand knot with a loop. It can be used to secure the ends of your rope to your pack frame, a tree or a post etc.

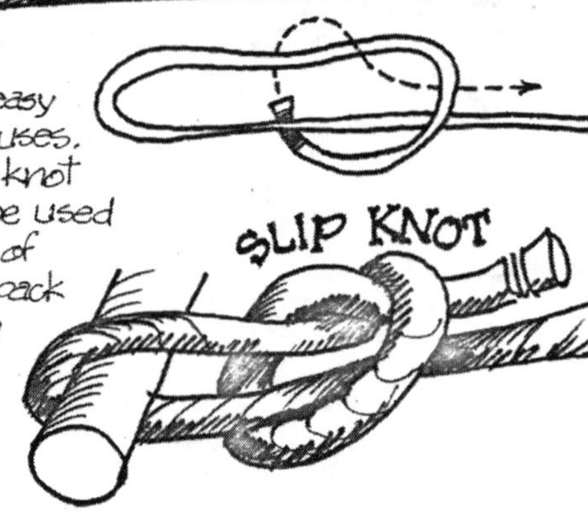

- The Square Knot is stronger than the granny knot which is the most commonly used but sloppy version of the square knot.
  - If you can tie a granny knot you can tie a square knot. Just pay attention to what you are doing.
    - The square knot is a good all around knot for joining two ropes.

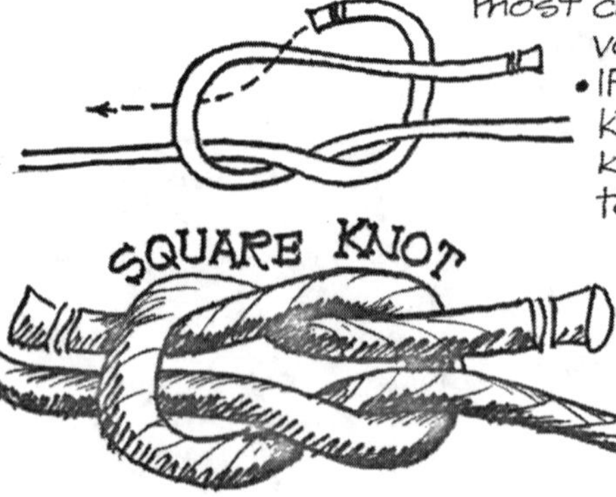

Terry's Epilogue

After Terry's travels in South America in 1973, he visited his family in Montana and returned to Guatemala to work with the Proyecto Lingüístico Francisco Marroquín (PLFM) in Antigua for four years. He provided cultural orientation and language training to several hundred US Peace Corps, Japanese, and United Nations volunteers, and to US Embassy and Canadian Embassy personnel who worked in Latin America. His early contributions in the creation of the PLFM continue to provide linguistic preservation and development for more than twenty Mayan languages which help Indigenes Mayans create grammar, alphabets, and dictionaries in their own languages.

In 1977 Terry established Xocomil Design, his first architecture practice and construction company in Antigua, Guatemala. For the next four years he remodeled a large Spanish Colonial home into a Spanish school and Mayan linguistic center and created a Mayan cultural center.

Terry married in Guatemala; his first two daughters were born in Guatemala City. After working in Guatemala for eight years, Terry and his family moved to the US in 1981. Along the way they explored

TEMPLE OF THE MAGICIAN
Uxmal, Yucatan
t. john brown ©

Mayan ruins in Guatemala, Honduras, and Mexico. Terry filled a notebook with sketches of Mayan architectural details that illustrate his book titled *Sketchbook on the World* (Sunstone Press, Santa Fe, New Mexico).

In 1981 Terry began an architectural internship with a prominent firm in El Paso, Texas. Later, he received a New Mexico architectural license and moved his family to Albuquerque, New Mexico and worked with three Native American architectural firms for the next twenty years. He focused on providing an improved quality of life for the Hualapai Tribe on the south rim of the Grand Canyon; the Quechan Tribe near Yuma, Arizona; the people of the ancient Southwest Pueblos of Santa Clara, Zia, Taos, Picuris, and Sandia; and the Oglala Sioux and Santee Sioux in South Dakota. He provided architectural services for Bureau of Indian Affairs schools, and for Indian Health Service health centers, public colleges, and schools across New Mexico and Arizona.

The massive 1976 earthquake in Guatemala marked the beginning of Terry's involvement in international disaster recovery efforts. Terry was toppled out of bed in Antigua in the middle of the night by the effects of a devastating 7.6 earthquake. A day later he assisted doctors in the local hospital. Due to the threat of aftershocks affecting the already weakened municipal hospital, he was asked to provide his architectural design skills to evacuate and organize bed layout in a temporary field hospital in a soccer field. He helped doctors with operations and cleaned wounds in this temporary hospital. He also helped create simple, self-explanatory picture booklets for Native Mayans and provincial farmers on how to build stronger homes with local materials to withstand earthquakes.

Many years later, after the 9/11 attack on the US World Trade Center, while serving as National Vice President of the American Institute of Architects (AIA) and Chairman of the AIA National Disaster Assistance Committee, he coauthored the first AIA *Handbook for Disaster Assistance Programs* and created the AIA national Component Response System, which together strengthened the AIA Livable Communities Knowledge Center. He facilitated disaster assistance training and education for more than one thousand architects and building officials across the US and Canada.

The hallmark of Terry's 12-year tenure with the AIA Disaster Assistance Committee was leading a team of architects, engineers, planners, and landscape architects to Sri Lanka after the 2004 tsunami that killed thousands and left the country devastated. Terry's team provided an interorganizational, long-term reconnaissance report on how to mitigate future damage.

Terry's history in Latin America was recognized by the president of the American Institute of Architects, which appointed him to represent AIA's 90,000 members for six years as liaison to the 100-year-

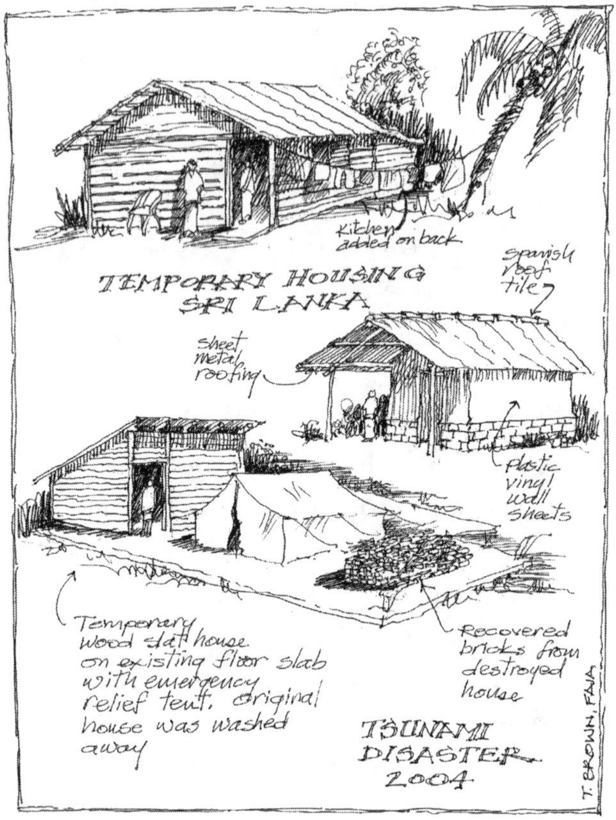

old Federation of Pan American Architect Associations (FPAA). This organization represents architects from thirty-one countries in the Western Hemisphere, from US, Canada, Central and South America, and the Caribbean. Terry's international leadership brought clarification to the AIA's international proceedings and guidance on issues that benefit architects in the Americas and the Caribbean. From 2000 to 2007 Terry represented the AIA in congressional meetings in Panama, Costa Rica, Ecuador, Brazil (three trips), Mexico, Honduras, Island of Guadalupe, Canada, Puerto Rico, and Colombia. He was elected FPAA North American Secretary 2004-2006.

In 2000 Terry was elevated to Fellow of the American Institute of Architects for his unique contributions to the profession of architecture. Terry is the first of two architects in the nation to be awarded both the AIA Edward C. Kemper Award and AIA Whitney Young Jr. Award (both national awards) for exemplary service to the profession. His Whitney Young Jr. certificate reads: "Dedicated to serving his fellow humans and his profession with respect, integrity, dignity, and compassion, his efforts to preserve the cultures of the Mayan and Native Americans and his disaster assistance efforts on behalf of Guatemalans demonstrate what a single architect can do to change the world and make the global community a better place to live."

Terry and his wife Sandra, a retired US Postmaster, are raising their adopted daughter and reside in Corrales, New Mexico. They are long time horse owners and trail riders. He is a leader in Scouting America (Boy Scouts of America) and has been recognized for distinguished service to youth with the Silver Antelope Award, Silver Beaver Award, and National Eagle Scout Association Outstanding Eagle Scout Award. He has mentored hundreds of youth and over 35 Eagle Scouts.

Late in life, Terry joined the Veterans of Foreign Wars (VFW) organization as a Legacy Life Member and is the VFW New Mexico Department Scouting Chairman. He is proud to have served as Post Commander and led the Post to All-American and All-State status three years in a row for the first time in its history.

Terry often reminisces about this journey and of his younger days hitchhiking through Europe with his twin brother to study historic architecture. After graduating from college, he returned to Europe to explore Southeast Europe, Turkey, Lebanon, and Greece. The US Army hurled him into the Vietnam war, and finally this 12,645 mile journey from Montana to the southern tip of South America gave him a unique perspective of life. Eventually, his combat boots wore thin, and he sensed it was time to begin a new chapter in life. Terry learned the important elements to a fulfilling life are to enjoy every moment, work for a good cause, and finding your greater purpose.

Danelle's Epilogue

I left Argentina in July 1973 and went to Paraguay via Foz do Iguaçu (Iguazú Falls). While visiting the Peace Corps office in Asunción, I met a female volunteer who had married a Paraguayan citizen. They had acquired land and built a homestead in one of the newer colonies of subsistence farmers and asked me to house-sit for them while they traveled to the US for a month. After that, I had two quite memorable trips in Paraguay: one to visit a couple of Peace Corps acquaintances, taking a train ride during which the front part of the train derailed on a bridge over a wide river; and the second (on my way hitch-hiking out of Paraguay to Brazil) in a pickup truck ride with two Brazilian brothers who had recently bought a ranch in Paraguay and took me to see it. (Longer versions of these stories will have to wait until I can write a memoir!)

I arrived in Brazil (or Brasil, as spelled in Portuguese) on my birthday in September 1973. I went to Jaqueparequa, a Rio de Janeiro suburb, where Jan S., another Peace Corps volunteer and friend of Terry's, lived. She was incredibly hospitable, invited me to stay as long as I wanted, and said not to worry since she had enough money for both of us to live on. Jim W. had made it from Chile to Brazil before I did and lived in Jan's neighborhood. He was the one who brought us the very sad news of the coup in Chile by General Augusto Pinochet Ugarte and his military forces on September 11, and of the deaths of President Salvador Allende, his press secretary, and many others. It was horrifying to think what might happen to the kind and generous persons Terry and I had known there. History would not find my fears unfounded! After years of investigations, The National Commission on Political Imprisonment and Torture Report, and others, found that at least 38,254 individuals had been imprisoned, the majority tortured, with another thirty having "disappeared" or known to have been executed.

While I was staying at Jan's house, I met Carlos M., also a Peace Corps volunteer, who worked farther north in Brazil. (He and his wife Sharon have been excellent friends to me ever since.) I was able to spend nine months in Brazil by going to Iguazú Falls every three months when my tourist permit expired. There I would cross the border into Paraguay, enjoy the Falls, then get a new permit when I crossed back into Brazil.

Most of my time in Brazil was focused on learning Portuguese (easy for a Spanish speaker), studying Afro-Brazilian and other "spiritist" religions, informally teaching English, and trying to adopt a child from the home for lepers' children where Jan did her Peace Corps work. I stayed off and on with a Brazilian engineer, her daughter Grace, and a housekeeper near the Ipanema Beach in Rio de Janeiro so Grace could practice her English. Grace and I took a trip north to Salvador, in the state of Bahía, near where Carlos lived and did his Peace Corps service in an "alagado" community, a slum built on stilts over a shallow bay.

We went to Salvador for Carnaval (the Latin American version of Madi Gras) which, unlike the glamorous parades in Rio, consisted of days of street dances with bands on floats going up and down the streets followed by crowds of anyone who wanted to dance while spectators were served drinks at tables lined along the edges of the streets. I spent some time at the dances with Carlos and Sharon, then at Carlos's house in the "alagados." After Carnaval, Grace went home to Rio, and I traveled north to see the new capital city of Brasília, the Sertao (a desert-like outback) where it was flooding, and the mouth of the Amazon River at Belém, before returning to Rio.

I wanted to spend more time in Bolivia before leaving South America. In May 1974 I took a freight train in which passengers had to pay a fee to ride in the back of empty, open freight cars, the shortest and cheapest way to get to Santa Cruz on the eastern side of Bolivia. The train crew permitted us to sit and play cards inside some Volkswagen vans they were delivering. Once inside the town of Santa Cruz, a traveling companion and I were stopped by police, taken to their station, and given the worst searching I ever had upon entering any country—except the US at New Orleans. I was granted a three-month visa anyway.

Bolivia was an extremely rustic place which totally fascinated me. Most of the natives in the Andean countryside still wore handwoven garments made "from scratch"; i.e., they raised the sheep and llamas, sheared their wool, and cleaned, carded, spun, and wove the cloth, sometimes dyeing it, and then sewed the pieces where necessary, knitting with the yarn. Although I traveled to other towns in Bolivia like Sucre, Potosí, and La Paz, I especially liked Cochabamba and stayed there in four different places. My favorite one had a view of the mountains and was next to the central marketplace. I made good friends there but was haunted by illness, including toxic hepatitis, so much so that my mother sent me a plane ticket and begged me to return home to Texas. In December of 1974 I flew there with quick stopovers in Central America, including in Nicaragua, where I saw Barbara and her babies, and in Guatemala where I met up with Juana and Carlitos again at the Hotel León. I distinctly remember visiting Terry in Antigua and buying a handmade guitar, but he doesn't remember this. Maybe that was a dream, but I don't think it was a dream because the guitar was stolen from my house in Houston three years later!

It took me a while to recuperate enough from my poor health to find a job teaching English as a Second Language in Houston, mostly to Iranians and some Latin Americans seeking entrance into Texas universities. I took a break in 1977 when I bought my first pickup truck with a camper shell and drove it around the perimeter of the US on my way to and from Alaska for almost a year. Right before the first winter snowstorm of 1978 in Utah, I moved there and worked for the Northern Ute Nation in one of their tutor programs until the fall of 1980, when I moved to the New Braunfels, Texas area (the southern edge of Hill Country). There, and in San Antonio, I worked at various jobs until I was able to save enough to make a down payment on some acreage at nearby Canyon Lake.

This is where I still live after almost 43 years.

During those years I became a para-professional librarian, later got a Master's Degree in library science, and spent the last 17 years of my career as the Spanish Language Materials Cataloger at the San Antonio Public Library. I was able to go to several book fairs in Guadalajara with side trips to the Pacific Coast, then on librarian exchange programs to Chiapas and Cuba. I returned to Panamá twice for Peace Corps reunions. After I retired, I made two month-long trips to Ireland, but other than that, have not often been out of the US.

In reading my Chilean journal after fifty years, it reminds me of how much I have forgotten and how much my life has changed. And yet it also reminds me of details I did not write down at the time but remember vividly.

It seems I will always remember how Mrs. T., in Santiago, would peel her oranges in a spiral and hang them to dry so she could make tea out of them since there was no black tea left in the markets.

Another was a conversation over my tiny writing in my journal. One companion analyzed it as arguing that it showed how neurotic I was, while another answered, "She's just trying to save paper!" It's pretty hard to read any way you look at it. And, by the way, I still have the good luck ring Maggie gave me.